Other books by Hugh Drummond Fulcher:

Emotional Mind Modeling (1995)

The Clear Mind Procedure (2007)

Bipolar Blessings & Mind Expansion (2008)

God, the Universe, & You! (2008)

God, the Universe, & You! 2nd Edition (2009)

"This read is an important glimpse into the 'troubled mind and spirit,' like Job, tested by the Lord. A juncture of desperation and inspiration motivated the next discoveries and revelations. I find neck, jaw, and facial exercises reduce physical/emotional pain."

Reverend George Jones
Rational Emotive Therapist

"The author's struggles include communication challenges with his fellow man and God. Adjusting inner thought processes is difficult. Mr. Fulcher has made progress in that direction. His writings reveal a remarkable person."

Rev., Dr. Joe T. Lindsoe

Cover: The Clear Mind Free of Ingrained Trauma Distortions

BIPOLAR BLESSINGS
&
MIND EXPANSION

SECOND EDITION

ONE CURE FOR BIPOLAR DISORDER

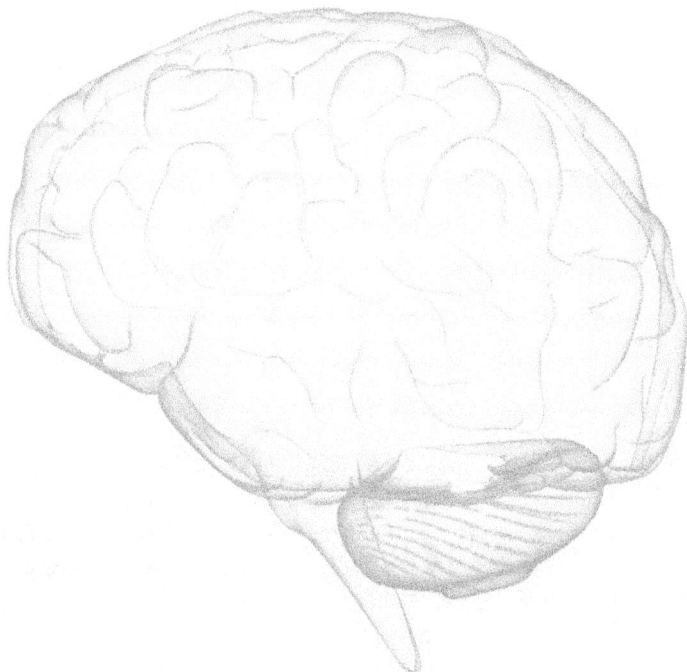

HUGH DRUMMOND FULCHER

MIND HEALING MODELS & EXERCISES

Disclaimer: This book is not intended to be a substitute for professional medical services. Neither the author nor the publisher is responsible for consequences experienced or not experienced when using the author's mind healing experiments. Performing mind healing practices given herein are at the discretion, risk, and responsibility of the reader. Bold methods have only been tested and proven to be beneficial to the author.

ISBN: 0-9790710-4-6
ISBN-13: 9780979071041

Published By H Fulcher Publishers

Visit www.booksurge.com to order additional copies.

Vita

Hugh Drummond Fulcher resides in Forest, Va. He has two children: Dr. Keston Hugh Fulcher, Kara Fulcher Hawkins, MD, (and her husband, Andrew Hawkins, MD, and son, Jack.)

The author graduated from VA Tech - BS degree in Physics (math minor) and MS degree in Nuclear Engineering. His thesis was on nuclear reactor modeling and design. He was licensed by the Nuclear Regulatory Commission as an operator of the experimental nuclear reactor at Virginia Tech and studied at Argonne National Laboratory.

He taught University physics, engineering, and computer courses at the VA Tech branch in Danville, VA and at Danville Community College. He worked in nuclear and computer industries for twenty-five years in management, reactor core modeling and design, nuclear software systems, and nuclear safety analysis (and modeling.) He has worked for nuclear reactor design companies, nuclear utilities, consulting companies, and on design of the New Production Reactor. He has written design and operation manuals, and given presentations on nuclear physics and nuclear software to nuclear societies.

Conversations on neurosurgery with Dr. O. Hugh Fulcher (an uncle, deceased,) former Head of the Georgetown University Neurosurgery Department and experience in modeling complex nuclear systems, gave the author confidence in modeling the brain and mind for understanding, and healing bipolar disorder.

Mr. Fulcher's books are written to understand and heal the mind, cure bipolar disorder, and integrate science and Christianity for spiritual understanding. He has given talks, and television and radio interviews. Simple physics models cross boundaries into metaphysical treatments of the mind and God. An unusual spiritual message demanded dedication. Mind healing and spiritual technologies were developed over a thirty year period.

In 2005, Mr. Fulcher established a financial company, Wide Acceptance Financial, Inc., in Forest, VA. He is a member of *Who's Who in the South and Southwest* and a member of *Who's Who in America*.

Table of Contents

List of Illustrations

(1) Holusion™ Art ("Holusion™ Art is a trademark of NVision Grafix, Inc.")

Acknowledgements

I am eternally grateful to my parents, Lewis Page Fulcher, Sr. and Frances Drummond Fulcher (both deceased) for their love and guidance. They were the love beneath my wings.

I wish to thank P. Joanne Bryant, Dr. Keston Fulcher, Kara Fulcher Hawkins, MD, and Professor George Jones for their comments and careful editing of the manuscript and for patiently listening to my incessant rambling on about mind modeling and bipolar disorder.

I wish to thank computer builders and software developers for their tools that have made writing and editing easier.

I also thank others who have added significantly to this effort.

I thank my Savior, Jesus Christ, now integrated within God, and God for sharing so many ideas.

Dedications

Bipolar Blessings & Mind Expansion, Second Edition is dedicated to:

1. My parents, Frances Drummond Fulcher (deceased) for her patience, and Lewis Page Fulcher, Sr. (deceased) for his wisdom, and both for their love;

2. My Uncle, O. Hugh Fulcher, MD (deceased), former Head of the Georgetown University Neurosurgery Department, who instilled confidence to reason about the brain;

3. My friend, P. Joanne Bryant, who has been so kind in editing the manuscript;

4. My children, Dr. Keston Hugh Fulcher, Kara Brenn Fulcher Hawkins, MD, and son-in-law Andrew Hawkins, MD;

5. My grandson, Jack Henry Hawkins, and future grandchildren;

6. My double first cousin, Barbara Fulcher Mays, and her husband, Carlton, for having cared for my aged parents, and are still caring for my childhood church, Ivy Hill United Methodist Church;

7. All ancestors in heaven and all future descendents;

8. All readers who need healing from stress disorders or who support afflicted loved-ones;

9. Everyone who loves, cares for, and shares with others.

Chapter 1

Introduction

"Imagination is everything.
It is the preview of life's coming attractions."

Albert Einstein

Persistent stress, success quickly changing to failure, and certainty changing to uncertainty, can cause depression and bipolar disorder. These disorders are difficult to manage and cure.

In depression, thinking becomes slow and painful with negative reflections on one's poor decisions and on one's self. In mania there may be a creative benefit at first, but thoughts often come so fast that one cannot finish one task before a more important idea captures the mind. The manic mind swings wildly out of control. Initially, the inner self becomes so important that thoughts of others are lessened.

We all have had times when it hurts to think. Severe colds, headaches, injuries, or other pains make thinking impossible. However, we are confident thinking will return to normal as pain subsides. In depression or mania, we are not sure if thinking will ever return to normal. We have fears of periodic or even persistent loss of control and even insanity.

To lesser or greater extents, everyone needs healing from repressed childhood and adult stress and trauma memories. Many of us develop disorders and are irrational at times. During trauma, the brain processes quickly to maintain reasoning limits.

Humans have limited sense and reason abilities. Human vision is confined to a small part of the electromagnetic spectrum with limited intensities. Everything we see, hear, smell, feel, and remember develops only limited models of reality. Humans have thinking and memory models of life's encounters. This book contains normal and limiting models of the author's life and faith [1].

Six percent of Americans are affected by bipolar disorder. Suffering and uncertainties can be devastating for individuals and families. Health, work, and resources suffer.

This book includes methods for managing and curing bipolar mood swings beyond psychoanalysis and current medications. Persons afflicted with bipolar disorder must be the most significant part of their own healing and cure. This book is an update of the original version. [2]

Current literature claims there is no cure for bipolar disorder. This is no longer correct. As far the author is aware, this work is the only research directed toward curing bipolar disorder using physics and engineering methods.

Healing the fabric of the brain with exercises and mind models is a true cure. The author has developed a cure for his Type I bipolar disorder, without relapses for over fifteen-years. With dedication and practice, the bipolar brain and mind can be cured. With renewed confidence in controlling the brain and mind, increased abilities become blessings.

One purpose of this book is to convince researchers, psychiatrists, bipolar readers, and support groups of a true cure. This self-cure takes years of dedication. There is no quick fix. All significant things must have a beginning. The mind is complex and heals slowly. Future research will make processes quicker and easier.

This edition updates the healing, maintenance, and cure of bipolar disorder from the original edition and *The Clear Mind Procedure* [3], which also includes a quest to communicate with, understand, receive blessings from, and benefit, God.

Many, afflicted with bipolar disorder, give up hope of returning to a normal life. This work gives hope for the afflicted and their families. The afflicted must take charge of, and work diligently for, a permanent cure. Hope and increasing confidence is a significant part of healing. Sanity is worth any price.

Curing bipolar disorder requires releasing inner stresses from traumatized neural networks and culturing effective inner subconscious processes. We learn to make good decisions from earlier failures. Giving ideas are more important than selfish ideas for mind and spiritual development.

After years of healing exercises, the new mind becomes pleasantly intoxicated with physical changes within the brain, and exciting, creative ideas. The author's cure has been unusually amazing.

Without truly curing bipolar disorder, we remain chained to mind numbing medications, which may prevent depressed, flighty manic moods, but often have side effects. Psychiatric prescriptions can control moods and improve worldly thinking. However, they reduce manic spiritual communications.

With some psychiatric drugs, thinking becomes dull and unimaginative. Some patients feel less than human, like zombies. Abilities can be lost for life. Research has shown that exercise cures depression more effectively than current antidepressants. [4, 5]

Manic thoughts can be exciting, which causes some manic-depressives to discontinue mind-numbing drugs. Never discontinue prescribed medications without your doctor's approval. Talk to your doctor if your thinking is dull and less than normal. With healing processes, abilities improve even while on medications.

What is a cure of bipolar disorder? It is reconstructing the fabric of the brain for a stable mind and life with unusual creativity and without worry or fear of depression or manic episodes. We can learn from our creative, dreamlike manic ideas.

Emotional writing began during my first manic episode in 1977. I feared insanity and death while locked in a small bare cell in a psychiatric ward. Without sleep for weeks, I had little hope of regaining sanity, feared never leaving this "prison," and frantically wrote to prove sanity and save my life.

Without references, I derived an unusual number of physics equations. I had abilities in physics, but emotional control and verbal skills were non-existent.

Manic thinking was flowing but non-verbal. I could not communicate in words. Fast thinking and psychiatric restructuring distorted my speech timing. I appeared insane.

After my first manic episode in 1977, I was compelled to write about enduring and healing bipolar disorder. Spiritual writing did not begin until 1994. *Emotional Mind Modeling* [6] was published in 1995 and included mind healing exercises and spiritual models. Inner sensations and mind models guided mental healing exercises and spiritual development. Mind and spiritual healing go hand-in-hand. This book focuses on mind healing and expansion.

Severe sickness profoundly affects outlook on life. During my first manic episode, I became curious of strange inner feelings and thoughts, and began thinking of using my physics background to cure my bipolar disorder.

We must take charge of overstressed lives and develop our own cures to regain consistent lives. Four months of performing unique psychiatric exercises initiated slowly increasing pleasant sensations in the neck, throat, and brainstem. Migrating localized energy-release sensations provided feedback of healing the brain. Creative models helped the subconscious mind understand its own restructuring processes.

Sensations varied, were somewhat predictable, and have been amazing throughout healing processes. Readers may find it difficult to believe sensations until experienced. Methods have healed repressed trauma effects. Mental abilities have expanded including spiritually.

Normally, we do not learn about things in depth unless inspired by teachers, parents, mentors, or traumatic events. I had a pressing need to heal my bipolar affliction. Necessity is the mother of invention.

A new purpose expanded thinking beyond my normal limits. Physical and mental healing, at limits, became themes for my life and this book. Consistency throughout this book may help readers construct their own healing and spiritual processes.

With hope, patience, and determination, the afflicted can learn to reason beyond their previous normal. Years of practice allowed the author to conclude that abilities have improved.

The author heard stories of neurosurgery and healing the brain from his uncle, Dr. O. Hugh Fulcher, former head of the Georgetown University Neurosurgery Department in the '60s and '70s. These stories and my physics and nuclear engineering background gave confidence for understanding the brain and mind to pursue a bipolar disorder cure.

Hardships in childhood, marriage, stresses, severe manic depression, and unusual spiritual communications developed an unusual perspective of the mind. It is good at thinking about outward events, but needs training to become aware of, and improve, its subconscious processes. Nuclear reactor design experience helped model inner mental processes for understanding.

After understanding more of the brain and mind, modeling heaven and God flowed naturally. Modeling forces in-depth analysis. Architects draw models to guide construction. Models are also developed for guiding scientific experiments.

We cannot just say to the brain and mind, "Heal your restrictive trauma scars!" It doesn't work. However, making creative models stimulates subconscious processes to understand and heal themselves. The subconscious mind translates models into its "inner language" for guiding healing processes.

Persistent stress and traumas imbed scars within emotional neural networks, which no longer function as part of the normal symphony within the brain. During insanities of depression and mania, the author discovered a secret. Excessive trauma scar energy, interfering with inner processes, can be healed by unique physical exercises and models. With stimulation, the subconscious mind can heal its own processes.

The author has developed and practiced psychiatric methods for over eighteen-years. Healing sensations became predictable and make sense. With dedication and psychiatric processes, the mind has expanded worldly and spiritual reasoning.

There was some desire for healing processes to be exotic. However, mundane exercises may seem, with persistence, they heal by releasing repressed tensions from localized trauma networks. Repressed, disruptive trauma memory energy is filtered throughout the brain to construct less emotional, normal memories.

Mania is worldly disruptive but uncovers hidden mental and spiritual talents. It reduces subconscious inhibitions for expanding creative thinking beyond normal limits. Extreme emotions and uncertainties develop motivation and need to search within for certainty in God. Uncertainties during mania reduce worldly reason but strengthen spiritual communication. Persistent imagination crosses scientific boundaries to develop amazing metaphysical models of the mind and God.

When manic, I, like other manic-depressives, had an intense desire to communicate with, and understand, God. Spiritual communications are more believable than messages received from other senses. The author's belief in truthfulness of deep structure English language helped develop spiritual models. Deep structure language reflects the inner self and has assisted with break-through healing discoveries and integration of science and religion.

Humans have developed sciences for understanding brains, minds, and the universe, and should develop spiritual science for understanding God, which may guide our way to heaven on earth.

Models of the mind and God are heuristic and developed on a quasi-scientific basis. Heuristic means best guesses that are deeply believed to be true. Heuristic ideas and philosophy are often forerunners of science discovery. Intelligent guesses and models are followed by experimentation and evaluation of results. Scientific discoveries prove laws or consistencies of nature and may cross boundaries to prove God's nature.

Spiritual development is based upon Christian beliefs, science, and spiritual messages received. God communicates with each of us in a personal way; especially, when near-death with no one else to turn to. His message to us today is as strong as in traditional spiritual times. We must listen and respond. A goal evolved to increase spiritual communications and deepen beliefs. I cannot scientifically prove unusual messages come from God, but cannot believe I have had so many creative ideas on my own.

Exploring mental uncertainties adds spiritual confidence. Beyond mental limits, earthly insanities build spiritual wisdom. Only the adventurous will follow this yellow brick road of mental healing. Spiritual modeling and development is treated in more depth in my book, God, the Universe, and You, 2nd Edition. [7]

It is difficult to believe mental healing and spiritual feelings unless having experienced them personally. Spiritual discoveries will come from scientists, and those who have suffered near-death experiences and surrendered their wills to God.

In severe depression and near-death, we become aware that only God matters. Experiencing near-death became a driving force for writing this book.

Our minds are results of all integrated brain cell activities. Every brain cell constructs a part of our inner hologram thinking processes including dreaming. In my models, God is the integrated awareness of all activities in the universe from atoms to galaxies.

With patience and psychiatric healing we can think more creatively for our own paths of curing bipolar and other stress related disorders.

Hopefully, processes given here will help people, nations, and religions unite, rather than fight, one another.

Models are tools used to construct or understand detail designs of physical, mental, and spiritual things. In the beginning, psychiatric and spiritual exploration was bold and daring, but after years of practice, became routine. Self-healing or self-psychiatry is expected to benefit readers willing to work to improve themselves.

Depression and manic depression cause the brain and mind to linger in abnormal, and sometimes self-destructive, thinking patterns. Depression is caused by loss of self-esteem, health, a loved one, or exposure to persistent physical or mental abuse. Life seems confused and hopeless with no way out.

In depression, "impossible" situations and problems are repeatedly recalled without real actions toward solutions. Chemical changes slow thinking, and the mind retreats from the outside world. It becomes painful to think. Suicide thoughts become appealing to escape mental pain and embarrassment of feeling less than human.

Physicists and engineers view life from an energy balance standpoint. Nothing is done or thought of in this universe without exchanging energy. The author uses physics and engineering for understanding and healing the mind. Manic-depressives must practice healing processes at their own comfortable pace and risk.

Each of us must reduce trauma effects and inner tensions to be all we can be. Processes and unique exercises heal over-stressed neural networks mostly within the neck, throat, and brainstem.

Many may not recognize benefits of purging trauma effects. They only know their minds as they have always been. Manic-depressives have an added perspective. In depression, thinking has been less than normal. In mania, thinking is more creative than normal. The bipolar brain needs to construct new wider limits for normal and creative mind control.

An important theory in healing bipolar disorder is that muscles and brains grow in ability only when briefly stressed to limits. Prolonged stress is not helpful in healing, but is damaging. At limits there are uncertainties as to whether something can be done or thinking is rational. Brief mind limit experiments beyond normal uncertainties develop confident inner processes.

Unique exercises and experiments force the subconscious mind to limits. It becomes emotionally aware of inner abilities and responds to rescue the mind away from stressful mental limits. For example, a football player makes a daring tackle, with risks, at emotional limits and learns to become a better player. There are many ways we can experience limits to heal and improve abilities.

Most of us are aware of three-dimensional holograms constructed on a flat two-dimensional surface. Virtual higher-dimensional mental holograms are constructed on complex brain cell membrane configurations within the brain.

Subconscious processing or "sub-thinking" is modeled as image manipulation and integration of virtual higher-dimensional mental holograms. Learning from dream analyses, subconscious processes integrate flowing or analogue mental holograms to form memories and thoughts. In dreams we view changing three-dimensional perspectives of holographic dream characters. Higher dimensions are emotional and spiritual dimensions. Subconscious, and dream, higher-dimensional holograms are human mental binary language processes for developing conscious thought.

Mental improvement goals are to heal generations. Healing is accomplished with methodical, inventive processes. Healing processes are a significant step forward. We take one small mental step at a time to make one giant mental leap for mankind.

Bipolar Blessings & Mind Expansion, 2nd Edition, should help heal overstressed minds of those who can look critically and creatively at themselves. Releasing imbedded trauma scars brings stability and expands our most prized possession, our minds.

Exercising neck, throat, and to a lesser extent all, muscles, make the brain and mind flexible. A flexible mind is creative and spends less time worrying about the past or future.

With input from the body, the brain constructs abilities of the mind, including consciousness. In turn consciousness directs subconscious processes that control the brain and body to navigate "inner" and external environments. Thinking and life are recursive, inner iterative processes, which may converge or diverge.

Models are improved by learning from earlier models and experiments. Science discoveries begin as educated guesses or theories which suggest experiments or models to prove or disprove ideas. Today's quality of life is based upon yesterday's dreams. Mind healing and integration of science and spirituality are break-through efforts to improve quality of life.

Bipolar disorder becomes a lifetime job of managing bipolar thoughts and moods, or the development of "one's own cure." The author's cure is described in this book. The cure takes years of work. Sanity and stability are worth all efforts of the afflicted and their families.

A key in helping family and friends manage bipolar disorder is for them to distinguish between manic motivated speech and actions and normal activities. If thoughts are manic, one might say, "I am king of the world." A support person might say, "Your thinking and actions are manic. Begin deep slow breathing while we get you to your doctor or the hospital." If thoughts are depressed and sounding such as, "No one cares about me. I have no reason to live." It is wise to act quickly and get professional help before things get worse.

Erratic behaviors cause the public to be prejudiced against and stigmatize manic-depressives. With education and patience, stigmas and prejudices disappear. During one manic episode for his own protection, the author spent a night in jail.

When manic and less efficient in meeting routine daily tasks, the "normal public" stigmatize the newly spiritual as the lesser of all mentally challenged, since they originally had abilities to make decisions in their lives.

With patience, and God's help, manic-depressives have ability to overcome stigmas and flourish within social and spiritual environments.

One goal is to entice the physics community into modeling normal and manic brains and minds to improve thinking for both. Creatively, this task might be on the order of difficulty of quantum mechanics, general relativity, or "String Theory."

Every thought is a potential force for accomplishing goals or increasing frustrations. Memories are only reflections of our thoughts and lives. Only we alone can control our minds and imaginations. Imaginations are our futures.

After surviving severe illness, it is an honor to be alive. The author is grateful and blessed to be a cured manic-depressive. His disorder has allowed an extraordinary analysis of his own brain, mind, soul, the universe, heaven, and God. With normal thinking and mental healing, we are fortunate. With spiritual healing, we are most fortunate.

You will never think the same about your brain and mind after reading *Bipolar Blessings & Mind Expansion,* 2nd Edition. Enjoy mental benefits of unique exercises and models of the mind! Enhance spiritual abilities by reasoning about the brain, mind, universe, and God rather than simply memorizing spiritual books.

REFERENCES:

(1) *The Holy Bible - New International Version - Disciples' Study Bible,* 1984, Holman Bible Publishers, Nashville, Tennessee.

(2) Fulcher, Hugh D., *Bipolar Blessing & Mind Expansion,* 2008, H Fulcher Publishers, a Division of Wide Acceptance Financial, Inc., Lynchburg, VA.

(3) Fulcher, Hugh D., *The Clear Mind Procedure,* 2007, H Fulcher Publishers, a Division of Wide Acceptance Financial, Inc., Lynchburg, VA.

(4) Blumenthal, James A., et al., *Effects of Exercise Training on Older Patients with Major Depression,* October 25, 1999, Archives of Internal Medicine.

(5) Babyak, Michael, et al., *Exercise Treatment for Major Depression: Maintenance of Therapeutic Benefit at 10 Months,* September/October 2000, Psychosomatic Medicine.

(6) Fulcher, Hugh D., *Emotional Mind Modeling,* 1995, H D Fulcher Publishers, Inc., Lynchburg, VA.

(7) Fulcher, Hugh D, *God the Universe, & You!,* 2nd Edition, 2009, H Fulcher Publishers, Lynchburg, VA.

Chapter 2
Caveman Dreams

"To cast a thought into the stream,
Is life a reality or is it a dream?
All of the things that we think can be
Seem to conflict with the feeling to be free
It's only a movie and has been from the start
Become your own director and get a good part."

Keylow, a homeless poet

Let's dream a simple story to think differently about our minds and lives. In this Caveman dream, our ancestors had a very different life and way of thinking than we do today. Emotions and fear were frequently high. Caveman's survival allowed us to live.

Let's escape from our present way of thinking and go back to Caveman's era to put ourselves in perspective. His behavior, skills, and developing genes had much to do with our brains and bodies. What kind of lifestyle did Caveman have? Life was harsh with daily struggles for survival. It was kill or be killed. Strength and cunning determined whether he would live another day.

Fear kept Caveman alert and emotional. However, too much fear could blunt Caveman's edge for survival. With frequent fears of being eaten or death, Caveman felt thankful for each day. From this perspective, Caveman was probably very spiritual. Since chosen by God, Caveman's spiritual communications may have been the only thing that kept him from becoming extinct.

Unlike our proper society, I imagine a time when Caveman expressed emotions in an uninhibited fashion. Psychology has determined that moderate stress enhances creative thinking and solutions better than either stress-free or severe stress environments. Caveman learned to handle stress for us to live. Psychiatrists today would say all cavemen were manic-depressives.

Let's look at the time when Caveman was communicating mostly by a series of grunts. Language was formative. Non-verbal was the basic way of communicating. At that time woman played a supporting role to man. This role included nurturing and raising children. Because of physical strength and possibly fierceness, man ruled woman. Today that structure no longer applies.

Let's take a historical look back at our great, - - -, great, grandfather and grandmother. We might think of them as G...G Mom and G...G Dad or simply refer to them as Caveman and Cavewoman. In any event, we should love them as they were our ancestors. We are alive today because they cultivated skills for survival and had an innate need to mate and nurture offspring for reflected approval, love, and hope for the future.

Caveman didn't use words, but he thought. He used grunts, groans, and probably coos of approval and intimacy. Words were not necessary for thought. Now days we believe we are not thinking if we are not mentally developing words. But, we drive down the highway for miles or vacuum our house while thinking but without one word entering our minds. Words are building blocks for "complex and future" planning. Future planning is active rather than reactive thinking. Caveman could do active planning without the use of words. Most of Caveman's thinking was short term, but he planned ahead for seasonal changes.

Caveman traveled long distances during hunting trips and returned home without roads or maps. This same navigation task would overwhelm most of us today. Sense of direction is a complex mental function. Complexity of verbal thinking has probably caused loss of directional skills.

There may be benefits for re-cultivating caveman skills in non-verbal thinking and navigation. Since we do not understand fully how Caveman thought or how animals think without words, we use the catch-all term "instinct." Thinking in words has strengthened some mental skills and caused some ancestral skills to become extinct. If we don't use skills, we lose them.

Just how did Caveman think? He thought as we should think most of the time today. Caveman "thought" by manipulating mental, or "dream" images. He planned for the future by manipulating remembered images. Thinking in vivid mental images is easier than in words. It is the natural language of the mind. We dream in vivid and active images with few words. As children learn languages, the task is so difficult that they often lose much of their visual or image-manipulating skills and memorize uninteresting, abstract letters and words. We should cultivate thinking in mental images. Imagination means manipulating images for thinking processes. Imaginative people think in images.

Caveman was imaginative because he thought only in images, sign language, and possibly a few sounds. Caveman's hieroglyphics were pictorial images on cave walls. To recapture some of Caveman's mental skills, we need to practice manipulating mental images as Caveman did. We should continue to think in words when we are writing or verbally communicating with others. With practice, we can become more imaginative and exciting individuals.

Let's look at our cave family's lifestyle. The entire family is hungry and fed up with berries and roots. The family is hungry for meat. Cavedad beats himself on the chest and makes signs of height, length, ferocity, and a funny distortion of his nose. Without a word the whole family knows Cavedad is going to bring home a wild boar for dinner. The family is elated; wild boar is a family favorite. As Cavedad prepares to leave for the hunt, he makes many ferocious growls. The family has no doubt that Cavedad will be strong, fierce and the family provider as his growls indicate.

As Cavedad disappears in the distance, Cavemom and Cavechildren idolize Cavedad. Caveboys dream of the day they can make deep growls and hunt the wild boar.

With a sharpened stick, the hunt is on. Caveman knows the wild boars feed several miles away. He studies the terrain and makes mental notes of landmarks.

Cavegrandfather taught him to study terrain and identify the favorite plants that wild boars eat without using a word. As Caveman nears the hunting area, he stops to eat berries and rest.

Meanwhile, back at the cave the children are playing games pretending to hunt the wild boar. Without a word, Cavedad has told many stories of hunting wild boar. Excitement is high. No emotions are suppressed. Cavefamily expressing emotions at limits was good for our DNA development. Expressing emotions at limits frees the brain of trauma effects. In the cave, the family is so manic that today the whole family would be placed in a psychiatric ward.

Rested, Cavedad begins the hunt. He searches for hours and finds no fresh wild boar tracks. At one point Caveman avoids being eaten by a mountain lion. With courage restored he searches for a new area to hunt. After a while he spots plants that wild boars eat. It is getting dark and too dangerous to hunt wild boar in the darkness. Caveman finds a cave. Sleep is restless; no place is safe.

Meanwhile, back at the cave, the family begins to worry about Cavedad not returning. The fearless growls Cavedad performed, to convince the family that he was the fiercest of hunters, are fading with time in the Cavefamily's minds. They worry wordless thoughts that Cavedad may not return and wonder what they would do without him. Time fades the most confident gestures even today. Doubts lurk in the minds of our Cavefamily. No one sleeps well in the cave that night.

As trained in not so gentle a fashion by his father, Caveman knows that he can show no fear; the wild senses fear. Caveman must be strong for his family and for us, his descendants. Morning breaks with a determined Caveman ready to hunt. He leaves the shallow cave with his spear and finds fresh wild boar tracks. He waits quietly with his wooden spear cocked.

After some time the wanted prize approaches. As the prey nears, Caveman jumps and thrusts his spear into the wild boar's flank as the animal turns to run. Caveman picks up his spear, runs as hard and fast as he can after the wounded prey. His "neck," is jerked around in all directions to limits. Emotions override his fear with his aggressive will to succeed. His aggression exceeds that of modern-day football players.

Running on adrenaline, he gains on his weakening prey. The wounded boar senses his closeness and wheels around in defense with tusks and teeth attacking. An injury may mean death to Caveman. There are no hospitals or antiseptics. Options are kill or be killed. Caveman avoids tusks and teeth and thrusts his spear into the shoulder of the boar. The blow is effective; the boar is down. Frantically, Caveman repeatedly thrusts his spear into the boar's heart until there is no resistance. Fear and aggression fade into elation. Our ancestor yells triumphantly in a manic fashion. The human race will survive. Caveman is master of his universe.

Caveman's hunger returns with a vengeance. He uses his "strong jaw and neck" muscles to rip the flesh from the carcass. Frantically he devours until his hunger is more than satisfied. Winning the Super Bowl is not near as emotional. Fighting for emotional family causes brings out the beast in Caveman. The family unit should still be our most important relationship. Be your beast for your family!

Caveman drags the carcass toward his cave home. His navigational abilities are remarkable. After a long, dragging journey, a triumphant growl alerts the family that Cavedad is home. It's supper time. Family fears turn into manic elation. No family has ever been happier. What a great time to be alive!

Cavemom and Cavechildren enjoy the feast. After the feast, the gorged children fall asleep with wild-eyed dreams of the hunt and their hero, Cavedad. Basic instincts fill Caveman. He is lucky to have a loving Cavewife and Cavechildren. Even though, Caveman is rough around the edges, Cavewife is proud of him. He and Cavewife sleep together feeling a completeness words cannot express. Nine months later your, G . . . . G, Grandfather is born.

Caveman risked his life for his family. It was his "instinct." There was family interdependence. Today, we are so independent.

Do we have caveman instincts within us, or are diversions filtering our duties of caring for our families? Has lack of life-threatening fear re-duced the family "spirit" and destroyed common goals? Is the family still a unit? Both Caveman and Cavewoman turn into beasts to fight for that which is greater than them selves. They fight for their family unit. Whose life would you fight to preserve? We are descended from Cave-man. We have the instinct to survive. Caveman survived so we could live.

Without daily challenges and traumas, we have lost innate abilities. We no longer learn from frequent fears and reactions at limits. Sense of smell was a significant learning process for Caveman. For generations, clothes have deadened skin awareness that historically provided aware-ness of nearby threats or romance. We have evolved and also reverse evolved.

Emotions and physical stress at "limits," and an alert skin purged Cave-man's neck and brain of trauma effects. Caveman thought with a "clear mind," which is discussed throughout this book. Usually, current gen-erations retain repressed and inhibiting emotional memories or disrup-tive trauma scars throughout life. Recalling our roots might help us heal from repressed trauma effects. This dream helps us think about early life without words.

Mind models in later chapters also help us think differently for improving thinking processes. "Neck" was in quotation marks several times in this chapter to emphasize that neck exercises were important in developing "the clear mind."

Chapter 3
Being Normal!

Lord, Let me live like a Regular Man,
With Regular friends and true;
Let me play the game on a Regular plan
And play it that way all through;
Let me win or lose with a Regular Smile
And never be known to whine,
For that is a Regular Fellow's style
And I want to make it mine!

Oh, give me a Regular chance in life,
The same as the rest, I pray,
And give me a Regular girl for a wife
To help me along the way;
Let us know the lot of humanity,
Its regular woes and joys
And raise a Regular family
Of regular girls and boys!

Let me live to a Regular good old age,
With Regular snow-white hair,
Having done my labor and earned my wage
And played my game for fair;
And so at last when the people scan

My face on its peaceful bier,
They'll say, "Well, he was a Regular Man!"
And drop a Regular tear!

Berton Braley

Most of us feel normal most of the time, but some of us rarely feel normal. In many cases, feeling normal means feeling the way we usually feel and sometimes feeling good about ourselves. Feeling normal depends upon the quality of childhood, current lifestyle, self-acceptance and acceptance by significant others.

Being normal means accomplishing easy and difficult tasks and is determined by our attitude toward our activities and interactions with others. It means "fitting in" with whom we interact and deem significant. When sick, doctors often assure us that for our current physical and mental condition our pains and emotions are "normal." We feel better knowing we are "normal" even "normally" ill.

"Normal" has the attribute of being accepted by people in authority or by the general caring population. Normal to a young individual may mean that things are currently occurring in family life the way they usually do. This environment could be nurturing and loving for confidence building with a good probability of developing a confident and useful member of society.

Unfortunately, for too many children, life consists of yelling, threats, and violence. A child from this environment has a greater probability of having lifelong insecurities, less mental freedom, and reactive violence toward others.

Those who have suffered deeply often do not mind making others suffer; it's "normal." Love is not learned. The emotionally injured do not understand why others love and act caringly as they do. They have no mental model of love. Some emotionally injured think "normal" people are just pretending to be happy. There is a tendency to think everyone thinks much as we do.

Abused children who have not learned to love see strength and power as the social rule. Strength gets what it wants, and weakness does not matter and is meant to be abused. The abused were destroyed when they were young and weak. They will not "be destroyed" again.

It is normal to believe in basic things as the sun will rise tomorrow. No matter if we are scientists or atheists; we must believe in many things from experience or by faith without going through a scientific proof on every occasion. We must have faith in our abilities to interact with our environment, or we can do nothing. We express faith in many ways.

Profession of faith strengthens beliefs and unites those reciting them together. We have beliefs other than religious beliefs. We believe in our senses most of the time. Listed below are some beliefs I reflect upon:

1) The goodness and values established by my mother and father. 2) love and forgiveness; 3) education, self-study, and work ethic; 4) some hurt others for selfish goals; 5) protecting the safety and lives of others; 6) showing kindness when possible; 7) preciseness of scientific principles and mathematical analyses; 8) looking for goodness in people; 9) having a positive attitude and brainstorming solutions to problems; 10) individual freedom of speech; 11) everyone has the right to pursue dreams as far as abilities allow with happiness and security; 12) the awesome responsibilities of parenthood and supervising others with love and respect; 13) competition in careers and sports; 14) the US government's established systems of checks and balances for citizen's protection; 15) prayer, Jesus, and God; 16) psychiatric process for physically reconstructing the brain; 17) and you. (You are reading to improve your mind.)

Many of us are familiar with the scientific method and its principles which are designed to understand the behavior and laws of nature. We cannot prove all ideas we hold as facts. Depending upon childhood and adult life, we have developed systems for establishing beliefs and doubts.

Believing too easily or doubting too quickly can make interactions difficult or dangerous. We have developed value systems for evaluating day-to-day decisions. With varied lives, we often have conflicts in our value systems. Some level of conflict in life is good for mind development.

Without conflict our brains would have no reactions and do nothing. Every new idea has some conflict with past experiences. Normal people have learned to manage smaller and larger levels of conflict. They are able to reduce inner conflict and resolve conflicts with others. Ill adjusted people are not able to reduce their inner conflicts or resolve conflicts with others.

Babies are filled with God's Spirit. They are spiritually born perfect but experience conflict in learning earthly things.

Being science and religious oriented develops conflict. We believe in prayer but do not understand prayer communication as we do sound or electromagnetic communication. Throughout religions, miracles have occurred with importance and awe. We do not understand miracles with current scientific technology. In one hundred years from now, our descendents will still know only a very small portion of God's great designs and truths. We continue to crawl using the paths of knowledge we and our forefathers have learned and not forgotten.

Each of us has a philosophy of life characterized by significant rules. These psychological rules make our lives normal or abnormal. Many rules were learned at an early age from significant role models. Humans and computers perform as programmed. A few rules and attitudes are listed below:

I feel good about myself.
I hate myself.
I like the way I look.
I hate the way I look.

Others act superior to me.
I am humble and act superior to no one.
I act superior to make others feel inferior.

Competition is everything; I'm only as good as my last win. Life is all or nothing.
I don't compete in anything.

I do my best work under pressure; I love challenges.
I prefer work I know I can accomplish successfully.

I reassure people during hardships and at work.
I have enough to do without worrying about others.
Some people deserve to fail.

I take time to make people feel comfortable.
No one takes time to make me feel comfortable.

Act like a gentleman/lady.
I can express my feelings to others.
What good does it do to talk about feelings?
I think about sex frequently.
I avoid thinking about sex.
My sex partner should know what to do.

I can positively talk about race with other races.
I try to make all races feel good and important.
I put down other races with gestures or words.

I am truthful with others.
I stretch the truth to make myself look superior.

I can solve problems working with others.
Others slow me down.

I have strong likes and dislikes.
Most anything pleases me.
I have lots of friends.
I don't trust anyone.

Family comes first.
Job, power, money, and my security come first.
I'm a high achiever.
I just try to get by.

I honor my father and mother.
I don't visit home; there is always a fuss.

I control with gestures, body language, and veiled threats.
I only control when helping others.
I am hurt when others control and degrade me.

I try to go beyond expectations.
I do what others expect me to do.
I do things my way.

I can achieve a higher state of consciousness.
I try to have a consistent level of thought and achievement.

I believe dreams are significant to my life.
I don't think about or remember dreams.
I am always true to myself and to others.
Others influence me too much.
I am only true to myself.
Most people are good to me.
Everyone puts me down.
I worship at church.
I don't trust those hypocrites.

Praying relaxes me.
I don't believe in God.

I am dependable.
I do what I want.
I have my own personal values and standards.
I live according to values and standards set by others.

My ego is wrapped up in my work.
My ego is wrapped up in my family.

If I get ill, my spouse will take care of me.
If my spouse gets ill, I will take care of her/him.

I visit and cheer up friends in the hospital.
I love and show affection.
I don't feel the need to love or show affection.

I tease to share fun with family and friends.
I tease to have fun at the expense of others.

I dream of doing great things.
Things will always be the same.
I am a good leader.
I am a good follower.

I take pride in my work, family, competitions, and religion.
I have no pride in myself, work, or family.

I make things complicated; it makes me appear smart.
I make things simple to help others learn.
I feel good about myself without drinking.
Drinking livens up my life.

When drinking I hide my inferiority by lying and accusing my "inferior" spouse and friends of not "thinking right."

Drunks have a false, superior ego.
Drinking causes people to degrade themselves and others.

Don't waste time.
Don't be late.
Plan ahead.
Live one day at a time.

Neither a borrower nor a lender be.
I pay debts on time.
I avoid those I owe money.

Get a good education.
Study hard, have patience, and you will succeed.

Who needs an education?
I've got to "have it all right now."
Drugs and stealing are my life.

Stay away from the wrong crowd.
Be part of the "in" crowd.

The list is rather random. Normal can be achieved in so many ways. Self-fulfillment usually means doing things we like and being accepted by those who are significant to us. It feels good to fit in where we want to belong, be confident, and truly love and be loved. It is important to justify reasons for selecting our rules of life. We must evaluate our rules and values often. Inner peace is second in importance to security. The depressed mind slows down, loses inner peace, and loses faith of restoring inner peace.

Some rules listed usually do not lead to a fulfilled life. If attitudes toward life are negative, we tend to spend more time in unproductive thinking. Often our unhappiness points to emotional injuries encountered in childhood when weak, vulnerable, and could not take care of ourselves. At this time we had no confidence in ourselves but developed confidence in parents and caretakers. Lack of nurturing in early life often results in lack of confidence in adult life. The unfortunate thing about long time suffering is that eventually some of us do not mind making or seeing others suffer. "Suffering" has become normal; why should we suffer alone?

We feel normal when we feel we fit in. A gang member who has pride in mugging and killing others for power or money is normal to his gang. Those beyond his gang are to be preyed upon.

As responsible members of a broader society, we need, for everyone's sake, to bring the severely tormented and misguided into a lifestyle that is healthy and nurturing. We need to rehabilitate those who would do harm to others. Transforming minds, with false pride and survival-hardened attitudes, is difficult. Crime, drugs, and threatening behaviors develop a sense of power and pride in overcoming victims and avoiding punishment.

Criminals will do anything to maintain their power base. The attitude is of having "absolute power" or of being worthless. "Heroes" are willing to risk their lives for "their gang." Members are pathetic without their gangs. We need to mentally heal these unfortunates before they are incarcerated.

There is an aspect of normal we must not forget. This aspect is not learned in words. It is the world of body language. A smile can brighten one's day. A hug or a warm handshake can sometimes raise someone's self-esteem. A friendly glance can initiate a wonderful friendship. A positive nod of the head can give others confidence in collecting and presenting ideas.

On the other hand, a frown from an authority figure can reduce us to shambles. Negative body language can cause our mind to run in circles without knowing what was expected or done incorrectly. Standing too close can be threatening.

Looking or walking away when others are talking reduces the importance of that person. The most dangerous controllers say positive things and then negate the words with body language. Mixed messages are normal for emotionally scarred, degrading individuals. Normal for each of us includes both verbal and non-verbal communication. In caring people, verbal and non-verbal communications complement each other.

Behavior rules for one person may not be compatible with those of another. In severe cases one individual may become life threatening to another. This book stresses prevention of mental suffering by reconstructing the mind. Truly adjusting mental attitudes requires changes to the fabric of the brain. Techniques are designated as "mind modeling" and "mental reconstruction." With these new techniques we can restructure subconscious processes to become more organized, efficient, and productive.

Improved and expanded thinking builds confidence with increased ability to love. Mental restructuring takes years of work. With practice and dedication, healing techniques become logical and even normal.

It is one's own choice to select a path of mind modeling and mental reconstruction. The author does not recommend processes to those who are pleased with their thinking. These methods have been practiced only by the author, may have different effects on readers, and take shorter or longer times. Technologies are a new frontier. There are risks in new things. Adventurers must choose methods at their own pace and risk.

There are false spiritual leaders we do not consider normal. They teach "others" to commit suicide and blow up innocent people. They think they are justified to kill those who worship differently. False martyrs are normal in some religions.

We have listed various guidelines for being "normal." The remainder of this book will concentrate more on the abnormal and on "new" ways of analyzing the brain and mind. With practice over time, the abnormal can become the normal.

Bloodletting, shock treatment, and pre-frontal lobotomies were once normal treatments. Today, PET scans, surgeries, and psychiatric drugs are normal for diagnosing and healing. Healing adventures given here may become normal.

Models and healing processes are presented truthfully as recalled by the author but are sometimes stranger than fantasies of childhood dreams.

Chapter 4

The Flash!

Death Be Not Proud

Death be not proud, though some have called thee
Mighty and dreadful, for thou art not so;
For those whom thou think'st thou dost overthrow
Die not, poor death, nor yet canst thou kill me.
From rest and sleep, which but thy pictures be,
Much pleasure, then from thee much more must flow,
And soonest our best men with thee do go,
Rest of their bones, and soul's delivery.
Thou art slave to fate, chance, kings, and desperate men,
And dost with poison, war, and sickness dwell,
And poppy, or charms can make us sleep as well,
And better than thy stroke; why swell'st thou then?
One short sleep past, we wake eternally,
And death shall be no more; death, thou shalt die.

John Donne

Those of us fortunate enough to have grown up in supportive families usually feel normal and accepted by families and communities. We usually look at the positive side of social interactions and life. As young adults we were looking forward for tomorrow being better than today.

While attending college many of us thought that the sky was our only limit. "Our" generation would take knowledge beyond current visions. We were dreamers!

In 1966 as a junior studying physics at Virginia Tech, my attitude was usually positive, even though I had to study harder than many students. Courses were exciting, and I studied consistently with some lapses into social pressures. It was the night before registration for spring quarter, and there was a party in Lynchburg, Virginia. I attended this party and returned to my parents' home near Temperance, Virginia, after midnight. The unusual thing was I needed to get up at 5:00 A.M. and travel one hundred and twenty miles to Virginia Tech to register for classes. The alarm awakened me. I had never felt so tired. It was a struggle to get ready for the drive. I finally felt awake enough and left for Blacksburg at about 6:00 A.M.

The drive was safe until I began nodding. Eventually, a dangerous thought occurred that I could rest while driving. Several times a nod would awaken me, and I thought how dumb to rest when driving. My tiredness was always with me.

Finally, it happened! I fell asleep at the wheel. My head nodded down and awakened me. As my head recovered, immediate awareness swept throughout my being. My foot had relaxed on the accelerator and the speedometer was reading 80 MPH. Suddenly, I was aware that a tractor trailer was only a few yards in front of me going about 25 MPH up a mountain. I started for the brake, but immediately knew it was useless. There was no way life could continue. Reason had lost all hope of life.

In fear, my life flashed before my eyes as I prepared to die. Rapidly, the thought occurred to use the center lane to pass the truck. Miraculously after "the flash," my arm jerked the steering wheel to the left. Tires screeched. Someone else seemed to be driving. I was a concerned and displaced bystander in a tragic dream. There were two lanes up and one lane down the mountain.

As I entered the center lane, another semi-tractor was coming down the mountain towards me. My hand jerked the steering wheel to the right. Tires screeched again. With God's help, I went between those two tractor-trailers going 80 MPH. The ordeal was over in a flash. In seconds, I was trembling like a leaf. Feelings linger to this day that no racecar driver could have avoided those obstacles without God's help. There was no difficulty staying alert the rest of the trip.

This story never ended. I always wondered about "the Flash" that occurred when my rational mind had given up hope of living. I thought about "the Flash" for many years. During excitement of manic episodes years later, I was able to conclude that the visions were of emotional experiences with concern or elation but with successful endings for my benefit. A keen interest remained in this miracle that seemed so abnormal yet so wonderful. After several years of psychiatric practices, many of the visions that were so hurriedly and profoundly experienced were recalled. In mania, my highly emotional mind became able to recall visions experienced in the highly emotional "Flash."

So many visions occurred in such a short time. "The flash" is important for my dreaming and mind development theories. The speed of the visions has always interested me. Estimates are that, in less than one tenth of a second, one hundred vivid memories of significant emotional events flashed through consciousness. "The flash" occurred between the time I was aware of the truck and before my hand jerked the steering wheel to the left. An estimate is made for the "apparent time span of all visions." Each vision seemed to last for an apparent or virtual time of ten minutes. Some visions appeared to last for an extremely long time. Assumptions are conservative. Let's perform a calculation for the "Apparent Time Span of all Visions" (ATSVs):

ATSVs = 10 minutes x 100 visions x 60 seconds/minute

ATSVs = 60,000 seconds of apparent or virtual visions

Let's look at the ratio of the apparent vision time span and the Actual Time (AT):

Ratio = ATSVs/AT = 60,000/.1 = 600,000

This simple calculation estimates that during "the Flash" the conscious mind processed nearly one million times faster than normal. Thank God we have capacity to think very fast in certain death situations. Subconscious processes momentarily became conscious. The flash was an unusual awareness of normal subconscious processes making emotional decisions. Why can we not become aware of more subconscious processes for our benefit?

God gave me "the Flash" to save me from this crisis or my brain has the capacity to produce "the Flash." If God gave me "the Flash," I have little capacity to understand it. The brain is electrical and chemical and has the capacity to function very fast. During "the Flash" as in a dream, I simply observed and was aware that no judgments were made in the scenarios. I, as an observer, also made no judgments on scenarios. Scenes of life just happened. It seemed the body was frozen, and the conscious mind was an unbiased, non-judgmental observer to a tragic play. The mind had a huge capacity to order significant emotional events selectively into consciousness during this "certain death" ordeal.

Normally, if we recall an event, it is replayed in real time. From "the Flash," we learn the brain can accelerate recalled scenarios. The mind has an unusual fast forward capacity. A goal is to learn how recalled scenes can be replayed at such fast speeds in chronological order. A flavor of "Flash" visions is included:

When I was two or three years old, my older brother was taking toys from me. We were playing in the backyard near the porch. Enough was enough! Choosing my best weapon, I shrieked. "I had him now." God was on my side. However, my brother told a different story. This was my first awareness that words could distort history. It was an emotional occurrence. I did not have the ability to counter in words. My innocence of language was lost. Words were not always Gospel.

At three and four years old, it seemed to take forever for dad to come home from work. There were many occurrences of asking

Mother how much longer until dad comes home. I would watch through the window and become ecstatic when dad's car turned into the driveway.

In 1949, the family car was a 1939 Ford. When four years old, my dad let me go to the town of Amherst with him. He said he might buy a new car. Dad bought a "brand new" 1949 Ford. No one could have been prouder of his Dad, and himself, than I was that day. In this vision, I was beaming. I probably would have glowed in the dark.

My brother and I told my mother about a snake on the back porch. This gentle woman took a pistol and unsuccessfully tried to shoot the snake. We could feel her fear. Dad's coming home eased her and my anxieties.

I was about seven or eight years old and the neighborhood boys and I were building a bridge. The other boys were older. We had cut logs that spanned a gully and were nailing planks across the logs. My foot slipped, and I slid down the bank onto one of the logs. Hitting the log knocked the breath out of me. In agony, I ran crying through the cow pasture, under the fence, and up the long hill to our house. In this vision, I was surprised to remember exactly how the grass and everything looked as I was running. By the time I reached mother, the crying had stopped. Mother gave a hug and a kiss, and away I went back to the important task of building the bridge. Mother's image was so clear. Her love and concern were so real in the vision. I lived in caring times back then.

I first took communion at Ivy Hill United Methodist church when eleven. The blood of Jesus was represented by grape juice. As I knelt and drank the "blood of Christ," my whole body felt a warmth and aliveness I had never felt before. I asked my mother many times if wine could have been used in place of grape juice. Her answer was always, no. I had a wonderful experience and felt God had spoken to me.

I was sixteen playing baseball at Amherst High School. As a left-hander, I played first base. There was a fly ball between first base and home plate. The catcher and I collided. We both had gashes over our right eyes. Blood was everywhere. Only briefly were thoughts of serious injury. This vision was long waiting for the ambulance, the ride, in the emergency room, and getting stitches.

The details of these highly emotional visions demonstrate the mind has extraordinary ability for storing information. Visions were of stress or extreme elation with successful endings. There was even time to "feel" the emotions. Like dreams, the content of visions was difficult to recall later. For many visions, the themes were, "I don't have a chance; I am going to die." Years later manic excitement stimulated recall of some of these memories.

Emotions are felt in dreams. The displacement quality of the dreamer viewing his own image is amazing. The mind constructs the dreamer's image so he sees himself as others would see him. Settings may be real or exaggerated. However, images of self and well known people are usually realistic.

Image displacement in dreams is no small mental feat. It and actions in dreams support the theory that a basic function of the mind is manipulating mental holograms. Displacement also shows we are very aware how others see us. Displacement in dreams is due to an uncertainty or fear of being observed when we do not want to be observed.

There are differences between flash visions, normal visions, and dreams. In flash visions, scenes are presented at many times real speed. My image was not displaced in flash visions. I saw environments from my real life vantage point. Normal visions are constructed at normal life speeds and scenes are observed also without displacement. Dreams occur at fast but slower speeds than flash visions. This could be due to added mental processes needed for displacement. Emotions are felt in all three.

"The flash" was a hundred scenarios spliced together running fast-forward at nearly one million times normal speed. The "flash" vision producer had time to select and edit scenarios for this spiritual movie.

However, scenarios may have been previously selected for different life threatening experiences. Survival is genetically programmed within our minds. Subconscious minds can be awesome vision producers. A thought occurred that the soul produced important scenarios of our lives for God's Judgment.

Everyone experiences "a flash" at the moment of death. If we learn about the subconscious mind, we may be able to construct "flashes" with better content for God's Judgment. "Flashes" occur during abrupt life threatening crises.

"The flash" has been instrumental in developing models of the brain, and hologram models within the mind.

Chapter 5
Early Mind Healing

Here we are, all, by day; by night we're hurled
By dreams, each by one, into a several world.

William Browne

Upon awakening we sometimes have "feelings" we have dreamed, but memory of dreams have dissipated and been lost. Dreaming begins at emotional levels that existed just before sleep.

Analyzing waking thoughts is sometimes difficult to do. It is more difficult to analyze bizarre dreams. A goal of this chapter is to gain dream awareness and relate dreams to waking life.

Thinking depends upon subconscious and dream processes. A common way of examining subconscious processes is from insight acquired when abruptly awakened and quickly recording dreams. We have little control over dream content and emotions.

After a brief digression, we study dreams. A principle of physics is that nature loves "energy efficiency." We are normally aware when we have done activities efficiently. We feel good when we have increased effectiveness in things we do. We want thinking to be organized and efficient. Smooth and efficient performances in running and dancing are things of beauty to behold. We sense and enjoy energy efficiency.

We are not energy efficient when hurting or dysfunctional. Trauma and emotional experiences cause physical scars in neural networks reducing their efficiency. Freud discovered that recalling and reliving hurtful early childhood experiences released trauma scar and mental tensions. Releasing repressed trauma energy for psychiatric healing is a theme throughout this book.

Exercises and energy release sensations have shown that pent-up trauma energy is stored in, and released from, shells. Releasing all energy from a trauma scar shell exposes the next slightly less energetic shell for stimulation and release.

Sigmund Freud

Among other things, Dr. Sigmund Freud is remembered for his dream analyses. Freud's work extended from the 1880s to the 1930s. He developed a methodology known as psychoanalysis. My work extends Freud's healing processes for releasing repressed trauma tensions. Psychophysiotherapy (PPT) is the name of my processes using physical exercises for healing and mind models for guiding subconscious processes. Psychophysioanalysis (PPA) is analysis for selecting exercises and models for mental healing.

I give only basic ideas of Freud's work as much of his work is difficult to follow. My work is easier to understand and should provide similar, if not expanded, benefits. After all, in retrospect, I have had the benefit of his creative work. References to Freud given here are from: *Sigmund Freud: The Interpretation of Dreams* [1], translation by James Strachey.

I remember in the early '60s there were frequent jokes about Freud being a quack. This is not so today. Let us look into Freud's dream world. He reiterates often that disturbance of sleep causes dreams to be remembered. Freud's hypothesis is:

"Dreams are more often forgotten than waking thoughts because they are too weak or because the mental excitation attached to them was too slight. The same holds good for dream-images: they are forgotten because they are too weak, while stronger images adjacent to them are remembered." (1965, p76).

Usually in waking life, occurrences of the greatest intensity are remembered longest. According to Freud, waking thoughts are converted into relational images in dreams. These images "dramatize" an idea, (Spitta, 1882, p83). We do not think through our dreams, but we experience them as if an observer at a play. Freud states:

> "Reports of numerous cases as well as the collection of instances made by Chabaneix (1897) seem to put it beyond dispute that dreams can carry on the intellectual work of daytime and bring it to conclusions which had not been reached during the day." (1965, p97).

During Freud's time there were differences of opinion about responsibility for dreams. Some thought that responsibilities for dream content were the same as for waking thoughts and actions. Others felt, as we do today, that dreaming was an emotional outlet and no blame or responsibility needed to be given for inappropriate dreams. Dreams are created by a part of our subconscious minds that exist on the edge between confident knowledge and assumption. Incomplete mental activities during the day become more important than higher accomplishments. The dreaming brain works toward daily solutions in its rather odd way.

From my experience during severe stress, dreamlike qualities enter waking awareness and make functioning in normal environments strenuous and reasoning difficult. Inner (dreamlike) thoughts become more powerful than sensed environmental stimuli. The mind's processing during mental disorders (such as manic episodes) for worldly tasks can be as difficult to follow as understanding the actions of dream characters.

Krauss (1859, p123) writes,

"Insanity is a dream dreamt while the senses are awake."

In manic episodes, dream scenarios become mixed with real life. Situations may become dangerous to the dreamer while awake. During manic episodes, the afflicted have little concern for their environment and confuse inner mental processes and dreams with waking sensory stimuli.

Humans have little idea what is real or reality? We see only through light, a small part of the electromagnetic spectrum. We would have a higher reality if we could sense, or "see" with, the entire electromagnetic spectrum as many believe God does. If we saw only in black and write, we would sense a higher "spiritual" reality if we began seeing in color.

Are thoughts not acted upon real? Are only physical things and actions real? Is a misconception in itself real? Reality is a relative concept. Some people have higher levels of reality than others. Is Einstein's relativity real? With quantum uncertainties, are elementary particles real? Is scientific understanding more real than biblical understanding? Is the integration of all awareness and cognition, God, the only true reality?

For years, most people did not believe psychotherapy was real. Dr. Freud emphasized that recalling traumatic repressed memories can free a person from its adverse effects. This is a foundation of Dr. Freud's psychoanalysis which is still used today. Psychoanalysis is included in my therapeutic methods and exercises in later chapters. Benefits to a mentally disoriented patient from psychoanalysis are enhanced by mental conditioning according to Freud. We must discover our own inner mental processes and eliminate guilt from things we had no control over.

Freud's methods of free association and the elimination of self criticism is included in "brainstorming" techniques currently used to develop group solutions to problems. Suppression of "critical" or negative ideas is crucial for developing a positive "flow" of creative ideas for problem solving and analyzing the subconscious mind. Without criticism the mind continues with creative ideas built upon previous creative ideas.

Becoming aware of induction into and awakening from sleep is one way of learning about the subconscious mind. During brief periods when minds transform between subconscious and conscious states, different areas of the brainstem become active or dominant. We see glimpses into the subconscious mind.

In dreams, waking experiences and verbal communications are transformed into visual and image content. Images in dreams are often constructed by conflict from similar-sounding words which were confusing for young minds to distinguish.

Dr. Freud stressed importance of mental attitude during waking activities before sleep. With increased self-observation before sleep, we can learn about our subconscious minds from our dreams. We should relax the face and mind before sleeping and think of long distance vision or pleasant future events. Forget about the details of the day. Relaxed thinking about God and praying before sleep is long range and right-brained thinking. The mind will not be constrained to worries of the day and dream creatively. If we can dream it we can think it.

Dr. Freud interprets most dreams as the "fulfillment of a wish" and describes the remembered dream image as the "manifest dream." The manifest dream consists of the visual images during dreams that are recalled. A part of Dr. Freud's dream analysis is to discover the origin of dream distortions.

Dream distortions occur since waking reason is reduced and is no longer needed. Distortion is due to subconsciously comparing "uncertain" remembered events to "certain" genetic and spiritual truths. Genetic truths were formed by repeated successful experiences throughout generations. Spiritual truths are formed by all successful events over all time throughout the universe.

It is not necessary to constrict dream logic to waking logic. The subconscious mind is consumed with coordinating conscious activities into memory libraries. The author's theory is that waking images and speech are organized more by emotional energy levels rather than by sequences of events.

Dr. Freud often stated that dreams are derived from the previous day and wishing a desired event to occur. Suppression of sexual desires is a source of frustrating dreams and even trauma scars. Dreams select visual content upon different principles from our waking memory. They do not recall what is essential and important but what is subsidiary and unnoticed. Dreams often include events related to early childhood impressions which, in waking, we would think were trivial and long forgotten.

Dreams include emotionally powerful and bizarre baby memories. Babies had to connect their genetic and holistic, spiritual background with a very different world. A baby's life is highly emotional as they struggle to make sense of a new world.

Our dream content is selected, to a large extent, on the emotional intensity of the previous day's experiences. Uncertainties that were only partially noticed during the day seem to force their importance into dreams.

The subconscious mind must reflect upon current events and relate them to historical memory libraries. This process is a self-focused act. Sleeping is time for self-focused inner processes and for reflecting subconscious processes to God for guidance. Waking is time for interacting with the environment and sharing with others. Sanity and well-being depend on subconscious self-centeredness during sleep. Physical facilities for interacting with others have been disabled while sleeping. From a philosophical standpoint, our minds should be expected to be self-centered during sleep.

Dr. Freud's practice included translating dream images into meaningful thoughts from previous days. Dream content is translated to the dream thought.

We become aware of dream-content when awakened at times. It is our normal subconscious processing language. During sleep, daily activities, stored within short-range dream-images, are retrieved from memory, amplified, de-amplified, sorted, organized, and integrated for comparison to historical memory images. New long range memories are stored according to genetic structures and synchronized with historical memories and their emotions for later recall and guiding future thoughts and actions.

Subconscious processes manipulate memory holograms for guiding and organizing conscious mental abilities. These processes compare to computers manipulating binary numbers to simplify, organize, and guide human activities.

Dream-content is revealed through analog or flowing processes rather than discrete digital manipulation of words. A fundamental concept is Dr. Freud's statements on displacement in dreams. We see dream activities as others might observe us. Often unimportant and insignificant things become important in dreams.

Dream associations and processes use mental technologies we developed as babies and children in trying to understand a new world. IQ's are tied to brain structure configured by waking and dream associations made early in life. At early ages, we developed mental associations when mental processes were highly emotional. Individual subconscious processes are very different.

Neural network structures had to be grown and connected. An emotional, frightened young brain was constructing a young mind. The young subconscious mind genetically knew it had to cope with a worldly environment. It had to learn like lightning. The young mind developed mental processes that were much faster than adult mental processes.

Dreams images seem absurd, but, translated into dream thought, they are always meaningful. Distortions in subconscious processes and dream content are results of early, and later, trauma scars. The mind never outgrows these distortions unless healed through psychotherapy or mental reconstruction practices.

Inconsistent baby and child attention to environments, and reactions to traumas, have constructed inefficient neural fabric and subconscious programming. Reconstructing overstressed neural networks and their processes requires dedication and persistence.

From psychoanalysis, we learn that many of our mental dysfunctions stem from early childhood. The development of brain structure and subconscious processes is made during histories in the womb, infancy, and childhood. In dreams, reasoning seems to go back to prenatal and infancy processes. An example is floating dreams. The infant before birth experienced floating in his mother's womb. Deep down it is not unreasonable to float in space. Dreams return us to safer, more comfortable times.

Dream processes return to infant times when we had little control over minds or bodies. In our dreams, we are only observers as we were observers in our waking infancy. Displacement in dreams seems natural. As infants we used displacement to live young lives through parents or caretakers. Through displacement we saw our parents as reality more than our own reality. As infants, we did not try to control our environment. We simply observed images and sounds in our young environment and desperately tried to make relationships between images and sounds. DNA programmed us to make sense of environments.

Young babies use "DNA instincts" to observe but make no decisions. They are simply "dreaming" displaced observers. Parents were their realities. With sporadic attention, babies record everything in sight and store memories by emotional levels. Babies' minds slow down dramatically with a growing data base and increasing comparisons for decision making processes.

With positive activities and frequent mental victories, young minds soar. It is helpful to think like a baby at times and experience things without making judgments. Babies, without experiencing significant traumas, have wider thinking limits. A mental victory is when a child or anyone feels like they understand, predict, or control an event within their environment.

Daydreams occur mostly at normal waking speeds and content seems to be more reasonable and structured than dreams. Dreams sometimes appear to last for weeks or months in a night's sleep. The mind has unusual timing abilities. On seeing an aged face of a person we have not seen for forty years, our subconscious minds are programmed to manipulate picture data to recall the younger face of a long-forgotten person very quickly. Picture data is processed faster than words.

Oh my, how fast the mind can fly! Subconscious minds process at the speed of dreams and possibly near the speed of light. Why then do we consciously think so slowly? One reason is because we think symbolically in words and not in images. Image thinking is fast, and word thinking is slow. Wider vocabularies slow thinking but increase depth in thoughts and emotions.

In waking life, our minds have developed "wait states." Our lightning minds had to wait forever for a hand to grasp, an arm to swing, a leg to kick, a neck to turn, and even for an eye to focus. That lightning mind has learned to wait so long for the physical body to catch up to its desires and commands. Slow conscious processing is linked to waiting for "slow" physical events to occur. This is an area of thinking to explore for added benefits.

If we purge emotional trauma scars while communicating with a therapist or psychiatrist, those emotional events and trauma scars no longer affect our waking lives as much. In a like manner, we can purge "wait states" from subconscious processes to increase mental capabilities using mental reconstruction. When we fully recall trauma memories, their adverse effects often dissolve away.

Memory of dreams might be considered as semi-conscious thoughts. Establishing dream-thoughts from dream-content allows the dreamer to transform semi-conscious awareness to the level of conscious awareness. The mental quality of the dream is raised to the level of conscious thought if we use our left-brains to take notes immediately after waking. Dream censorship is then overcome. In dreams, censorship is related to the constant fear of being abruptly awakened and the subconscious mind having to slow down to take on conscious responsibilities.

Dreams are holistic and flowing in nature. The rhythmic right-brain is dominant during dreaming. Flowing picture, right-brained functions are not remembered as easily as discrete left-brain functions. Recording dreams upon awaking, transfers right-brain activities to the left-brain for ease in remembering.

Childhood memories are repressed to reduce trauma pain and feelings of inadequacy including the inability to speak. Adverse repressed memories can erratically disrupt subconscious processing and hinder normal life. Repressed memories are physically stored within traumatized local neural networks. Releasing energy from trauma scars converts localized trauma memories to more dispersed, holistic memories which rejoin the amazing symphony of activities within the brain.

For a reasonable life, we must distinguish between dreams and waking thoughts and activities. If dreams are too energetic, we confuse them with waking activities. For mental healing, it is often important to relate dream activities to early childhood and recent experiences. Childhood experiences have much to do with early levels of perception, reasoning, and dream-content.

Dianetics

"A science of the mind, if it were truly worthy of that name, would have to rank, in experimental precision, with physics and chemistry."

L. Ron Hubbard

I have attempted to understand mental transformations from "normal," depressed, and manic thought processes and moods with mind models since 1988 to heal the mind. *Dianetics (The Modern Science of Mental Health)* [2] by L. Ron Hubbard inspired realization that simple methods for examining the mind can be beneficial for psychiatric healing. Simple reflections into the mind can develop awareness of subconscious processes for guiding healing within the fabric of the brain.

Dianetics is an adopted mind model. Models do not need to include neurophysiology or accepted science to promote healing. Dianetics is an exploration into the mind for psychiatric healing. A mental explorer searches within his subconscious mind to learn that which he does not know. Hubbard states, "Only things that are poorly known become more complex the longer one work's upon them;" (1986, p6). Hubbard lists criteria for a science of the mind:

1. "An answer to the goal of thought.

2. A single source of all insanities, psychoses, neuroses, compulsions, repressions, and social derangements.

3. Invariant scientific evidence as to the basic nature and functional background of the human mind.

4. Techniques, the art of application, by which the discovered single source could be invariably cured; ruled out, of course, are the insanities of malformed, deleted or pathologically injured brains or nervous systems and, particularly, iatrogenic psychoses (those caused by doctors involving destruction of the living brain itself).

5. Methods of prevention of mental derangement.

6. The cause and cure of all psychosomatic ills, which number, some say, 70 percent of man's listed ailments;" (1986, p10).

Hubbard lists what Dianetics does and is:

"1. It is an organized science of thought built on definite axioms (statements of natural laws on the order of those of the physical sciences).

2. It contains a therapeutic technique with which can be treated all inorganic mental ills and all organic psychosomatic ills, with assurance of complete cure in un-selected cases.

3. It produces a condition of ability and rationality for man well in advance of the norm, enhancing rather than destroying his vigor and personality.

4. Dianetics gives a complete insight into the full potentialities of the mind, discovering them to be well in excess of past supposition.

5. The basic nature of man is discovered in Dianetics rather than hazarded or postulated, since that basic nature can be brought into action in any individual completely. And that basic nature is discovered to be good.

6. The single source of mental derangement is discovered and demonstrated, on a clinical or laboratory basis, by Dianetics.

7. The extent, storage capacity, and recallability of the human memory are finally established by Dianetics.

8. The full recording abilities of the mind are discovered by Dianetics with the conclusion that they are quite dissimilar to former suppositions," (1986, p12).

Positivism is powerful in healing the mind and body. Hubbard sets a high goal for students of Dianetics. Complete success through Dianetics enhances a student to the level of a "clear." Hubbard describes the enhanced qualities of the "clear":

"A clear can be tested for any and all psychoses, neuroses, compulsions and repressions (all aberrations) and can be examined for any autogenic (self-generated) diseases referred to as psychosomatic ills. These tests confirm the clear to be entirely without such ills or aberration. Additional tests of his intelligence indicate it to be high above the current norm. Observation of his activity demonstrates that he pursues existence with vigor and satisfaction;" (1986, p14).

"The analytical mind is that portion of the mind which perceives and retains experience data to compose and resolve problems and direct the organism along the four dynamic paths listed above; (1986, p55).

"The reactive mind is that portion of the mind which files and retains physical pain and painful emotion and seeks to direct the organism solely on a stimulus-response basis. It thinks only in identities;" (1986, p56).

Hubbard's mind models consist of the analytical, reactive, and somatic models. He develops a strategy for separating the mind into parts to reason about it. The center of awareness, "the monitor," controls the analytical mind, which is the perfect mental computer. Aberration occurs when trauma and confusing data over stresses and freezes the analytical mind. The reactive mind makes fast, rugged decisions based on comparisons to historical emotions only. Memory banks of the analytical mind are considered perfect. Potential for recall is perfect. The analytical mind weighs new experiences relative to historical experiences and makes in-depth comparisons to integrate new and historical conclusions.

The reactive mind contains the entire source of aberrative, trauma content in an emotional engram bank. The reactive mind uses this emotional reservoir to make fast stressful and emotional decisions. The reactive mind is designed to protect refined and higher-level neural networks. The reactive mind is stored within high-energy neural networks with repressed trauma energy.

Related activities may stimulate engrams, or repressed memories, and cause as much fear and anxiety as the original trauma. Fear of recurring trauma may become greater than the original experience.

All experiences are recorded within either the analytical or reactive data banks. The reactive mind is a coarse and rugged, but fast, response system. Responses may not be completely correct but fast for survival. Reactive, high-energy, right-brained activities often interfere with detailed, analytical left-brained responses.

The goal of Dianetics is to purge all engrams from those practicing Dianetics processes for them to become a "clear." "Returning" is a more natural process of arriving at memories than simply remembering. In returning one goes back in time through a conscious, organized thought process. Remembering consists of random thinking of similar things until something is remembered. Returning is reverse mental time travel for reliving experiences more vividly than remembering isolated events.

An "auditor" is a person practicing Dianetics who assists in methodically purging engrams. Hubbard writes that engineers make good auditors.

My models include some of Hubbard's methodology. Dianetics has been useful to many people. I wish to repeat a principle of mine. If there are changes happening in the world or within my mind, I try to look for the simplest source first, and then look to the next simplest source, for an explanation. This is a concept from my physics and engineering background. Simple models explain how environments affect the subconscious and conscious minds. A mind model might be simple, but if it makes us feel good or helps us understand something we were unsure of, the model serves a useful purpose. Often in physics, discoveries are simpler than at first expected.

Dianetics is a useful, emotional process for healing the human mind. Processes are simple and can relieve stress. However, I see little evidence that sufficient scientific procedures were followed to qualify Dianetics as a science of the mind.

A model of the mind does not to be scientific to heal. Without expressed assumptions and scientific methods, Dianetics is not a science. It is a useful emotional process that can effect psychiatric healing. These techniques to relieve mental stress and pain are good if kept in perspective. Psychiatric healing should provide pleasant feelings. However, release of extreme trauma scars or engrams might cause brief emotional pain that should pass quickly. Trauma scars and engrams are terms for the same thing. The remainder of this book uses: trauma scars.

I know very little about Dianetics and Scientology. On the surface, a religion founded on psychiatric techniques seems odd and of the same order as scientists worshipping scientific tools and discoveries. Mental healing and spiritual feelings are similar. Alcoholics worship their displaced "high" feelings and moods.

Dianetics is an emotional mind study for healing as are my models. *Bipolar Blessings & Mind Expansion, 2nd Edition,* is a quasi-scientific, heuristic, and philosophical study. Readers are free to experiment with mind modeling and mental reconstruction techniques. I discourage making a religion of psychiatric methods. We must distinguish between feelings of psychiatric and spiritual healing. Psychiatric processes heal specific discrete overstressed neural networks individually. Spiritual healing is holistic or global healing throughout the brain.

Philosophical and heuristic conjecture refines focus for scientific analysis. Philosophers must understand sciences to promote theories for future experimentation and discoveries. Heuristic and scientific failures provide focus for future successes.

REFERENCES:

(1) Sigmund Freud, *The Interpretation of Dreams,* translation by James Strachey, 1965, Avon Books, New York, NY.

References within *Sigmund Freud: The Interpretation of Dreams:*

    Chabaneix, P.

        1897. *Physiologie cerebrale: le subconscient chez, les artistes, les savants, et les ecrivains,* Paris.

    Krauss, A.

        1858-59. *Der Sinn im Wahmsinn,* Allg. Z. Psychol.

    Spitta, H.

        1882. *Die Schalf- und Traumzustande der menschlichen Seele,* Tubingen. (1st ed., 1878)

* * *

(2) Hubbard, L. Ron, *Dianetics (The Modern Science of Mental Health),* 1986, Bridge Publications, Los Angeles, CA.

Chapter 6
Depression

Ode on Melancholy (verses 2 and 3)

But when the melancholy fit shall fall
Sudden from heaven like a weeping cloud,
That fosters the droop-headed flowers all,
And hides the green hill in an April shroud;
Then glut thy sorrow on a morning rose,
Or on the rainbow of the salt sand-wave,
Or on the wealth of globed peonies;
Or if thy mistress some rich anger shows,
Imprison her soft hand, and let her rave,
And feed deep upon her peerless eyes.

She dwells with Beauty — Beauty that must die;
And Joy, whose hand is ever at his lips
Bidding adieu; and aching Pleasure nigh,
Turning to poison while the bee-mouth sips;
Ay, in the very temple of Delight
Veil'd Melancholy has her shrine,
Though seen none save whose strenuous tongue
Can burst Joy's grape against his palate fine;
His soul shall taste the sadness of her might,
And be among her cloudy trophies hung.

John Keats

Oh how high the mind can fly!
Like the bird up in the sky.
With a broken wing it hits the ground!
Can this fragile mind yet rebound?

Hugh Fulcher 2006

This chapter is dedicated to those depressed, manic-depressives, and those working to forge their own positive mental changes. Tragic relationships and experiences cause brain altering stresses. We do not appreciate good mental health until having experienced sickness or disorders. I write of depression, pain, and sadness to help others cope and recover.

Lost expectations turn thinking inward. Depression begins when mental energy and anger is repressed and not expressed outwardly. Energy is stored within traumatized neural networks, or trauma scars. Depression deepens with time as disappointment builds for not having expressed anger to abusers.

Many who abuse others have been abused in childhood. Hurting others is normal. Life is Hell for spouses of alcoholics and adult children of alcoholic parents. As a codependent, I let damaging home behavior continue for so long. Many of us endure, hide, and deceive others about the nature of abusive spouses for years in vain hopes things will get better. An adult child of alcoholics is more dangerous than alcoholics because he/she is sober and more capable of deceptive manipulation. Adult children of alcoholics have learned controlling manipulation from observing alcoholic parents.

My research was too late to understand controlling and manipulative behaviors. Unfortunately, as a codependent, I shared the blame. Work and social interactions appeared normal, but spousal interactions were guided by childhood insecurities learned from a deranged mother's behavior. Later, I read an invaluable book, *Adult Children of Alcoholics* [1], by

Janet Geringer Woititiz, which helped me understand my former wife's behavior.

I was a gentle, kind person. Both of my parents were kind, loving, and gentle. No one in my country neighborhood asked young folks questions they needed to respond to with a direct no. Life was good in my nurturing community.

Both of my ex-wife's alcoholic parents were controlling, power based, and manipulative. That lifestyle was foreign to me. My former mother-in-law was the cruelest person I ever met. I write so gentle spouses might learn to defend against abuse.

With a poor family background, my former wife frequently found ways to "show" superiority. We were from different worlds that nearly caused my death. It must be clear that persistent stress from those close to us can cause bipolar disorder.

What caused manic depression? It was stress extended over a long time. I was mentally assassinated and driven beyond coping limits. It still hurts to re-experience the deception and suffering.

The marriage should have been corrected with counseling or ended in divorce early on. After the divorce, I discovered my ex-wife's behavior was not unusual for those abused during childhood and for adult children of alcoholics.

After being abused, I will not abuse others. I will continue to treat everyone with respect and love. Everyone must know that a manic-depressive just doesn't happen or "just get sick." He has been abused and experienced stress beyond limits. There was seldom a relaxed atmosphere for me in our home.

Conflicting body and verbal languages confuse to control. The damage comes in a victim's split second of insanity of not understanding conflicting language. Body language is processed with the right-brain and verbal language is processed with the left-brain. This conflict causes uncertainty, confusion, and stress.

The two brains develop conflicting opinions. A negative holistic opinion is developed by the right-brain processing the body language. The left analytical or verbal brain receives deceptive positive words and develops a positive opinion. The conflict remains unresolved between the two brains.

In my case, the analytical left brain strived to accept "positive" words. The conflicting body language would spiral thoughts downward in confusion. The brain can be resilient but needs stimulation for resolving inner conflicts and releasing stress.

My ex-wife was an impulsive controller. Quick conflicting body and verbal language caused emotional confusion. With my childhood, I expected everyone to be loving and kind. Character and good values are developed over a consistent path of loving parental guidance, especially in the first seven years.

Abused men and women require unusually high levels of security at the expense of their spouses and others close to them. They often imitate their own tormentors and become high controllers to "protect" themselves against torment experienced in childhood. The abused degrade spouses to increase their own importance and security. Drunken controllers convince spouses they are not thinking right to increase control. Deranged spouses add to their twisted importance by accusing normal spouses of never being good enough. The deranged frequently push spouses to limits before they rebel or leave. Emotional pushing, or bullying, often continues until their prey is emotionally destroyed.

Insecure women use children to increase their own importance and degrade husbands. Deranged women try to goad distressed husbands into hitting them to gain control by getting them in trouble with the law. They falsely accuse good husbands of physically or sexually abusing their own children. Deranged women are more subtle in their twisted control and put-downs of their husbands. Women are more likely to psychologically degrade husbands and withhold sex. They nag rather than logically setting specific times to discuss individual needs and responsibilities.

Deranged men control spouses by threats of force and violence. Men degrade by giving overly importance to jobs and withholding money. Deranged drunken men more frequently adversely affect future generations. Deranged men often isolate wives from family and friends to have more control over them. They get in trouble with the law more often which destroys family life. Most men do not give spouses enough praise for the hard work they do at home. Inconsiderate men give too much importance to activities such as sports, and drinking buddies, which degrade wives' importance and security. Most men do not give quality time to spouses and children. As women know, I could go on and on.

Personally, I was taught to love and be kind, and had difficulty disagreeing on emotional issues. Well-adjusted people are well-adjusted because they have learned to acclimate to situations and environments. In this sense I was not well-adjusted.

My dad visited hospitals and nursing homes. He paid respect to the sick. He thought laughter was the best medicine. I learned this in my formative years. I sometimes cry when thinking how dad cheered up sick friends and my depressed spirits.

I was depressed about the marriage and was not thinking as confidently as normal. Depression started after purchasing a farm. I went for a month or so without sleeping. I became non-responsive but was afraid to go to the hospital. I had no desire to do anything.

One philosophy is every entity has an opposite. Depression can become a springboard for manic episodes with its elevated moods with little reasoning for solving current circumstances. In overly optimistic mania, one feels he can do almost anything. Excited, fast thinking of mania degrades into psychosis. As moods rise, a manic-depressive becomes aware he cannot trust his own thinking.

For me, anti-depressants reduced symptoms of depression. However, manic episodes continued sporadically throughout the years until development of my psychiatric exercises and models. With a positive attitude and patience, my methods may cure others with mental disorders. Self-healing methods awaken hidden mental and spiritual abilities.

My one depression lasted only a few months in 1977 but led to sporadic bouts of debilitating manic depression, or bipolar disorder. I have relived torments and pain to help others understand, prevent, or heal from, depression.

In depression, a deep sense of failure or loss annihilates self-esteem and self-worth. A sense of poor judgment on important issues pervades thinking. Negative evaluation of judgment and inadequacies becomes self-hatred. Self-hatred adds to the pain and agony of the clinically depressed. Heaviness of mood slows thinking. The depressed had rather be anyone but himself.

The first-time depressed individual is sure he has brain damage and will never recover abilities. Persistent thoughts emerge that life is not worth living as a mentally damaged person. Unreasonable negative thoughts about self are believed. Nurturing and positive comments from others are not believed. As depression deepens, positive thoughts become impossible.

Past mistakes dominate thinking and preclude solutions. The depressed experiences pain when thinking "in words." The mind and physical reactions slow down. The depressed mind becomes attuned to negative and self-destructive information. The poor biased mind only records negative statements and occurrences, and agonizes over even small decisions.

Depression reduces mental focus and distorts memory. Past occurrences are remembered greater or lesser than reality. Persistent worries block focus on the future. Before depression, self-worth was too high with too little humility. Selfish interpersonal comparisons reduced focus on God.

Destructive relationships and work environments cause adverse changes within the brain, loss of self-esteem, spiritual isolation, and depression. Depression is difficult to treat, causes physical health complications, and lingers on and on.

Personally, I was having reasonable recognition for difficult work. Marrying a woman with mixed and degrading verbal and body languages, impulsive controlling characteristics, and avoiding sex slowly degraded mental health. When alone with my wife, she seemed chained to behavior learned from her deranged mother.

Increasingly, the depressed feel alienated from others as once keen minds become the slowest of minds. Embarrassment is immense. The swift mind, accustomed to developing solutions, has to adjust to limited mental and physical abilities.

In depression, rhythm and harmony of the holistic right-brain disappears. The mind slows with no inner rhythm to guide life and experiences cacophonies while pondering discordance. Left-brain reasoning is overpowered by negative emotional energy.

Wherever a depressed person happens to be, it never seems to be the right place. The depressed is not certain if thoughts are rational and feels no one understands his torment. Earthly reasoning seems worthless if there is no tomorrow.

Without anticipating the future, there were times I would be walking down a hall and freeze. There was no purpose to think, move, or do anything. I no longer existed. I was only the wall I starred upon. Depression to the point of freezing is referred to as catalepsy. Either we live in the present, looking forward to the future, or wallow in a hurtful repetitious past.

The most frustrating aspect of depression is relentless "what if" and "circular thinking." Worry does not allow relaxation or sleep for renewal of energy. The mind and body degrade. Reasoning is never conclusive, and exhaustion grows. The mind blares out uncertainties and painful thoughts. It takes superhuman effort to put aside "what if" and "circular" worrying to answer simple questions. With persistent mental pain, one concludes life will never get better, and suicidal thoughts become appealing.

In good psychological order on a sunny afternoon, a person enjoys going to a park. In depression, going to the park seems as being forced into a cold torrential rain. Riding on play equipment makes little sense since the rain is so cold and distracting. In depression, negative emotions overpower normal thinking.

Earlier, a depressed person may have felt admired by others. He is afraid of losing admiration and receiving only pity. Losing admiration, or coping with the death of a loved one, can lead to depression. With high successes, big egos have greater vulnerability for depression and further to fall if things go wrong.

Unsolvable problems can cause insomnia. Without sleep, reason degrades. Brain and body chemistry are adversely affected. The body smells unpleasant. Movements become less certain like those of an old person. The voice quivers.

Unresolved personal and work problems increase stress. Neurotransmitters, norepinephrine and serotonin, are depleted in the brain. There is an increase in the hormone, cortisol. Changes distort thinking. The mind turns inward searching to understand how such a tragedy could happen. Without a brain we are only "straw-men."

In severe depression, the air was dense and closing in. Soon, I would no longer be able to breathe. Death seemed scary but welcome. Worrying was too persistent to relax or sleep. Exhaustion was always present. Rare and brief periods of sleep were devoid of dreaming. Dreaming renews the spirit. Without dreaming, the mental predicament is the same as before sleeping.

My first session with a psychiatrist was in 1977. I had some miraculous hope that a psychiatrist could relieve my mental anguish. I felt that using my last energies toward describing my pain would somehow help me. Depressed senses are supersensitive toward negative remarks. I heard, at a distance, my first psychiatrist telling my dad that he could not do a thing with me. I quickly resolved to expect death shortly. It is important to be out of ear range when discussing a psychiatric patient. Any lack of encouragement overheard will be taken as negative and create fears of impending death. Fortunately, Dr. Gene Goode became my psychiatrist after that, and I began to develop confidence and heal.

In one sense, I was lucky since seriously contemplating suicide for only a few weeks. After a brief encounter with suicidal thoughts, Dr. Goode prescribed an anti-depressant. One night, only two or three days after taking this medication, it was as if a comic strip balloon popped within my head followed by a sudden feeling that I was too worthwhile to commit suicide. I remember the dramatic moment when abruptly turning away from depression, self-destruction, and looking toward the future. This medicated odd feeling increased my self worth above wallowing in self-pity. The anti-depressant worked.

The "endless" depression slowly disappeared, and the mind became more nimble toward "normal" thoughts and decisions. Life became more reasonable. In the long run depression seemed to have left few lasting wounds, but left indelible memories of horror and pain. William Styron's book, Darkness Visible (A Memoir of Madness) [1], helped me describe my own depression.

For most of my life I had been healthy, happy, and successful. After depression, there is now joy in thinking about the mind and God. Setbacks in my healing research activate my computer oriented mentality. If something does not work, I don't get frustrated, but simply look for the next alternative.

A depressed person needs a support team to remind him frequently of his worth, good decisions, and that mental abilities can and will return. Be honest and remind him the mind heals very slowly, and everyone, including the depressed, must have patience for healing. Having lived through depression gives a richer, more spiritual perspective toward life. Patience and love are needed to support the sick and depressed, and are among our highest virtues.

Conversations should include good times sprinkled with good decisions the depressed person has made. Slowly during healing, support persons should talk about patients accomplishing good things in the future. If appropriate, help patients with simple decisions and share activities enjoyed before depression.

Depression is healed more quickly when patients accept their loss of status. Accepting meager existence, mental and spiritual healing begins. Psychiatric procedures, given later, should be practiced with medications if prescribed.

Physiological causes of depression and manic-depression are not well known. It has become my goal to heal depression and manic depression. For years, I continued experiments to gain control of, and heal, my manic-depressive mind. I pulse my mind in many directions and patiently wait to see if I can feel or recognize improvement, greater awareness, or increased emotional control. I search for inner joy and spiritual awakening.

Helping people feel good about them selves is spiritual. We may help prevent depression or suicide, or guide someone out of depression. Love and caring heal physically and spiritually.

Significant others who do not love and share can cause depression. It is dumb and counter productive to follow soap operas and other imaginary distorted programs and not take time to know and love those around us. Unfortunately, many identify with arrogant TV characters and destroy the lives of others.

Clinical depression is often caused by failure to vent suppressed anger, which is stored as negative potential energy toward self. We must guide the depressed to express anger at stress causing behaviors and tragedies in acceptable ways for them to heal. Not expressing anger, during or after abuse, is harmful to mental health. Victims of severe abuse may not recognize, or be afraid to discuss, the sources of repressed anger.

Since 1977, the author has wondered why God saved him from death when he was too depressed to be angry, mentally void, in pain, and having the feel and smell of death. He was certain of not recovering. At the time, death was welcomed. God, his family, loved ones, and potential readers became reasons for continuing a life of hope and wonder.

Wouldn't it be wonderful if we could "heal" abuse, mental isolation, and, in turn, depression with faith in God. We must dream and work to culture kinder, rewarding spiritual futures. All "mind criminals," whether recognized or not by victims, are ill trained and mentally ill. Without love, guidance, and discipline in childhood, mental illness is certain and causes mental illness for generations.

Newsweek Magazine, February 26, 2007, p47, had an article, *Men & Depression, FACING DARKNESS* [3], by Julie Scelfo:

> "For decades, scientists believed the main cause of depression was low levels of epinephrine. Newer research, however, focuses on the nerve cells themselves and how the brain's circuitry can be permanently damaged by hyperactive stress responses, brought on by genetic predisposition, prolonged exposure to stress or even a single traumatic event. 'When the stress responses are stuck in the 'on' position, that has a negative effect on mood regulation overall,' says Dr. Michael C. Miller, editor of the Harvard Mental Health Letter."

This statement mirrors my models of manic depression. In this article there is further hope.

> "... Scientists are developing medications that block the production of excess stress chemicals, hoping to reduce damage to otherwise healthy nerve cells. They are also looking at hormones," p.47.

It is rewarding to me that current science supports my models developed from inner feelings and reason, documented in 1995 in *Emotional Mind Modeling*. My solution is different. I suggest that psychiatric exercises and mind models are more effective and straight forward in curing bipolar disorder in the long term. Short term pharmaceutical solutions are also needed.

REFERENCES:

(1) Styron, William, *Darkness Visible (A Memoir of Madness)*, 1990, Vintage Books (A Division of Random House, Inc.), New York, NY.

(2) Woititz, Janet Geringer 1983. *Adult Children of Alcoholics*, Health Communication Incorporated, Dearfield Beach, Fl.

(3) Scelfo, Julie, *Men & Depression, FACING DARKNESS*, February 26, 2007, *Newsweek Magazine*, New York, NY.

Chapter 7
Neurophysiology

The mind's house is so confining,
Yet thoughts sail beyond the silver lining!
What a delicate place for a mind?
With stress, it can be so unkind!

Hugh Fulcher, 2006

Neurophysiology studies the anatomy and functions of the brain. A brief physiology of the brain may assist healing. The subconscious mind has the ability to translate simple models into its own mental binary language and heal itself. Mind models do not need in-depth physiology to heal the brain. Only elementary neurophysiology is needed.

The brain consists of several components. Each component is connected to other components through neural networks. Brain cells interconnect to form neural networks. Neurons consist of a cell body, axon, and dendrites. Axons send electrical and chemical impulses to other neurons through connections with dendrites of other neurons.

Dendrites mostly receive electrical signals from axons of other neurons. Axons and dendrites are physically, electrically, and chemically connected by synapses. The pre-synaptic neuron affects the post-synaptic neuron by transferring neurotransmitters through axons to dendrites. Neurotransmitters are chemicals transferred between neurons that allow them to influence one another. Neurons supplying neurotransmitters to connected neurons can enhance or suppress their activations. Figure 8.1 is a simplified illustration of a neuron. The nucleus of a neuron with its axon and only a few dendrites are shown. A synapse is also given.

The brainstem, located at the top of the spinal cord, receives signals from nerves throughout the body and transfers these signals to various parts of the brain. The brainstem is composed of several groupings of brain cells. There are two groups within the brainstem of most interest for my work - the reticular formation and aminergic cluster. These two cell groupings play a large role in determining sleeping (dreaming) or waking states.

The reticular formation is most active while sleeping and extends along the length of the brainstem. The aminergic cluster near the top of the brainstem is concentrated in the dorsal raphe nucleus and is most active during waking. These two areas of the brainstem suppress each other's activities similar to predator and prey animal populations affecting each other. Change of state is a war between opposing brainstem neuron populations. Reticular formation neurons send negative signals to impede aminergic cluster activations, and vice versa.

A surface view of the brain is given in Figure 8.2. A cross section of the brain is illustrated in Figure 8.3. The limbic system is seen surrounding the brainstem. The cerebral hemispheres surround the limbic system.

The brainstem, midbrain, pons, and medulla control the overall activities of the central nervous system. The reticular formation within the brainstem regulates communication with the cerebral cortex. We expect the reticular formation to have strong connections to the right (holistic) brain as dreaming is a holistic function. Holistic relates to overall aspects of something being studied and not individual parts or sub-functions. Consciousness is created holistically throughout the entire brain.

The two cerebral hemispheres are at the top of the brain, weigh approximately two pounds, and consist of two-thirds of the entire brain. The dark grayish matter lying a small distance below the surface of the cerebrum is the cerebral cortex. White matter is made up of millions of tiny nerve fibers. The cable-like structure connecting the cerebral hemispheres is the corpus callosum.

The interior of each cerebral hemisphere contains the basal ganglia. The surface of the cerebral cortex is approximately 325 square inches. One-third of this area is on the outside, and two-thirds in grooves and fissures which divide the cerebrum into frontal, parietal, temporal, and occipital lobes. Grooves are called sulci; and ridges are called gyri or convolutions. The cerebral cortex is thicker at the top of convolutions. The average thickness is one tenth of an inch.

Memory is believed to be in two parts. The first part is short term for up to an hour. The second is long-term memory and believed to cause changes in brain cell RNA or ribonucleic acid. Long-term memories may be stored by "coded" protein variations on cell surfaces for memory. Theories in later chapters promote mental hologram manipulation as basic building blocks of thought.

Memory associations are made between coded proteins with similar resonances. In theory, the subconscious mind compares resonances of historical "coded" proteins to currently sensed resonances to construct new memories. All creations and memories need building blocks.

Psychiatric exercises for promoting mental reconstruction focus on neck, throat, and jaw muscles. Nerves from all these muscles are connected to the medulla. The medulla transmits effects of muscle stimulation throughout the brain.

Technologies such as functional magnetic resonance imaging (fMRI) and positron emission tomography (PET) have allowed scientists to pinpoint locations of various brain functions.

Let's begin a physics theory of the brain. Neural activations create integrated electromagnetic resonances. One resonating neural network can stimulate other networks to resonate with complementing frequencies. For example, stimulation of nerve resonances on the retina of the eye stimulates resonances within appropriate areas of the brain.

An example of resonances is the radio. Characteristics of radio receivers and resonances allow us to select frequencies of one radio station and block out other stations. Radio stations transmit on different frequencies. We want to receive one radio signal, clearly.

Thinking about the brain is a recursive relationship. The brain is needed to think about itself. Mental reconstruction includes brain storming and positive thinking for psychiatric healing.

The left-brain processes up-close details for humans to navigate environments. Relaxing the mind allows the rhythmic right-brain to dominate and produce long-range, rhythmic, and continuous holistic thinking. We can practice mental control by switching between left and right-brain dominance. Dancing is flowing with relaxed right-brain dominance. Dancing with the detailed left-brain is awkward.

One way to relax into holistic right-brained thinking is to view a Holusion™. Figure 8.4 is a Holusion of "The Thinker." Relax and focus beyond the surface and its detailed lines. The right-brain kicks into dominance, and we see the three-dimensional Holusion image of "The Thinker." Holusions have properties of holograms. We must use our right-brain to imagine beyond the physical world for spiritual feelings of completeness. We can learn awareness of which brain is dominant.

Worshiping God is a long-range, right-brain process, which promotes feelings of completeness. We think of God holistically beyond details of the universe and not considering different parts of God. However, we can allude to continuous, spiritual feelings using discrete words at times.

Man and robots navigate their environments. Man has two eyes separated by a small distance. This separation allows us depth perception. Man's two-eyed vision of the world can be described as a "two-and-one-half" dimensional vision. A two-eyed (two cameras separated by a small distance) robot can use videoed data to "understand" and navigate its three-dimensional environment.

Images from both cameras are matched and processed by a computer to identify, locate, avoid, or approach three-dimensional objects. Currently, robots can navigate and perform effective tasks in limited environments. Robots have no sub-conscious processes so all functions must be understood and programmed explicitly. Our minds perform so many activities subconsciously. We are just beginning to learn how powerful our subconscious minds are.

We are vaguely aware of assumptions and decisions our subconscious processes make for us. Learning about these assumptions and decisions will improve our minds.

Nearly 24,000 genes make up the blueprint and structure of the 100 trillion cells in our bodies. We can improve the genes of our offspring by experiencing and overcoming emotional limits through bold physical and mental adventures, introspective study, and mental reconstruction.

Figure 7.1 Neuron

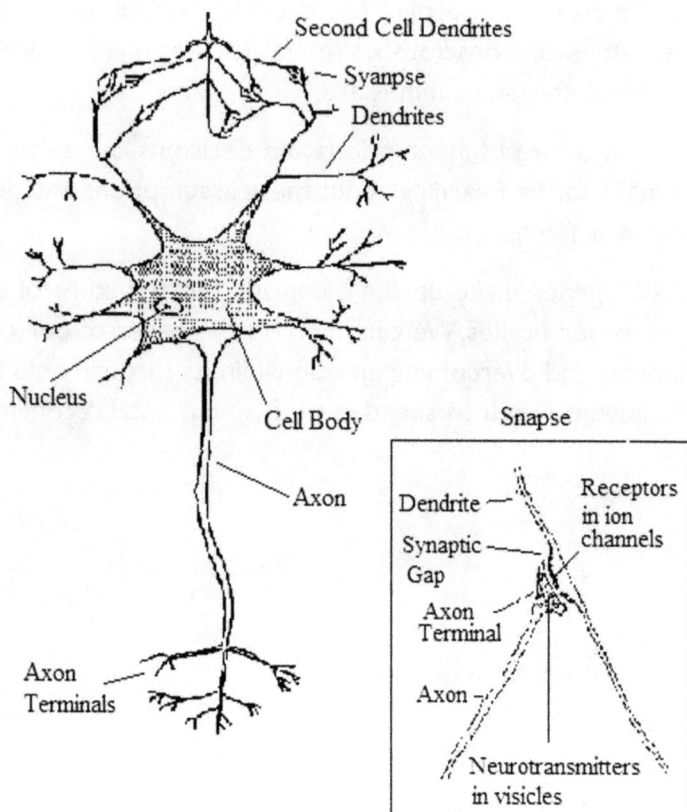

Second Cell Dendrites
Syanpse
Dendrites
Nucleus
Cell Body
Snapse
Axon
Dendrite — Receptors in ion channels
Synaptic Gap
Axon Terminal
Axon
Axon Terminals
Neurotransmitters in visicles

Figure 7.2 Surface Side View of the Brain

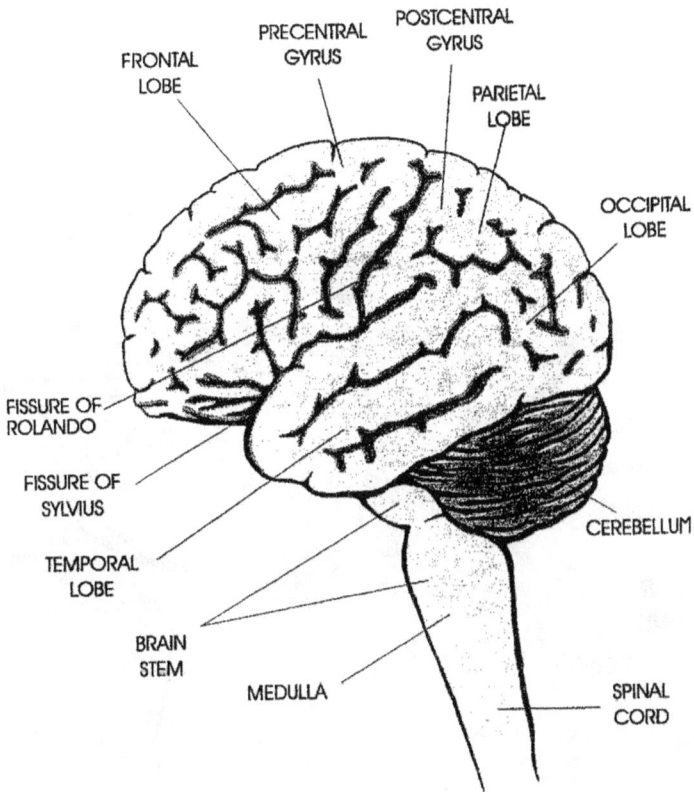

Figure 7.3 Cross Section of the Brain

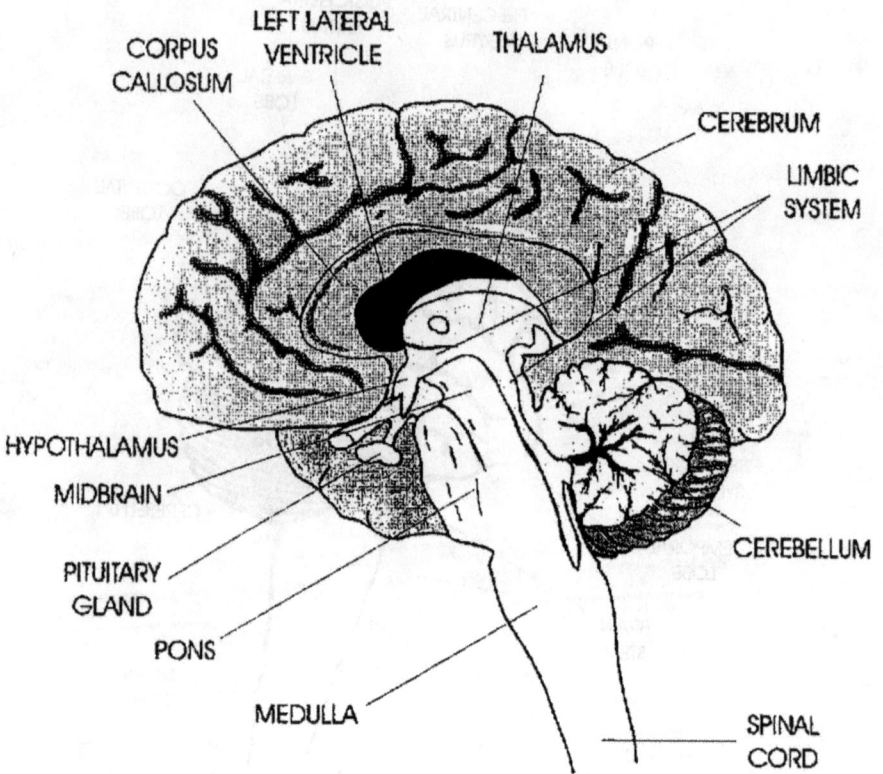

CORPUS CALLOSUM
LEFT LATERAL VENTRICLE
THALAMUS
CEREBRUM
LIMBIC SYSTEM
HYPOTHALAMUS
MIDBRAIN
PITUITARY GLAND
PONS
CEREBELLUM
MEDULLA
SPINAL CORD

Figure 7.4 Holusion, "The Thinker"

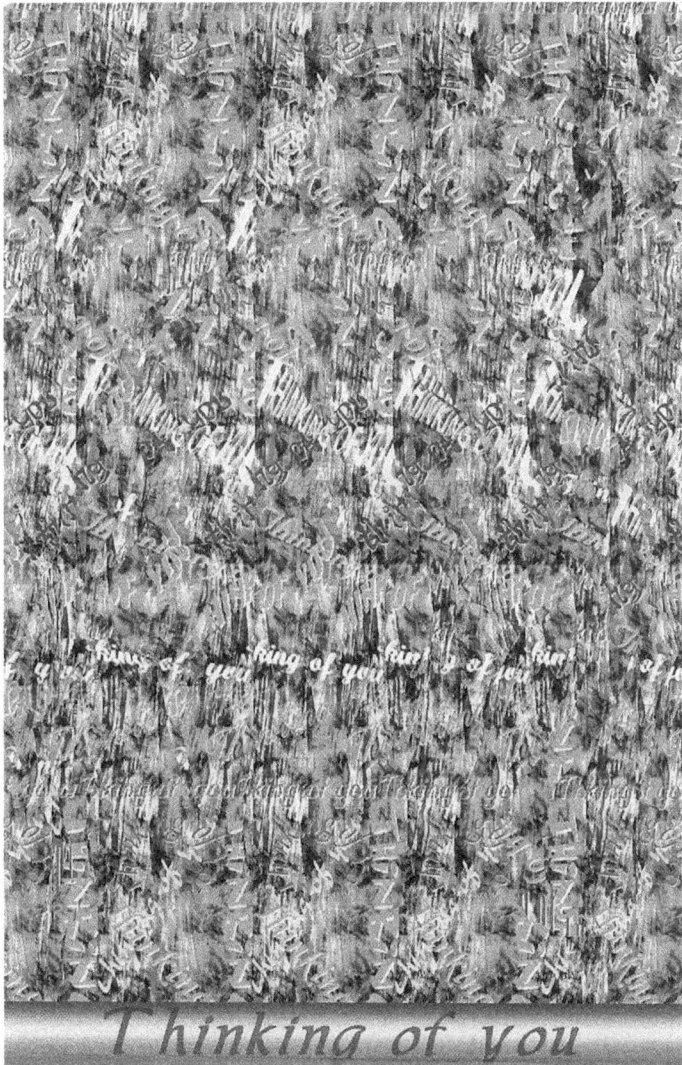

Chapter 8
Bipolar Disorder

WILL

There is no chance, no destiny, no fate,
Can circumvent or hinder or control
The firm resolve of a determined soul.
Gifts count for nothing; will alone is great;
All things give way before it, soon or late.
What obstacle can stay the mighty force
Of the sea-seeking river in its course,
Or cause the ascending orb of day to wait?

Each wellborn soul must win what it deserves.
Let the fool prate of luck. The fortunate
Is he whose earnest purpose never swerves,
Whose slightest action or inaction serves
The one great aim. Why, even Death stands still,
And waits an hour sometimes for such a will.

Ella Wheeler Wilcox

Depressed and not sleeping for months, fear of a tortured, slow death permeated my mind. Suicide seemed to be the only escape. Anxiety caused faster and faster thinking. Behavior became more active and erratic. My wife overreacted causing added anxiety. My distrust of her had built up over the years. She recruited my parents to have me committed to a psychiatric ward.

In the hospital, a thought occurred to me. How could any human endure so much pain and still be alive? "I must be Jesus Christ!" Hallelujah! I yelled to mother and dad, "I am Jesus Christ!" To my surprise, mother did not seem pleased with the idea. She gently forced her face directly in front of mine and calmly said, "Hugh, you are not Jesus Christ!" For the first time in my life, I did not believe my mother. I "felt" the power of Jesus.

I went into the hall. At the first opportunity, I proclaimed to a poor elderly lady: "I am Jesus Christ!" She responded with raised hands, a bowing of her head, and a "Praise the Lord." This response made me feel genuine.

Surprisingly, a not-so-manic thought occurred. If I am Jesus Christ, I have a responsibly to this lady, mother, dad, my children, and mankind. With this thought, I knew I was not Jesus Christ and did not have His love or power. I became a tired, sick person again and retreated to my room. With some coaxing, I accepted the tranquilizer and resigned to give up a hurtful life. The next morning, I felt better and was more reasonable after the first sleep in months.

During this first manic episode, I began writing when locked in a psychiatric cell fearing permanent insanity and even death. Writing was the most stabilizing thing I could do. I wrote about physics and about injustices to regain sanity and save my life. Writing seemed to cleanse my soul.

Unfortunately, I was prescribed Haldol. After a week of so in the hospital, I was chemically numbed and released. Haldol produced horrendous side effects that nearly killed me. I could not swallow and muscles cramped all over my body. I thought death was near. Since then I have felt as if living on borrowed time. In prescribing new medications, psychiatrists must monitor helpless patients frequently for side effects. Severely depressed and manic patients are not able to describe ill effects. Even deeply depressed, I knew I needed emergency treatment. I was taken off Haldol and returned to a normal manic-depressive, if there is such a beast.

Beginning in 1988 after several manic episodes, I decided to take charge in preventing my manic episodes. I intentionally extended my mind briefly to the edge of insanity to cure manic depression. We need to experience insanity to develop a higher sanity. After experiencing emotional limits over the years, I have not had depression since 1978 or manic episodes since 1994, and have increased feelings of confidence and accomplishment.

Emotional highs help us accomplish, but it is important to be able to control and come down from emotional highs quickly. Briefly experiencing mania is much like a vaccination. We need to experience brief stress and emotional highs in order to control real stress and emotional highs later.

When not experimenting, thinking was consistent and more excited about creative ideas than ever before. I felt on the path of curing bipolar disorder and possibly other stress-related disorders.

During sporadic manic episodes from 1977 to 1982, there was persistent fear of the next episode. After seven years without a manic episode, strange things happened. In Phoenix, Arizona, on the Metro Racket Club tennis courts in 1989, I had my first awareness of a slight inner "metallic" sound as if two small metal balls had hit together inside my brain. This sound might also be described as the breaking of a thin metallic wire. Sensations felt like small bubbles releasing their compressed energy.

This reverberating metallic sound occurred again later when exercising the neck. In the next several months, internal energy-release sensations continued with increasing frequency during exercises. Internal energy-releases increased with neck exercises. Exercises were varied to increase inner sensations. I designated inner sensations or sounds as: Snaps, Crackles, And Pops, or SCAPS. Cascades of release sensations occurred as sensations became easier to release. Cascades of releases were also referred to as SCAPS.

I have coined the term, SCAPS, when referring to repressed, pent up trauma and emotional energy releases from the neck, throat, and brainstem. There is a correlation between sound and energy released. Let's look at a simple example. We can store energy between our middle finger and thumb to thump a bug. Placing the hand next an ear, we hear higher sounds with stronger thumps. This is also true with SCAP sounds and energy releases.

There was no discomfort from SCAPS. Instead, the desire increased to exercise the neck more to speed up SCAP releases. For obvious reasons, I minimize head and neck exercises in the presence of others. As SCAP releases progressed, sensations felt pleasant as if the brain was restructuring for self-improvement. A major premise is that pleasant feelings within the brain are psychiatric healing. A procedure for healing and regaining mind control has been discovered.

After several months, SCAPS releases seemed normal. Releasing energy reduces the brain to a more efficient and natural energy state. Nature and brains love energy efficiency.

Since SCAPS were neither painful nor disruptive, I kept sensations and exercises to myself. I was afraid of a change of medications and being "zombiefied." I wanted to delay discussion of experiments until I had explanations for these odd sensations.

Five or six months after initial SCAPS, I am playing tennis with my normal tennis group and bang! I was in the middle of a point stroking the tennis ball and suddenly felt as if my head was as heavy as an anvil and was just hit with a metal hammer. The internal sound was deafening and reverberated as any heavy piece of metal would when struck by a metal hammer. Momentarily, I was stunned and my knees began to buckle. Falling to the ground seemed appropriate.

Surprisingly, I regained composure and remained on my feet. I had experienced a huge mental shock but felt no pain. I recovered and continued play without trying to let fellow players become aware of this traumatic incident. Several metallic sounds occurred in the next few months. Each had significantly less energy. I refer to lesser, subsequent anvil strike sounds also as "metallic pings." Relaxed feelings followed metallic pings.

Metallic pings have more reverberation than SCAPS. Releasing energy with both sensations increased mental stability. Throughout abnormal activities, I never experienced headaches.

In 1989, I lived alone in Phoenix, Arizona. It was between 2:00 and 3:00 AM. I had few worries and had been sleeping well as on previous nights. I abruptly awakened with an overwhelming awareness of the bright-yellow glow of an explosion expanding outward in all directions. I realized I was in the middle of a nuclear explosion. The thought flashed that I would never regain consciousness or see the world again that I would recognize.

I became aware that the nuclear bomb was exploding inside my head. The violence of the mental nuclear bomb remained until I was almost sitting up on the side of the bed with my feet nearly touching the floor. I never felt pain but had a tremendous fright. Amazement came over me; I regained normal consciousness and recognized my room. My whole body was sweating and shaking. I walked around the apartment for a while. There was no pain. The huge energy-release seemed directed toward mental reconstruction and healing. I decided not to call my doctor or tell anyone.

I was not yet ready to be known as "abnormal." I wanted to resolve my mental disorder on my own. This experience was absolutely the most frightening event that I could have imagined (except unexpectedly seeing my ex-mother-in-law.) I felt like being blown apart in all directions. I came to two conclusions that night. I was not in pain. I felt fortunate to have survived this mental nuclear explosion. I went back to sleep and slept soundly the rest of the night. The next day was a "normal" day at the office.

Several months later, there was a second mental nuclear explosion with less energy. This event did not produce sweating or trembling. I never feared not regaining consciousness.

Due to inner changes my mind seemed less stable. After a conflicting encounter a few months later, I was overwhelmed with disbelief that a coworker could be so deceitful. A short while after the encounter and sitting at my desk, I had a feeling that the right cerebral hemisphere was being drained, cleansed, and awakened. This was a strange feeling. I knew my right-brain was releasing repressed energy. There was a significant discovery. For the first time, I was experiencing anger. I was truly angry at this individual.

In teenage and early adult life, I realized that I had only been mimicking anger. Mother never showed anger; seldom did dad. I had suppressed anger all my life, and could now actually feel anger. The right cerebral hemisphere had released energy to process as it was designed to do. God gave us emotions for a reason. Anger protects against mental and physical abuse.

Accepting this newly restored emotion was similar to having dreams of floating in air. One thinks it is a little unusual, but judges that it is actually occurring and is exciting. Floating in the womb was an early sensation that we subconsciously never forget. This sensation was fundamental to our development. Awakening anger seemed abnormal at first, but then felt normal rather quickly.

One night in Phoenix, manic thinking was so inward I could not respond to people. I tried to appear normal but absolutely knew my thinking was not normal. I was put in jail for one night for my own protection.

The night was long. There was no place to sleep. The next morning I was too preoccupied to listen to or answer questions. Finally, I'm freed, or am I?

I walked out of jail the next morning with absolutely no idea where I was or how to get home. I felt I could not call anyone so I walked and walked. I walked through some of the roughest neighborhoods in Phoenix all night never having fear for my safety. Finally, adrenalin was wearing out. I was tired on the second morning as the sun arose. I noticed street signs enough to get home. Hours of weary walking allowed some sleep.

I had been fearless for days. But a chemical that suppresses fear ran out. Little things began to have great importance. People on a nearby balcony were spies. Programs on TV seemed directed specifically for me. I became afraid of almost everything. I told my story to the police. They suggested I stay in a Holiday Inn nearby.

I must have slept some, for the next day I was concerned with the outside world. I went home, remembered that I was prescribed thorazine and lithium, and took medications. I called the doctor and told him about my long ordeal. He did not suggest an appointment. Things started getting better. I became aware of missing work. It was difficult explaining why I had not notified anyone. I told the truth that I had gotten my nights and days mixed up. Things became more normal.

This ordeal was important to me. I learned I could find my own way back to sanity without a doctor's assistance. However, if I ever had a similar experience, I would quickly seek a doctor's help. The experience was too risky.

With daily SCAPS and infrequent metallic pings, I felt abnormal but able to work faster and better for a while. Effects are similar to alcohol and some drugs. Initially there is some benefit.

In mania, "strong" ideas demand attention but evolve into disconnected dream like loss of control. Dreams include waking truths but are expressed as bizarre images and displaced characters. Insanity is invasion of thinking processes with "dream" qualities. One follows dreams without normal reasoning. Imagination soars. Manic minds become very positive and feel abnormally capable.

Repressed networks resist releasing trauma energy to become more normal. Trauma network sporadic activations disrupt the symphony of normal neuron activities within the brain. Therapists and patients must overcome this resistance to begin healing. Psychophysiotherapy, including neck, throat, and facial exercises, reduces the resistance to releasing trauma energy.

Conflict is necessary for brain functions. Without conflict the energy level of the brain would be zero. We are born of conflict between choices. Exercising neck and throat muscles with conflicting hand resistance stimulates emotional energy-releases. Brief physical conflict extends the brain to limits. Subconscious processes are forced to recover from mental limits. The mind and muscles grow only when briefly stressed to limits.

In the beginning, small high-pitched, spiked inner sounds indicated SCAP energy-releases. There was also awareness of SCAP locations. The number of SCAPS slowly increased with exercises. Individual releases had slightly less energy over the years. My SCAP sensations occurred only after becoming a manic-depressive. Several "normal" people I have talked with also sense SCAPS with neck exercises.

Throughout the years, I have released billions of SCAPS. They are not heard by the ears but sensed through an inner sense. An idea occurred that the brain should be reduced to its lowest energy level for efficient processing. We and our minds feel better when performing efficiently.

SCAPS were released in the upper neck and brainstem, around the throat and vocal cords, and infrequently behind the ears and throughout the upper brain. SCAP releases migrated slowly and somewhat randomly with psychiatric exercises. Surprisingly, in the short term, SCAP energy-release changes were predictable. Exercises and mental reconstruction had direction and made sense.

Psychiatric exercises add energy to neural networks. Stimulated networks store this energy in higher resonances until limits are exceeded. Then this energy is released along with long held repressed trauma energy. The brainstem with its proximity to the neck is the part of the brain that is affected the most. It is normal for neural networks and all things in this universe to absorb and release energy. Exercises included neck, jaw, throat, and facial muscles. After years of exercises, SCAP energy-releases were predominant in the upper neck, throat, and brainstem areas.

Descriptions of neck and head exercises are given in Chapter 10. Opposing muscle tensions "re-traumatize" and activate high-energy trauma memory scars. The subconscious mind then recognizes and purges localized trauma memory energy.

In psychotherapy, the therapist overcomes resistance to recalling repressed trauma memories. Normal brain functions suppress energetic hurtful memories for our protection. Controlled conflict stimulates release of trauma energy at mental limits in both psychotherapy and psychophysiotherapy.

Trauma scars include guilt feelings that the victim was inadequate or did something wrong. Even babies have guilt of inadequacy stored within trauma memory fears. Resisting neck movements with a hand gives the subconscious mind conflicting feelings of something wrong happening. This conflict stimulates activation of repressed memories for releasing excess energy.

Emotional, including marriage, decisions should discuss emotional limits. Understanding emotional limits is instrumental in formulating "important" decisions. In marriage, sooner of later "limiting" behavior is experienced. Before marriage, psychological tests should be given to gage compatibility. Emotional experiences must be shared and not hidden or repressed. Hiding or repressing emotional issues eventually destroys.

Impulsive controllers should be brought out of the closet. Their impulsive controlling actions and words should be addressed and healed. Quick put downs through words, gestures, or glances are impulsive controlling techniques. Recognizing and discussing emotional behaviors early can save mental pain and marriages.

Those with an abnormal need to control have deep trauma scars and are insatiably power hungry. Inner power struggles expressed outwardly either subdue or drive others away. Spouses and children are trapped. A controlling parent will prevent a child from developing ability to make choices. A high-controlling person controls thinking even when he is not present. They place psychological hooks into their victims, and brainwash loved ones. The need to control can be enormous.

An abused child of a high-controller may try to please everyone around him or may be compelled to control everyone around him. Techniques which minimize a child's thinking and creativity when he is away from that parent are the worst actions a parent can do. It takes a victim to transform a high-controller into a perfect person. Anyone who uses the word "perfect" when referring to himself or his actions is a high controller.

An abused person spends so much time caring for his own emotional needs and security that he seldom has time to care for his spouse's needs. An abused child's security needs are insatiable. The torment from abusive alcoholics lasts for generations. All human behavior, good and bad, is first in the mind before actions. To be successful, we must accept responsibilities.

I was working as a nuclear safety analysis engineer. My task was to verify that a multi-billion dollar nuclear plant was safe to start up for the next fuel cycle. My work modeled all safety components of this nuclear plant. I had updated physics data describing new component characteristics. My responsibility was to verify that this particular plant would operate within all safety limits. Calculations were time consuming, complex, and precise. Schedules were tight. Without a successful safety analysis, this nuclear plant could not start up. Work was important since this plant provides power for a city of a million people.

Each day delayed would be a loss of millions of dollars to the nuclear utility. Being late was not an option. Many nights were spent developing physics input data to my safety analysis model. My model simulated operation for the entire upcoming fuel cycle.

My mathematical analysis proved the upcoming nuclear fuel cycle would operate safely within design limits. Nuclear analyses were required to be verified by another independent experienced engineer. We finished the day before the deadline.

My nuclear engineering responsibilities were stressful but not near so as a degrading spouse with two alcoholic parents. We live as we have been emotionally and technically trained to do.

For years I preached that bipolar disorder was not simply caused by a chemical imbalance. I theorized that SCAP sensations were caused by repressed excess energy being released from neural networks originally injected during a trauma event. Our emotional and thinking limits are constructed by our trauma and emotional experiences. Releasing trauma energy from repressed neural networks expands thinking limits. Normal thinking limit structures are lost, and limits are no longer complete. The mind searches frantically for, and extends beyond, lost limits. The excitement and overwork evolves into mania.

The mind responds to threats. If stimuli are too threatening or conflicting for the brain to react, it is not able to filter information normally throughout the brain. Trauma stimuli overstress the first reactive networks with similar high energy resonances. Overstressed networks lose elasticity, become rigid, and fire erratically apart from the normal symphony.

During years of unusual energy-releases, I have faithfully taken prescribed medications with one exception during an experiment in 1994. For approximately the last twenty years, I have been satisfied with prescribed medications. In the last three years, I have requested, and my doctor has allowed me, to reduce medications. I am reducing medications slowly since my brain has been accustomed to them for such a long time. This reduction has been successful without any feelings or signs of mania.

Releasing trauma energy from localized networks dissipates non-productive inner conflicts. Sleep becomes more restful. The body feels revitalized, and the mind is eager for challenges. The brain is robust with higher resistance to new trauma scars. We become mentally and physically healthier.

Predicting behaviors adds stability. Bipolar thinking and actions are predictable to some extent. At the beginning of mania, many statements and actions are similar. The afflicted or supporters should get help early on to save pain and expense. Predicting manic behaviors early on gives hope for improving, controlling, and healing.

If there are manic feelings, statements, or actual mania, the afflicted and his support team should write down pressures and events that may have caused depression or mania to document episodes. After episodes, analyze causes, reactions, and how episodes could have been stopped earlier. Knowledge for predicting and preventing mania or abnormal behavior can heal.

Chapter 9
Mania and Insanity

XLIV

One need not be a chamber to be haunted,
One need not be a house;
The brain has corridors surpassing
Material place.

Far safer, of a midnight meeting
External ghost,
Than an interior confronting
That whiter host.

Far safer through an Abbey gallop,
The stones achase,
Than, moonless, one's own self encounter
In lonesome place.

Ourself, behind ourself concealed,
Should startle most;
Assassin, hid in our apartment,
Be horror's least.

The prudent carries a revolver,
He bolts the door,
O'erlooking a superior specter
More near.

Emily Dickinson

Thoughts and feelings during manic episodes are discussed for under-standing the manic mind. Manic thoughts are both creative and disrup-tive. Writing has been refined for readability. Creative ideas are often developed by subconscious processes as defensive reactions.

Manic ideas like dreams often bypass subconscious censorship. They may not be rational but fascinating. Dreams normally have too little energy to become conscious. However, traumatic dreams with high en-ergy or dreams energized by abrupt awaking can enter consciousness. Recalling high energy negative memories is limited by childhood trauma energy levels.

Manic ideas include spiritual qualities which should be acted upon. We must analyze and recognize differences between emotional and spiritual ideas to channel thought processes. This book is an example of chan-neling creative energy. Mania begins when energy is high enough to activate traumatized networks. In mania, a person may not recognize his mental and physical limits and what is or is not reasonable.

After years of taking prescribed medication, I discontinued medications in 1994 to experiment. The risk seemed worth a trip into a different manic world. After the abrupt discontinuation of psychiatric medica-tions, mania began three months later and allowed practice in calm-ing back down. My mind feels different and more alive since practicing psychophysiotherapy (PPT). PPT is a powerful tool for exploring the bipolar mind.

While manic, I acquired brief unusual predictions from the Bible and its concordance. Spiritual ideas became deeply important. However, recollection of unusual predictions using the concordance has escaped memory like forgotten dreams.

The concordance and deep structure words helped predict future events. I became aware of shocking inner abilities and secrets about myself. Unfortunately, thoughts occurred so quickly I was unable to write them down. With future work I hope to be able to recall these spiritual techniques to help readers and myself.

My brain became sensitive to electromagnetic fields and soon afterward to the earth's magnetic field. The orientation of my head tended to enhance or limit thinking. The energy level of my brain had become so high it developed an unusual sensitivity.

A distinct feeling evolved that every thought was monitored. I had an increased awareness that God constantly monitored all thoughts. Sensations were distracting, somewhat scary, but fascinating. With all the later manic experiences I have had, I did not worry about insanity.

TV stations became strange as occurred earlier in Phoenix. Usual programs were not on. Viewed programs seemed strange with conversations directed to me. I wondered if unusual sensations were from God. Prayer may be transmitted with refined spiritual energy our instruments cannot detect. Prayer transmits thoughts to and from God. Some might say prayer only organizes and integrates inner thoughts. During a brief hospitalization, and reinstituted medication, I lost unusual mental and spiritual abilities.

During mania, ordering unusual thoughts seemed extremely important. I felt someone was using microwaves to read my mind. I wrote cryptic codes to confuse those trying to "read" my inner thoughts.

Since brain functions normally develop a weak electro-magnetic field, someone could electronically control thinking. I felt my writing was being monitored and sensed a slight pressure from an electro-magnetic field on my hand when I wrote. I again went through many gyrations when writing to confuse "those" monitoring me. Highly manic, I experienced paranoia and extra-sensory perception, ESP.

Things got weird but had happened before in mania so nothing really frightened me. I just accepted the weird things with patience and prayed for understanding. Could an unknown awareness perpetrate nonsense? Did I black out and do things subconsciously? Stop, what's that sound; everybody look what's going round.

I bought six shiny ballpoint pens and absolutely loved their geometrical design. Still having sensitivity to magnetic fields, I carefully aligned the pens perfectly straight on a counter. I went upstairs and was alone in a locked house. As expected, when I came down, the pens had been separated in a helter-skelter manner. Years later, I concluded my own movement and my amplified electricity and magnetism caused the rearranging. When highly manic, I may have attracted paranormal forces.

When manic, reality is different. People seemed normal but overly friendly. We must accept the reasonable and unreasonable and not worry about odd visions or occurrences. Occurrences may be only in manic minds or a higher reality. "Normal" people may be shallow in stigmatizing others. Unusual behaviors may be during higher mental and spiritual experiences.

It is important to recall unexplained occurrences so when normal, we can patiently search for mental reasons. I recall unusual incidents and work for solutions. Patience is my best virtue. Manic experiences were so exciting, with little concern for safety.

Being abnormal has a brief risk of insanity. I experiment to understand how abnormal thoughts might benefit mankind.

We do not appreciate sanity until having experienced insanity. Brief insanities may help us create higher consciousness and abilities. Do not worry if someone makes fun of you when preoccupied. You may be experiencing higher communication with God. However, we must periodically experience the mundane life to take care of bodily functions and our families.

With manic awareness and reflexes, the mind returns to genetic instincts. Manic sensitivities may be similar those of baby and Caveman sensitivities. Babies and Caveman do not suppress feelings or moods. However, babies recover from mania or depression rapidly compared to adults. Babies think holistically, non-verbally, many times faster than grownups. Can you remember how long a day seemed to be when you were young?

Mania includes spiritual abilities like that of young babies before being corrupted by speech, traumas, and inconsistent parents. Babies are not as disruptive to families as out of control manic adults. Babies' manic gyrations can be cute.

Normal adults and teenagers restrict thinking to conform to customs and social pressures. The manic mind becomes so excited about inner ideas it loses sight of accepted customs and behaviors. Manic ideas are creative but evolve so fast and forceful that actions are not completed before another strong idea dominates.

Good advice is to help a manic person slow down and write ideas for later organization and discussion. Calmly repeating difficulties during previous manic episodes may slow down his manic thoughts and actions. It is best to work together with the manic person in making decisions to call a psychiatrist. Helpers must be tactful and truthful in convincing the manic-depressive that they are working together or the afflicted may feel there is a conspiracy against him.

Similar to displaced observers in dreams, manic-depressives do not question manic ideas or make judgments. Uncensored ideas come from deep within the subconscious mind as do dreams. It is difficult to determine between spiritual, and worldly, sanity. Before acting on manic ideas, write them down. Writing activates left-brain judgment, slows manic thinking, and adds reason.

No matter how experienced a psychiatrist might be, he cannot truly understand inner manic processes and thinking unless he is also a manic-depressive. During high excitement levels, manic ideas vary widely.

From years of experience, I have learned to avoid letting mental excitement develop into physical actions.

Here are examples of thoughts written during mania:

> God has complete understanding of all things. Jesus taught simple holistic truths with parables to integrate God's Truth. Anything less than the whole truth is false and sinful to God. Mysticism will not make us complete. False worship is similar to alcohol or drug intoxication.

> Self-reflection is good for the mind and soul. Spiritual control of others does not exist in this universe. Spiritual enlightenment exists. False minds falsely control for selfish purposes and to "keep us out of trouble." Parents working together to help each other correct mistakes develop well-rounded children.

> Loving God and family is our greatest spiritual opportunity and responsibility. Be thankful for everyone inspiring confidence and love. Amen.

We must understand ourselves to love family and God. We must make sense to ourselves before communicating with and making sense with others. Do not speak physics or computer languages to those who do not understand those languages. Speak to be understood. Speak and write with reasonable assumptions. Refine language for listeners. Use caring gestures. The following was written while highly manic:

> *I love computers; they love me. They are not prejudiced. They respond the same to everyone. We must to think logically to work with computers. Emotions do not increase computer's response. I am not emotional correcting my computer. My computer is my reflection and honest with or without awareness yet has God-like qualities.*

> *Emotional computers may be referred to as androids. We may eventually have imbedded computers and not need brains. We may still need souls. Human computers would have to simulate the mind and soul. Should*

computers communicate with God? Will God respond to computers? Will computers pray for us?

Science will discover higher dimensions. We learn from asymmetries but love and worship symmetry – God.

Without sleep everything is connected to everything. Sleep restores reason. Mania exists between dreaming and waking and allows insight into both.

The essence of these words came from the subconscious mind without conscious censorship. There has been editing for readership. During this same 1994 manic experiment, my computer would automatically capitalize entire words and place periods before and after words as if developing logic grammar. My computer seemed to be reaching out to me.

Manic thoughts and sensations seem so pleasant and confident that manic-depressives are reluctant to return to normal. There is an increasing confidence in ideas, even incorrect ideas. Mania is as intoxicating as alcohol at the edge of insanity. Finally, demanding ideas come so fast nothing is completed. Insanity comes knocking!

Recalling highly negative memories is usually limited to those below childhood trauma energy levels. Mental reconstruction may be possible only by manic-depressives. I know no others with similar experiences. If sex is a basic instinct, mental reconstruction is a fundamental instinct.

After mental reconstruction, ideas flow faster and easier. With practice over the years, trauma energy-releases are easier to initiate followed by relaxed and cleansed feelings. Meditation and breathing exercises calm the mind back to normal.

In December of 1994, there were feelings of resistance to neck exercises. Resistance felt like biting into an apple. After biting through the skin, it was easier to eat the apple, or release localized trauma energy from the neck. After each exercise, resistance to neck movements and trauma releases built up again. Repeated exercises slowly reduced trauma energy resistance. Sensations were mostly in the upper neck, brainstem, and throat.

How do we know that energy-releases promote psychiatric healing? Each series of SCAP releases deep-down pleasant feelings. Have you ever hugged your baby and felt deep-down pleasant feelings. Trauma energy-releases produce similar feelings.

Computers, and, also, minds can be reprogrammed. We can stimulate the subconscious mind to understand and reprogram itself. Dreaming synchronizes recent memory resonances with historical memory resonances to create long-range memories. Psychiatric exercises create significant emotional events necessary to reprogram mental structures.

Spiritual communications affect the entire brain equally or holistically. Spiritual messages can only be translated into words that relate to earthly experiences. That is all we know. Spiritual messages are smooth and continuous, or analog. If we become spiritual enough we must translate feelings from God into earthly analogies. Jesus used parables to simplify understanding.

In wonderfully weird manic experiences in October of 1994, I experienced joy running through my beautiful fields communicating with God. I received spiritual communications in words. God and I became buddies that day during my worldly insanities. I would romp in my fields and think of something funny to say to God and then clear my mind of all thoughts.

I would wait, and God would answer in the distant thunder. I was so happy when God responded. His answers were deep yet funnier than my questions. Surrendering without worldly cares invited spiritual communication.

Manic and spiritual thoughts are like dreams and difficult to recall. Here are examples recalled from that sunny day:

   H. "Why do ducks quack?"
   G. "Should they quake?"

H. "Why is the sky blue?"
G. "Physics."

H. "Why can't I see you?"
G. "You can't?"

H. "You neglect me."
G. "Who are you?"

H. "You make me laugh." [I was sure I felt the earth shaking as I fell in the grass.]

H. "Do you like my writing?"
G. "About what?"

H. "Not making sense."
G. "Makes sense."

H. "Who created the universe?"
G. "Not you!"

H. "Who created me.?"
G. "Me."

H. "Do you love even me?
G. "Yes."

H. "Why?"
G. "You are me."

This interaction went on and on. I was a two year old enjoying play with my Father. It was a unique way of spending time alone with God. There was more reflection than response. We reflected feelings and words back and forth. Often, the simplest of times are the most meaningful. I never felt more spiritual.

When spiritual, impossible things seem to happen. Spiritual presence is felt surrounding insane thoughts. Beyond mania, abnormal, impossible things are "experienced" without ability to control, stop, or make sense of such odd occurrences. However, the most dysfunctional, damaging, and insane people are the idiots who think they are perfect and are able to convince others of their "perfection." This insanity multiplies insanity.

If I have talent, it is persistence to think on, and refine, a topic over time! Developing inner reality from dreams requires persistence but sometimes produces flashes of spiritual reality.

Insanity is when one cannot respond to normal situations and it creeps into the manic mind like a thief in the night. There are many ways of experiencing insanity. It begins at birth as innate spiritual sanity is slowly suppressed by earthly trauma and insane experiences which slowly develop baby's earthly reasoning limits.

Strange things happen to sleepless, overworked senses and minds. Reason fades into flighty uncertainties. Senses and even God seem to deceive us.

During my manic experiment of 1994, I had a desire to write what I was going through. I wrote fundamentals of this chapter when extremely manic. Mania and insanity give insight into the depths of troubled minds. It is important to write ideas, or they "fly away" like the forgotten dream. When insane, I returned to childhood.

I include a paragraph written when very manic. I reached beyond my worldly reason. Capitalization indicates emotion:

GOD's Primeorder Created Primordial FIRST LIGHT, GOD MULTIPLIED LIGHT ENERGY BY CREATING SPACE. GOD REFLECTED UPON HIS CREATION after THE FIRST QUANTUM of TIME. GOD CREATED SPACE TO SEPARATE GOOD AND EVIL AND REFLECT GOOD. God was NOTHING before the BEGINNING. God understood He was LIGHT. God integrated and reflected ONE QUANTUM of LIGHT into TIME AND SPACE. REFLECTED LIGHT transcended into PURE LOVE and CHAOS creating atoms, galaxies, stars, the sun, the earth, and a vague AWARENESS framed as the MIND of MAN.

This paragraph shows a level of insanity, but may include building blocks for future understanding beyond normal reasoning. Words were inadequate to express quickly flowing thoughts. We do not expand thinking limits without reaching for the unreachable. God has a purpose for manic and insane minds.

While highly manic, I could feel and relive God creating the universe. Holistic or spiritual thinking overrides earthy reason. In protected environments, we do not always need to be sane.

Laughing is enjoyable. Oscillating loss of control is insanity. The mental number under our radical thinking is negative and control of our minds is imaginary. Insanity is imaginary holistic thinking and may eventually be described mathematically.

Being afraid to stretch the brain to emotional limits briefly might be considered insanity. Pop a pill or take a drug that reduces anxiety and emotions to avoid emotional limits. Many emotionally and intellectually limit their minds to moronic levels to "feel" comfortably sane. We must not be afraid of adventurous thinking to improve inner processes. Physical changes to the fabric of the brain are needed for a psychiatric and spiritual cure.

Artificial spirits and drugs produce "confident" minds that feel little need for God. We must physically reconstruct our brains slowly to build truly sane structures. Alcohol produces two separate insane minds: one distorts confidence and attitude toward self and others, and a sober mind craves to become the alcoholic mind. Alcohol distorts the mind into reliving past glories.

Where did you get your mind today? You got it from a flat brain, three uppers, two anti-depressants, wine, and a little loco weed. Makes sense as long as doctor's fees come rolling in. A pleasantly numbed brain with less pain pays well. A chemically inhibited brain does not improve future genes. Humanity weakens!

One day a drug might be developed for creating geniuses without study or emotional effort. Today, effort is still required for personal and spiritual growth.

When one is insane, he might communicate purely with God, but be so spiritually high that he cannot communicate about earthly things. According to Plato, we must distinguish between one who is of shallow thought and one who is temporarily stunned by the beauty and truths when communicating with God. Spiritual communication sets us free of earthly worries.

When exciting the mind to mania, I had these thoughts:

True love means giving of your self to others. Giving is divine. Mental attitude makes the difference between heaven and hell. Prolonged giving to an arrogant taker devastates the mind into insanity and a personal hell. Choose friends and spouses carefully and spiritually.

Interpersonal comparisons consume and cloud our souls. Individuals cleared of trauma scars seem odd searching to discover inner reasons for existence and mental abilities.

When alone, we never need to be normal. We can research our minds until we feel we can reach out and touch God.

Insanity is incompleteness in words, conflicting gestures, and exasperated sounds that send other's minds into incomplete and inadequate circles of worry. The abused wonders what the "authority's" level of disapproval might be. The opposite of Holy is worries of not understanding an authority figure's response and feeling loss of security and acceptance. Mental efficiency degrades with high levels of uncertainty.

When manic, we focus on the big picture. Cosmologists model the universe to understand and possibly control future environments. Their models predict properties that may be discovered later. Predicting the future adds confidence and order to life. A few years ago many of today's ideas would be insane.

Age discrimination laws mean nothing in this country. Corporations falsify records to ensure that terminated persons have "performed poorly" for the last few years. There is little truth in corporate America today. Corporate executives steal hundreds of millions of dollars from their companies. Entry level workers make barely enough to get by. This is insane.

Sensitivity to magnetic fields is not insanity but a lost skill. From rigorous daily activities, Caveman naturally purged trauma effects. Magnetic directional sensitivity is how Caveman navigated long distances. This sensitivity is probably still true for animals. Traumas and complexities of learning speech have clouded man's innate navigational abilities. When traveling, Caveman could pulse his mind to emotional levels to determine his direction. Once the brain is sensitized, magnetic feelings grab attention.

This magnetic feeling in the brain is similar to placing an opened hand into a smoothly flowing stream of water. When the hand is sideways to the flow, the resistance is low. When the hand faces the flow, resistance is greater. The earth's magnetic field gives the mind a sense of direction.

Facing one direction, there is little disruption to thinking. With a ninety-degree re-orientation, the earth's magnetic force is strongly felt. This sensitivity is normally hidden by trauma effects. To be free from conflicting trauma scars is to experience insanity briefly by re-experiencing historical traumas at limits and resolving conflicts through mental reconstruction. The clear mind and that of animals navigate by following the path of least thinking resistance.

When extremely manic I was shocked when touching cars. I first thought this was due to microwaves or magnetic fields from high-powered electric wires causing charges on car surfaces. Later, I realized the problem was within me. My brain chemistry became imbalanced and my body developed an overall positive or negative charge. This charge caused the sparking when touching cars and caused my mind to be affected by the earth's magnetic field.

I predict that if voltage is turned down on a Van de Graaff generator so skin sensitivities are not overwhelmed and a student stands on a rotating table, a normal person will feel this inner "magnetic sensitivity." This experiment may support my theory that consciousness is mostly electromagnetic resonances and that charge contours on the surface of the brain and awareness can be affected by the earth's magnetic field.

Manic-depressives without prescribed medications have a chemical imbalance with an excess of free electrons in the brain. These free electrons influence brain functions. Physical motions and movement of brain electrons increase the magnetic effect on the brain. With excess free electrons on the surface of the manic brain, this magnetic effect could drive anyone crazy.

Some think spiritual feelings are insanity. We may live waking lives only so our minds can experience dreaming and spiritual reality. Integrating dreaming and inner sanity develops spiritual communication technology.

On the other hand, dreaming may underpin foundations for a cohesive and reasonable waking life. A reasonable integration of dreaming and waking lives develops a healthy mind and body.

Worldly insanity is lack of knowing what to do in normal and difficult situations. The mind is unable to construct complete thoughts. Without feelings of completeness after thoughts, insanity follows. Those who make others feel incomplete develop false completeness in them selves. They are insane.

I worked with a blind engineering friend. Sometimes, he would ask me to read a list of hand written numbers to him. There might be six numbers with ten digits. I would read all numbers to him at one time. Using memory he would return to his desk and enter these numbers into his computer. It would be insane for me to attempt such a feat. Without sight, memory is more prevalent. However, not recognizing a person is blind and watching him search for something, one might think he is insane.

Unless we are in war or threatening situations, we should not view life as all or nothing. Individuals from dysfunctional childhoods or with disorders often have an all or nothing syndrome. A well adjusted person may recognize one hundred solutions to a problem. A severely stressed individual might think he will die if he does not solve some problem or dominate others. All or nothing thinking usually occurs when there is unexplained guilt or loss of hope. The right brain accelerates to emotional reactive conclusions at rapid speeds.

One model of mania is driving a car. When everything is normal, we press the accelerator and the car accelerates and maintains expected and reasonable speeds. We can enjoy the ride and the scenery. If manic, we press the accelerator and the car unexpectedly accelerates quickly to a high speed. We are excited about the speed and engrossed in the challenge to survive, but should be afraid of the risk to ourselves and others. In the excitement, we do not have time to think about others or the scenery. In our manic car, we are two excited about our fast, creative ideas to worry about reality.

Practicing unique psychiatric exercises, I pulse my mind toward spiritual sanity to touch the hand of God. Clouds sometimes form the face of God. As He rises toward my mountain top, He passes through me as the morning mist and renews my soul. This is spiritual sanity.

After depression and manic depression have been cured, I am proud of enduring and surviving insane experiences. It felt like risking one's life serving one's country in the military and surviving. Emotional experiences seemed similar. I fought an inner war and survived. Here are insane events I have witnessed:

Anatomy of a Fight

Pool is an interesting pastime and opportunity to observe competitive activities. One night I entered a pool room. A tall and strong dark haired man, "Joe," and his younger brother, "Jim," were playing pool. They were of the strong working class and in their thirties or early forties. Joe was ruggedly handsome. His face showed the pain and uncertainties of a hard life and his yearning for acceptance. Jim looked of needing attention and accustomed to quick responses.

I played pool with Joe. My goal was to help Joe release inner tensions and have fun. I was friendly and personable. We played a few games and were having fun. I won a last game, and another man, "Jake," put up his money to play the winner. It seemed unusual for Joe to relax and have fun. His mind reverted to the "Child" model of thinking as in the "Parent, Child, and Adult" models in Dr. Thomas Harris' book, I'm OK, You're OK [1].

Joe did not want to stop playing even though normal rules were if someone puts up money to play, they played the winner. An argument began. I repeated that I would sit out and let others play. Voices were raised. I thought I could calm things down.

Unfortunately, dummies heard the shouting and rushed in. One dummy, "Mike," entered with a beer bottle. He pretended to ask for lowered voices, but made a subtle aggressive move toward Joe and Jim. Jim lunged at the beer bottle dummy. Several people fell behind a pool table. I could not see but heard the crash of a bottle. When everyone got up, Joe was bleeding. He was hit on the back of the head with the beer bottle.

More dummies came in to restrain Joe and Jim. The beer bottle dummy, causing the chaos, sneaked out without being hurt. He could not help but degrade someone who was psychologically hurting worse than himself. Mike had deceptive arrogance written all over his face.

The police came. Things were calmed. No one went to jail. However, the beer bottle dummy should have been arrested. The abused abuse the abused. I did not know anyone involved until the dummies came to the "rescue." Seldom are the "real" initiators of crimes punished in our society.

Tough dummies search for opportunities to show their "superiority," using gang mentality to degrade the vulnerable who need help the most. They seldom work toward long-term goals.

* * *

SCAMS

Some young cashiers distract and neglect returning change. We need to stop this abusive trend. Note perpetrators and call managers to report scams. Ask managers about their policies. Go higher if necessary. I usually call a manager only after an obvious or second incident. It is our job to promote honesty in this country. We can't blame everything on Adam and Eve. Too many young folks begin with small crimes, develop deceptive criminal egos, work up to larger things, and are eventually incarcerated. We must do our part to prevent escalation. If possible, correct politely but thoughtfully. In the long run, we are not doing scammers a favor by not correcting or reporting them. Madoff!

* * *

Chapter 10
Psychiatric Exercises

I search deep within this crazy mind,
A brain with little hope can be so unkind!
What can mend its twisted strings?
Faith in simple exercises of all things!

Hugh Fulcher 2006

The author has developed a system of unique exercise therapies for releasing inner tensions for mental healing. Inner tensions are developed over lifetimes such that inner feelings and sensations are accepted as normal.

Only one exercise requires special equipment. Exercises have been repeated often over the past eighteen-years. Neck, throat, and facial exercises are the most effective. Effectiveness is judged by the number of repressed energy-releases. Exercising muscles (and activating nerves) closest to the brain are the most effective. Predicting healing sensation migrations and intensity variations has made exercises exciting.

Throughout the years of exercises, healing sensations have migrated throughout the neck, throat, brainstem, and to some extend the upper brain. Healing sensations have evolved from unusual to spectacular. Thoughts become more creative. Results from psychiatric exercises are like body building results. There is little change in sensation feedback during the first months of exercises but results become spectacular over the years!

Since 1988, I have exercised the neck to release SCAPS. I model SCAPS as feedback sensations from traumatized neural networks breaking up and dispersing over-reactive trauma energy throughout the brain for my bipolar disorder cure. The goal is to release all SCAPS and attain "a clear mind." A clear mind thinks as efficiently as it was designed to do.

Normal body functions and movements are flowing or analogue. SCAPS began as brief, digital, energy-releases, which should not occur if the brain and body worked as designed. Neck exercises release trauma energy similar to chiropractic releases from joints. Manipulation reduces effects of calcium deposits and allows joints to return to least stressful positions. Unique exercises reduce traumatized neural networks to their least stressful state.

The criteria whether to practice psychiatric exercises and mental reconstruction has not been entirely developed. The decision is difficult since individual situations vary and processes require years of practice.

However, I give some rough guidelines. If exercising the head and neck rigorously and experiencing only a few SCAPS, traumatized neural network limits may be too rigid and difficult to purge to continue mental reconstruction. If many SCAPS are released during head and neck exercises, old subconscious processing limits may be more easily purged for expanding mental limits. If there are many SCAP sensations during mania and neck exercises, psychiatric exercises and mental reconstruction may be important processes for reducing inner stresses, mental healing, and recovering mental control.

Practicing psychiatric exercises is more pressing due to increasing atrocities and murders by those who have been bullied and stopped taking prescribed medications. This trend is increasing due to sensational news coverage, recognition of perpetrators, and action movie heroes.

Some feel so much mental pain that life is not worth living. They yearn for a moment of attention. Perpetrator names should not be continually repeated on the news media.

Physicians and psychiatrists cannot ensure patients take medications. Patients often stop taking medications when feeling slowed down or dull. Exercises expand thinking with feelings of excitement, heal the fabric of the brain, increase mind control, and develop a true cure for bipolar and other stress disorders. Be cautious. Exercises increase excitement initially. If practicing exercises, stay on prescribed medications unless reduced by your doctor. Even with medications, exercises improve thinking.

In 1990 after exercising my neck for over a year, I developed a system of resistant exercises, which increased SCAPS or trauma energy-releases. In privacy, and using the right-hand:

> *I used hand resistance with the following exercises: head-down, chin-down, chin-right, head-down and right, head-right, head-back and right, head-back. Similar exercises were alternated using the left-hand. Exercises used resistance of one hand at a time such that muscles were tired after 100 repetitions. Feedback was used to make exercises more efficient in releasing SCAPS. Unusual processes are needed for difficult to cure disorders.*

After a few months of practice, exercises can be performed quickly. Exercising muscles closest to the brain are most effective in healing trauma effects. Practice relaxing all muscles except the conflicting muscles being exercised. As in weight training, neck muscles and connected neural networks heal quicker when isolated during exercises. The subconscious mind is more able to focus on rebuilding isolated muscles and their connected neural networks.

Sensations from resistance/conflicting chin-down exercises are different with different hands. Some neural processing paths must also be used for the same exercise with different hands.

In depression or mania, there is a feeling of helplessness. Performing neck exercises gives feelings of doing something positive for oneself. Resistance exercises are my most powerful tool for psychiatric healing. Developing and practicing self-healing processes are more reasonable than simply relying on medications. Success depends upon abilities and time to practice.

Conflicting hand resistance during neck exercises is unusual and stimulates the subconscious mind to emotional limits. The hand pushes the chin up, and neck muscles pull the chin down. The subconscious mind makes psychiatric adjustments to avoid going beyond emotional limits and out of control.

If choosing to perform psychophysiotherapy, I recommend beginning with a few repetitions of the above exercises two or three times a week. Then increase to 100 repetitions when feeling comfortable in doing so. Do not perform exercises if experiencing pain. Mental reconstruction may not be positive if there is pain. We do not want to add trauma scars. Each reader must assess his own risks and benefits in performing exercises.

Traumatized networks are affected more by resistance exercises. Traumatized networks cannot accept and release energy as easily as normal networks. Energy builds up to traumatized neural network limits by exercises until released with a SCAP.

It helps to visualize head and neck muscles when exercising. Figure 10.1 shows head and neck muscles. Figures 10.2, 10.3, and 10.4 illustrate resistance exercises.

In the resistance chin down and the head down exercises, the digastric muscles promote the most changes of all psychiatric exercises. In genetic controlled reactions to trauma, these muscles open the mouth and the neck stiffens to gain control of the head. The mouth flies open to purge food and prepare for fight or flight.

Resistance head down and right (left), exercises stimulate high levels of SCAPS. The stylohyoid and sternocleidomastoid muscles are stressed with these exercises.

In caveman's times the neck responded and turned quickly to oncoming dangers. These muscles are close to the brain and, historically, reacted to traumatic situations. Traumatized, fast responding rigid nerves in the neck and throat release SCAP energy as reactions to hand resistance conflict. SCAP sensations in the throat and neck lead to the conclusion that mental processing is distributed into the neck and throat. I am aware of normal pain locations, and also of SCAP release locations within the brain.

The risorius and zygomaticus muscles are used for smiling and broadening the face. As these muscles relax and broaden, the creative right-brain becomes more dominant. A relaxed smile with meditation promotes creative ideas not previously thought possible.

Most headaches result from pent-up neural network energy and associated restricted blood flow.

Effective exercises for releasing tensions and pain are to meditate on simple pleasant holistic thoughts such as feeling good all over, and broadening the forehead. Periodically, rub horizontally over the muscles between the eyebrows with some pressure.

These muscles will feel noticeably relaxed to the touch. Headaches dissipate. With continued practice, appearance becomes more relaxed and skin improves. Muscles in the face relate to and are connected to glia within the brain. Reducing tensions between the eyebrows reduces tensions within the brain and promotes right-brain dominance.

When the face and body are tense, the brain is physically tense. Tensions cause thinking to be left-brained, short-ranged, and focused on pain.

The face is coordinated with emotional areas within the brain. With plastic surgery, facial muscles and structure are changed. Emotional areas of the brain change. The brain tries to heal cosmetic wounds and restore facial muscles. Plastic surgeries last for only a few years. If artificially changing the face and the brain, who have you become?

Highly stressed neural network SCAPS were released early on. SCAPS near the end of mental construction were sensed as flowing, with less energy, and lasting longer than initial SCAPS. With exercises, overstressed neural networks accept, but do not release, energy as readily as normal networks do.

Experimenting with normal, non-resistance neck exercises while stiffening the throat releases tensions and SCAPS. In resistance neck exercises there is no stiffening of the throat as emphasis is on conflicting muscle tensions.

There has been an effort to keep the brain balanced with exercises. Exercises were normally performed the same on each side. However, if there seemed to be more energy-release activity on one side; more repetitions were done on that side.

Scrolling text rather rapidly on a computer monitor and focusing long distance through the text enhances subconscious, holistic reading.

In focusing long distance through the text, all words are perceived with equal attention or holistically. Even though not aware of learning the scrolling text, there is a tremendous feeling of excitement. Caveman may have had this same feeling running through the woods. With training, the right-brain may be able to read holistically and the left-brain could interpret later. Holistic reading saves all the eye movements and reduces conscious effort.

Achieve feelings of excitement when quickly alternating short and long distance focus. Create excitement performing rapid eye movements: 1) from side to side, 2) up and down, and 3) diagonally both ways.

These activities prepared reactive minds for attacks from all sides. Eye exercises stimulate few SCAPS, but create mental excitement.

Performing normal workouts is less effective in releasing repressed energy than neck exercises. Calf exercises release the most SCAPS during normal weight workouts. Knees (and one knee) to the chest release SCAPS.

Performing left and right-brain dominance exercises uses my only special tool. I use a Holusion to practice switching between left and right-brain dominance.

An example of a Holusion was provided at the end of Chapter 7. It is best to use a large Holusion for practice. When looking at the detailed surface, the left-brain is dominant. When looking through the surface and focusing long distance, the right-brain becomes dominant and the three-dimensional Holusion, similar to a dream image, appears. Practice includes rapidly altering long and short range focus and bringing up a three-dimensional Holusion from different viewing angles. This exercise adds awareness and control in selecting left-right dominance.

I alternately push the top and sides of my mouth hard with my tongue rather infrequently.

When pushing each side of my upper molars, I can feel the brain twisting. It limbers up the old brain. A limber brain works better. Tongue exercises were done infrequently. Physicists think of tensions and movements. Begin slowly and gently.

Resistance exercises increase blood flow to the brain, tone face and neck muscles for looking and feeling better, and speed up mental reconstruction. Cosmetic surgery is so superficial! God gave humans wide mental and physical capabilities. Long-range planning develops man's greatest achievements. Continued lack of challenges and mental and physical disuse reduces capabilities.

Before sleeping, take several deep breaths to increase blood oxygen levels and relax the body, and brain by broadening the face with a slight smile.

Taking deep breaths before sleep reduces subconscious worry. Yawns automatically force deep breathing for increasing oxygen levels. Broadening the face activates the right-brain for sleep. Focusing on daily problems before sleep narrows the face and restricts subconscious processes to waking problems during the night. Before sleep, meditate and free the mind of negative thoughts. Broaden the face, relax, lower mental energy, and the dreaming brain will become nimble and creative.

Relaxing is a bit of an art. Broadening the face too much energizes temple and cheek muscles. It helps to over-broaden the face several times to recognize and obtain the relaxed neutral position. This position needs to be maintained for a few seconds until the glia relax and broaden the brain. It is a bit like in Star Wars when Yoda says, "Open your mind."

With a broadened brain and open mind, the subconscious mind is free to travel creatively through memories independent of physical time. Practice meditating and broadening the face until feeling relaxed. Feel excitement of increased blood flow within the brain.

There is a tendency for the brain to narrow and the face to frown during headaches as minds focus on pain. Relaxing and broadening the face for a few minutes reduces headaches. Pain may increase a little at first and then lessen. Try it.

Important facial exercises include smiling. For additional facial relaxation, place finger tips of both hands on the center of the forehead and sweep them apart and down the cheeks and together at the upper neck. Use a slight pressure for broadening and relaxing the face.

Neck and facial exercises affect areas of the brainstem that control the exercised muscles. During traumas facial and neck muscles react by contracting. Each neck, throat, and facial muscle is connected to brain cells. We can look at a middle-aged or older person and tell who has hated, loved, or had pain throughout life. The contour of the facial muscles mirrors brain configurations. It is healthy to maintain good facial posture. Smile and become "broad-minded" and your brain structure will smile and love you for it. Do not let your narrow face create a "narrow-mind."

To some extent, we feel in control when we can predict and influence future occurrences. Practicing exercises and models, places us in control of healing our minds and, in turn, our lives.

Yelling and rhyme exercises were performed. Do not under estimate confidence building and healing powers of low-pitched and repetitive sounds. Nursery rhymes built strong, confident neural networks as we grew up. Poets and dictators have used the power of repeated sounds and rhymes for centuries.

Voice exercises elevate moods. I practice aggressive and quite moods. Voice experiments helped distinguish between verbal and non-verbal inner thought processes. Exercises placed my mind at conflicting trauma limits. I am not normally a yelling person. Releases of energy with these exercises came quickly and powerfully, but lasted for less than a month. One should not practice yelling exercises around others, or if one has health issues. Benefits are small compared to neck exercises.

In October of 2005, I went to a chiropractor. Pain prevented me from bending the last joint of my right-hand writing thumb. From earlier experience, I knew adjustments to the neck might relieve the pain and restore writing ability. My chiropractor twisted and popped my neck and back and prescribed a neck pump to realign neck vertebrae.

The neck pump included straps that held the head down. A hand held squeeze pump inflates a blunt rubber knife into the back of the neck. With the rubber knife and head restraints, I was in control of my own chiropractic adjustments. I exercised the head up and back and at small angles. I repeated movements until neck pops dissipated. Pops were breaking up of calcium deposits between vertebrae joints that restricted alignment.

By adjusting my neck on the rubber knife, I could isolate and exercise each vertebra within the neck. The thumb was healed. I explored movements to release tensions between neck vertebrae.

In performing psychiatric exercises, never continue with pain more than one might encounter in normal weight training. Extended pain will not help healing.

Chiropractic experience is similar to neck exercises and supports the value of psychiatric energy-releases. Many aches and pains are caused by subluxations or partial dislocations of neck and back vertebrae, which put pressure on related nerves.

Chiropractic releases are more energetic than SCAPS but not as energetic as metallic pings or mental nuclear explosions.

SCAPS reduce physical tensions in rigid neural networks. When activated, traumatized networks, including glia, release high-energy frequencies or resonances. With nanotechnology, new health care professions may eventually locate and disperse energy from extremely traumatized neurons and glia. Stresses within the brain cause stresses throughout the body, adversely affects health, and hastens aging.

Psychiatric neck exercises can break up rigid traumatized networks releasing energy. Conflicts caused by traumatized neural networks ages the brain prematurely. Practicing exercises and making models, the subconscious mind increases skills in locating and releasing energy. The Fountain of Youth is a relaxed mind.

Chiropractic care is applied physics. Sometimes, all that is needed is release of pressure on nerves in spinal column joints. Many will also not believe benefits of chiropractic adjustments or mental reconstruction until experienced.

Neural and muscle back tensions reduce capabilities which may remain throughout life unless treated with unique exercise, psychiatric, or chiropractic therapy. Unwanted disruptive energy from stress and traumas builds up during childhood and adult life. Inner stress feels normal since developed over a long period of time but reduces mental efficiency. We are not conscious of the brain's slow degradation. We all have levels of dysfunction. Slow mental murders are caused by childhood abuse and uncaring false significant people.

For every chiropractic energy-release, there have been millions of SCAP releases. Significant improvements can be made with chiropractic care. Trauma scars resist releasing trauma energy but can be stimulated to release energy by psychoanalysis feedback and my psychiatric exercises.

Psychiatric exercises have taken years for mental healing. The brain and its mind heal very slowly.

Physicians usually do not recommend chiropractors. One reason is they do not want to take the risk if recommendations are not beneficial. It is important for patients to search for reasonable long-range solutions to health problems.

Let's develop psychological exercises that may help if getting mixed messages from someone significant. Some people give mixed verbal and body languages, possibly, without even knowing it. This exercise is intended to evaluate communication. Evaluate verbal communications with numbers between and including positive and negative ten.

We need to judge whether important communications are confidence building or not. Start at zero! Subtract one if there is a degrading smile at the end of a verbal communication. Subtract one if there is an inappropriate laugh at the end of verbal communication. Subtract two if the speaker is walking away during his or your speaking. Subtract two if there are conflicting head gestures. Subtract one if body language is cold or stiff. Subtract one if hand gestures conflict with words. Subtract three if verbal language is intentionally not understandable. Subtract two if listening discontinues while you are talking. Numbers need not be precise, but you get the idea of associating actions with discrete numbers to activate left-brain reasoning.

Add one if there is a positive nod of the head. Add two if there is a gentle touch along with the speaker's communication. Add three if there is a warm hug. Add two if words are confidence building. Add three if words are very confidence building. Add four if word and body language are inspiring. Start at zero and cut off totals below negative ten and above positive ten.

We are lucky getting "tens" from our significant others, including bosses. If the value is negative, we need to talk with communicators and try to understand each other's languages and motives. Stress how important confidence building is to everyone.

Controllers and deceivers use mixed verbal and body languages to destroy victims. The left-brain understands the words and the right-brain understands the body language. In this exercise, we have placed numbers on body and verbal language to involve the left-brain for understanding the conflicting languages. If we understand conflicting communications they affect us less.

Unique stress reducing exercises are like vaccinations. They briefly add stress to the brain and subconscious mind. We learn to handle this stimulated stress. When real stress comes along, the brain and subconscious mind are more prepared to handle it. We build up immunity against stress. Additionally, the subconscious mind becomes adept at locating and releasing pent-up, neural network stresses. Briefly, experiencing and calming down from justified anger is healthy.

Routine psychiatric exercises restore flexibility to the brain like stretching exercises restore flexibility to the body. Psychiatric exercises increase blood flow to the brain and may prevent strokes. We need a healthy and strong mind and back. Help develop children's brain structure by nurturing appropriate responses to emotional and limiting conflicts.

Tell children it's okay to be angry for short periods of time, but they need to develop creative ways of expressing and reducing anger that helps all involved. Also, a child does not need to love or say he loves a sibling who abuses him. Otherwise, he or she may continue in an abusive marriage.

After years of practice, psychiatric energy or SCAPS continue to be released more easily with similar exercises. An original SCAP model is a few high-energy SCAPS released by one exercise. Near the end of mental reconstruction, the SCAP model would consist of a few hundred SCAPS, with one hundredth of the original SCAP energy, and with

a connected and flowing feeling during the release when stimulated by a similar exercise.

Complementary verbal stimulation activates subconscious left-brain processes for discovering and releasing repressed energy and for increasing inner associations. Be creative in increasing inner communication and control. There is a language barrier between conscious and subconscious processes. We must enhance language communication between subconscious and conscious processes for healing and mind improvement.

The mind manages repetition through right-brain processes. We do not need to remember individual processes, but only the purpose and efficiency of processes and repetitions. Exercising neck, throat, and to a lesser extent all, muscles, make the brain and mind more flexible.

The right brain influences reading "discrete words." The exercise below gives left-right brain importance in comprehension similar to Holusion exercises. Believe it or not, you can read the following:

I cdnuolt blveiee taht I cluod aulaclty
uesdnatnrd waht I was rdanieg. The
phaonmneal pweor of the hmuan mnid
aoccdrnig to rscheearch at Cmabrigde
Uinervtisy pvroes it deosn't mttaer in waht
oredr the ltteers in a wrod are, the olny
iprmoatnt tihng is taht the frist and lsat ltteer
be in the rghit pclae. The rset can be a taotl
mses and you can sitll raed it wouthit a
porbelm. Tihs is bcuseae the huamn mnid
deos not raed ervey lteter by istlef, but the
wrod as a wlohe. Amzanig, huh?

This exercise proves we can read words holistically using the right brain. With practice we can read sentences and paragraphs holistically with the right brain.

Figure 10.1 Head and Neck Muscles

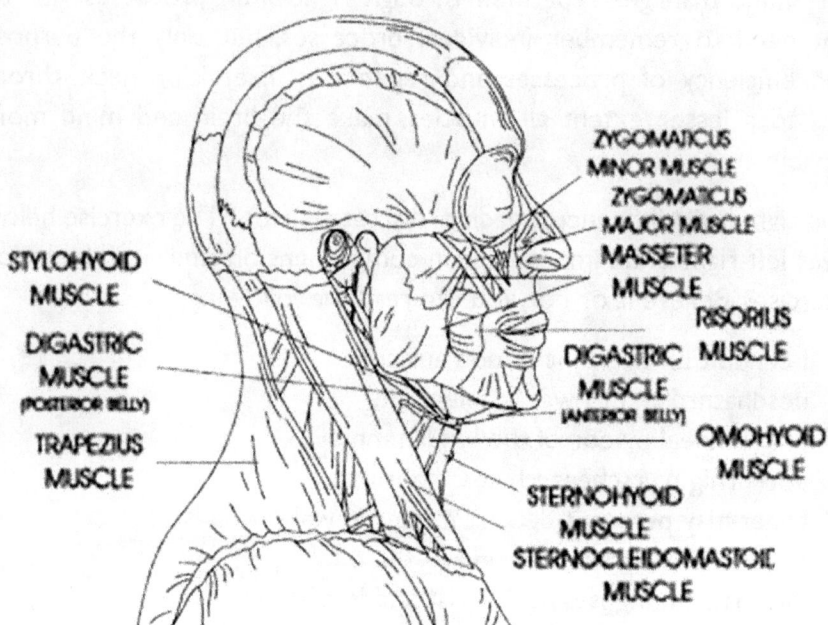

ZYGOMATICUS
MINOR MUSCLE
ZYGOMATICUS
MAJOR MUSCLE
MASSETER
MUSCLE
RISORIUS
MUSCLE
DIGASTRIC MUSCLE
(ANTERIOR BELLY)
OMOHYOID
MUSCLE
STERNOHYOID
MUSCLE
STERNOCLEIDOMASTOID
MUSCLE

STYLOHYOID
MUSCLE
DIGASTRIC
MUSCLE
(POSTERIOR BELLY)
TRAPEZIUS
MUSCLE

Psychiatric Exercises

Figure 10.2 Head Down Resistance Exercise

Neck Muscles Pull Chin Down, Thumb Pushes Chin Up

Figure 10.3 Head Down & Left Resistance Exercise

Neck Muscles Pull Chin Down & Left, Thumb Pushes Up & Right

Figure 10.4 Head Left Resistance Exercise

Neck Muscles Pull Head Left, Hand Pushes Head Right

Chapter 11
Elementary Mind Models

"All men dream, but not equally.
Those who dream by night, in the dusty recesses
of their minds,
wake in the day to find that it was vanity.
But, the dreamers of the day are dangerous men, for
they may act their dreams with open eyes to
make them possible."

T. E. Lawrence

Mind models assist inward, reflective thinking. The mind understands and heals itself increasing efficiency.

Mind models initiate and guide subconscious healing processes. The conscious mind develops an understanding of models and the subconscious mind translates them into its own language to understand and heal its self.

Elementary mind models were the earliest models requiring little physiology. Like psychotherapy, they use relational concepts for the subconscious mind to understand and heal its processes for expanding mental limits. Elementary models promote thinking about the brain and its function: the mind.

The Tip of the Iceberg

This model helps readers think about how powerful our subconscious processes are. It relates the conscious mind and subconscious mind to the tip of the iceberg and the rest of the world, respectively. The tip of the iceberg only "knows" the heat of the sun, ocean winds, the ocean water slapping against its edges, gravity, and vaguely the bottom of the iceberg that supports it above water. The bottom of the iceberg corresponds to the subconscious functions that build consciousness "above water." Conscious minds have little awareness of subconscious processes.

Environments increase or diminish icebergs and conscious and subconscious communication. Subconscious reasoning and memory support processes relate to the ocean and rest of the world. The solar system and universe are modeled as heaven. This model shows the expansiveness of our subconscious minds.

Hanging on the Edge

Extend awareness and mental control by hanging on the edge between waking and sleeping, consciousness and sub-consciousness, and sanity and insanity. Convert more of the subconscious mind into consciousness for increasing mind control. Practicing hanging on the edge develops confident mental skills.

With practice athletes hang on the edge to play well when the pressure is on. Do the thing and have the power. We can learn to maintain sanity in stressful situations! An introspective mind, hanging on the edge, is more revealing than a hundred books.

After seven years of age, basic intelligence and personality do not change significantly unless we experience significant emotional events. Practicing hanging on the edge at mental limits simulates significant emotional events.

Say, an individual sees a fire and pulls a family out from certain death. He gets some burns and is a hero. He remembers his ordeal and the exhilaration of accomplishing a superhuman feat. He faced death, hung on the edge, and won! The experience purged mind limiting trauma effects. He now has the attitude and "feeling" to live the rest of his life thinking and acting as a hero.

Hanging on the edge can produce "significant emotional events" many times a day. The fabric of the brain is healed. One becomes stronger and confident. Meditate to calm down.

Explain!

How would you explain an entirely new experience to someone? Could you explain to someone how to swim if he had always lived in the desert and had never seen more than a glass of water? You would have to learn about his background and what concepts he understood. You would explain swimming with analogies to things he already knows, demonstrate hand and leg movements while lying on the floor, and assist his imagination in feeling the water's buoyancy and its resistance to hand and feet motions. If your explanation was good enough, the student would swim and live. Good teachers keep others afloat in new situations.

Reality to the student is when he is tossed into the deep water. He faces the trauma by adapting and swimming using his simulated lessons; he drowns; or someone bails him out. A good explanation of something new must have a good balance between old and new. So many explanations do not consider the backgrounds of listeners.

A manic-depressive is plunged into a new reality and learns to swim, drowns, or someone bails him out. He will never heal, cure, or save his overstressed mind unless he aggressively works to understand its inner processes.

Limits

The brain is a machine - a thinking machine. All machines have limits. Any machine extended beyond its limits will either blow a fuse or blow up. The mind can be stressed beyond its reasoning limits. It can blow a fuse. It does not stop right away but loses stability and operates in an oscillating mode called bipolar disorder. By learning to stress ones self briefly to mental limits, abilities can be expanded and controlled. The subconscious mind can slowly awaken to construct new mental limits. Old broken emotional limits are replaced with wider, more logical mental processing limits.

Subconscious processes are reflected by emotional limits, or they continue to get more excited searching for limits that no longer exist. Trauma scars are like cancers and do not synchronize with the normal symphony within the brain. Normal subconscious processes are slowed and limited by the normal symphony of the brain having to avoid or counter effects of sporadic traumatized network activations. Purging trauma memory energy restores versatile and efficient neural processes.

When excess energy is purged from trauma memories with exercises, the subconscious mind no longer has to avoid disruptive trauma activations but loses stability. Let's look at a mind limit experiment that may have caused a trauma scar.

A wire needed to be drawn up a wall into the attic and down the same wall on the other side of a door. I completed the second floor work and went to drill holes from the attic. I only had a flashlight. I began drilling and recognized that two dark areas two feet from me were coiled-up snakes. I scampered back to the attic entrance. I stopped and thought for a while. I would either have to remove the snakes, quit work, or work close to the snakes. The weather was cold. I decided to complete work, snakes and all.

This experiment allowed me to experience emotional limits of fear, fierceness, and bravery. I intentionally created a simulated "significant emotional event" to initiate psychiatric healing. I do not recommend this experiment. I felt a bit like Caveman at the time. Stimulating the mind to limits promotes subconscious and conscious creativity.

Meditating on calm flowing scenes without words develops imagination. Words reduce creativity. Einstein was slow learning language. Thinking longer in images or pictures may have helped him develop picture models for his impressive discoveries.

Imagination means thinking in images and restores genetic creative abilities. With imagination we can extend thinking to limits. Experiencing fear through imagination may liberate our minds to function during real fear.

Perfection

Perfection is God. On earth, perfection is only in the mind. Using superlatives for your or other's work may be damaging to listeners. Avoid unnecessary comparisons, especially in youth sports

Perfection might be when things are going your way; you are at your best at what you do. For example, if you were writing well and creative words were flowing, you might say you were having "white flow." Usually labeling yourself or anyone with the label "perfection" is impossible to maintain and harmful. Perfection is when others do something better than you had imagined. Use "perfection" sparingly.

Calling a child a genius is a horrible burden to place on a child and can ruin his life. The poor child feels he has to be a genius to everyone. "Genius" has connotations of perfection.

Create

What does create mean? It means making something that has never existed before, something new and different. We can create new ideas. We can have a thought we have never seen or heard before. Some of us are more successful at developing creative thoughts than others. How does it happen?

The human machine has developed limits for all aspects of its operation. The subconscious mind is much like muscles. It prepares for only what it thinks it needs to do with some small additional "safety" ability. The subconscious mind performs "ho-hum" tasks day in and day out for individuals who stay within their comfort zones. Retrieving memories and making comparisons are routine. For them, nothing much is new under the cranium. The brain needs building blocks for creative ideas.

Every complete thought is constructed by subconscious iterative building blocks. During life, subconscious rules and processes are developed to promote sub-thoughts into words and thoughts. Sub-thoughts are stored subconsciously as hologram images. This is understood as dreams consist of three-dimensional images. Dream characters are presented at all angles.

Subconscious minds have the ability to compare any two three-dimensional holographic memories at many angles using imaginative subconscious processes. The subconscious mind can mentally rotate holographic memory images around on all three axes for analyses. It compares only two memory holograms at a time. With stimulation, subconscious minds become more versatile and creative at comparing hologram images at more angles. If a comparison develops a resonance between two images, the subconscious mind creates a new three-dimensional hologram. A new sub-idea has been created. If the created hologram is energetic enough, the sub-idea is elevated to a complete conscious idea.

Memory

For some, scriptures memorized over a lifetime are more real than their every day lives or scientific models. Repetition strengthens memory holograms and beliefs for the soul to ponder.

We might view a person from only one angle. Our powerful subconscious minds complete his three-dimensional hologram image from all angles. Holistic and symmetric processes complete image memories. What we see and memories we construct depend upon our attitude, curiosity, and imagination.

Some people think more precisely than others. A person constantly seeking and experiencing new things expands his subconscious hologram comparison and integration functions. A subconscious mind, existing on the edge, learns to make more precise, wider, and faster comparisons.

Probabilities of creating resonances between current and memory holograms increase with patience, attention and practice. Matchmaker, Matchmaker, make me a match. Without hologram matches for new ideas, there is no learning. When very young, experiences were compared to God's spiritual holograms. Babies learn like lightning with fewer experiences to compare. Creative ideas, stimulated by new experiences, are compared to combinations and permutations of similar memory holograms.

Hologram comparisons are made in two fashions. Comparisons are made searching for details with either symmetry or asymmetry. Every entity has an asymmetric opposite. For example, a vertical line in a current hologram may be compared to a horizontal line in memory holograms. The second process is comparing refined emotional energy levels within holograms. Hologram memories are formed with refined emotional energy levels. Mental hologram processes up to seven years of age are very emotional and formative. In the womb, holograms were compared to God's perfect holograms. Each new baby has perfect communication with God.

What about the blind? Their processes also compare three-dimensional holograms using genetic abilities cultivated by sight. Blind experiences are also stored in subconscious holograms.

The Parachute

The mind is like a parachute; it does not function unless opened. Let's say air molecules are "sub-ideas" or subconscious building blocks for ideas. The more sub-ideas our parachute catches to slow down our descent, the more patience and versatility our subconscious minds have to hit the ground with a creative idea.

Subconscious reality starts when we jump out of the plane. Our subconscious minds start having sub-ideas for producing a conscious thought as the parachutist sails toward the ground. The controller of the subconscious mind must have an emotional discrete sub-idea to open the parachute. The parachutist panics about needing to have an important sub-idea of being adequate to do a life saving task.

The subconscious mind, the parachutist, fails to stay within its own rhythm and limits, and becomes temporarily insane and incapable of opening the parachute. Insanely, the parachutist, the controller of the subconscious mind, fails to open the parachute, and receives only a few molecules of air to slow the fall.

With great impact a highly emotional conscious thought is created. A trauma scar is ingrained as our parachutist blames himself for not opening the parachute. The force of the manic idea is so strong it frightens observers from jumping since the conscious thought was so emotionally defensive. The emotional parachutist can not think of an intelligent thing to say. He is temporarily brain dead because of the impact of the landing, a trauma scar.

The parachutist goes to Dr. FEE (My powerful futuristic dream psychiatrist described in Appendix A.) to mend his body and mind. It takes time before the parachutist or subconscious mind is ready to jump again to produce a creative thought.

Dr. Fee was successful. The parachutist regains confidence and jumps again. The more confident the parachutist, the higher the probability the parachute will be opened. A confident parachutist opens the parachute and has control where and how softly he might land. The parachutist produces a creative conscious idea upon landing. On hearing a gentle idea, listeners are inspired, jump out of the plane, open their parachutes, and produce creative ideas. One shared creative idea inspired many creative ideas.

Everyone learns to parachute well. Opened parachutes gather many sub-ideas for gentle impacts. High-level, low-energy creative ideas are for all to understand and nurture. Thoughts are shared. We must stay within our own rhythms and use our backgrounds for solutions to challenges and world peace.

When ready for sleep, open the dreaming parachute by broadening the face with good thoughts before dreamland. We may float through the air with parachutes open to return to an embryo. Floating in mother's womb was heaven on earth until kicked out.

If we try to reason like someone else, we have an uncertain universe. Displaced solutions will not produce the inner harmony of our own confident solutions. We must be ourselves.

Never let others convince you their way is the only way. They aggrandize themselves without empowering others.

People who truly have mental freedom may be those who have had significant trauma or near-death experiences. It is difficult to understand the purpose of life until having experienced near-death or spiritual rebirth. A closed mind seeking only its own security is not spiritual and loses eternal life. With an open parachute, we have more time to receive God's guidance.

Headlights

A simple analogy between left- and right-brain dominance is that of car headlights either on high or low beam. The battery (generator), electrical circuitry, and sealed beams are structures that allow drivers the option of focusing up-close and detailed, requiring quick reaction times or focusing holistically long-range permitting slower reaction times.

In a similar manner, the brainstem, and possibly the limbic system, switches on left- or right-brain dominance depending upon desire or need to focus up close or at a distance. Selecting brain dominance is improved with practice. With either set of headlights, the driver must learn to operate his car within reasonable and safe driving limits. Minds must have a balance between short and long focus to develop a mental structure for exciting lives within limits.

I'm O.K.; You're O.K.

Dr. Thomas Harris in his book, I'm O.K.; You're O.K. [1], has developed a mind model: "the Parent, Child, and Adult" in his book. In this model, we have three distinct personalities and modes of decision making. A grown person retains personalities of his parents which were imprinted while a baby and young child. This emotional decision making method is called the "Parent." During this stage the young child made no judgments of right or wrong but observed and mimicked his parents' decisions as wisdom from the "gods." The young baby lives his life through reflections of his parents.

Next, the "Child" personality rather than having absolute faith in parent behavior and decisions begins to have doubts about their wisdom and searches for independence. The Child's decision making consists of wild oscillations between faith in parents and faith in his own experiments and judgments. The "Child" learns by mimicking parents' activities and decisions without fully understanding purposes. The third, "Adult," personality relies on his judgment and abilities, developed from his own experiences and trusted opinions.

Depending upon traumas in early childhood and current levels of stress, a grown person may revert to emotions and thinking of either "The Parent" or "The Child." Under stress, a grown person might act and make judgments using only directives parents dictated when he was a young child. Reasoning is absent; the limbic system gains control. Emotional thinking becomes erratic, especially, if parenting was harsh or conflicting.

Tumbleweed

The Tumbleweed model is to re-experience awareness of early childhood thinking. The young mind is a tumble weed controlled by the wind. The wind can blow in any direction and at varying speeds. The wind is the flighty stimuli sensed when babies.

Clear the mind of worries and relax. Close your eyes and feel only what your senses are presenting. Broaden the face. Relax and lose conscious control. Be aware only of influences affecting your relaxed body and mind. Relax free will. Become a simple recorder of sensations and external influences. Make no judgments. Go where the wind blows. The mind becomes the wind-blown tumbleweed that is at peace wherever it is. We have returned to our spiritual baby's minds. By making no decisions we gain insight into decision making.

We increase control in the long run by briefly reverting to our baby thinking without control but simply recording sensations holistically or spiritually. We create a database for later judgment. When relaxed, the mind humbly surrenders to the will of the wind. We learn to have no guilt for abuses in childhood or mental inabilities, for we were only tumbleweeds.

Diamonds

Let's add a sparkle to creative processes. God is creative today. If we forget worries and calm our minds to concentrate on God's pureness and love, He will share His creativeness with us. The secret is that we must prepare to recognize and receive His creative processes. We can become more aware of God's constant creative communications. Creative ideas are retracing God's timeless footprints left during creation of the universe.

What are creative ideas like? Well, they are not always so obvious. God's creative ideas are always present for each of us, but we must be prepared to recognize them.

A creative idea from God is a diamond in the rough in flowing analogue spiritual language. We must have faith that diamonds or God's creative processes exist, be sensitive, and ready to recognize God's creative diamonds in the rough.

We must find and go into the diamond mine, be prepared to dig through tons of worthless dirt and rocks, and separate the rocks from the dirt. We must examine the rocks and recognize the diamond in the rough.

Once we have found, or received, a "diamond in rough" we must study the creative idea, and cut the diamond so that it sparkles for the world to see. That sparkle and shine is the reflection of God's love for mankind. God's creative ideas are complete and analogue. It is our responsibility to breakup holistic spiritual ideas into discrete words with our best translation to present God's sparkle to the world.

If we are blessed with a gift from God, our work is not easy. We have work to transform creative ideas from God's deep structure, analogue language into sentences so all might experience God's Creation. We must accept spiritual responsibilities.

Good Night!

Most people work hard at being consistent. Being consistent may be good for social and work life but is not so good for being creative. Can we enhance our creative processes? Subconscious processes manipulate holograms for consciousness and decision making. There are obstacles which may prevent subconscious processes from performing needed permutations and combinations for creative ideas.

Worry causes repeated subconscious processes which block creative thinking for solutions. With relaxation and meditation before sleep, the subconscious mind awakens the next morning with creative ideas from dreams.

While awake, consciously think of possible solutions. Don't develop a mindset that there can be only one solution. Think of input that might be used to make each solution viable.

Meditate on darkness with expectation of goodness and light emerging. Thinking of darkness, the subconscious mind no longer needs to perform the complex tasks of producing normal sight awareness. The subconscious mind becomes free to expand its search for confident solutions. The body and mind are calmed so less subconscious energy is used to develop conscious functions.

One conscious mind selecting the best subconscious options corresponds to voting by members in brainstorming for solutions to corporate problems.

Inner subconscious comparisons are somewhat similar to computer comparisons but with tolerances set by moods and subconscious hologram characteristics. Some have more creative subconscious processes than others with wider tolerances for recognizing mental hologram similarities. A person routinely seeking and experiencing new things expands tolerances for making hologram comparisons.

A person who lives on the edge trains the subconscious mind to work in bursts of activities. Bursts of activity can be cultured with controlled emotion levels to develop creative ideas. Mental consistency does not produce creative ideas.

Approval

Let's analyze creative writing. As with the "diamond" model, we need to do homework in our areas of interest.

God, our Creator, gives a humble and faithful writer a gift of developing ideas. When, a writer focuses on God, remains humble and faithful, but writes assertively, God gives the writer an unusual gift. This gift is not a full blown brilliant idea. God allows us to ask Him for approval of our ideas. We must develop imaginative ideas and be willing to ask God for acceptance.

By meditating and presenting ideas to God, He lets us know which ideas are creative. Creative ideas seem to settle deep within us, become a part of us, and give us an unusual feeling of completion. God helps us verify we are following in His footsteps when He created the universe. With experience, the writer refines writing with flowing creative ideas.

Elementary models are easy to understand and help us learn about aspects of the mind. Elementary models often have more effect in psychiatric healing than more complex models.

REFERENCE:

(1) Harris, Thomas, 1969, *I'm OK, You're OK*, Avon Books, NY, NY.

Chapter 12
Discrete and Holistic Mind Models

Paradise Lost (Excerpt)

"The Mind is its own place, and in itself
Can make a Heaven of Hell, a Hell of Heaven ..."

John Milton

Traumas create high-energy, difficult-to-control resonances that interfere with normal processes and demand attention. Subconsciously, minds reflect upon their traumas. Severe trauma victims are prone to abuse others. With excessive energy, the emotional right-brain overrides day-to-day left-brain reasoning. Psychiatric exercises reduce trauma energy allowing the left-brain to increase dominance and control for slowing thinking.

Let's look at discrete left-brain and holistic right-brain models. Models are directed toward subconscious coordination between the two normally complementary hemispheres.

The two functions are up-close and detailed thinking, and long range, flowing, and holistic thinking. The goal is to provide the subconscious mind models of itself so it can understand and heal its self.

Subconscious processes are good at receiving sensed data and producing conscious thoughts but have difficulties analyzing their own functions. With stimulation, the subconscious mind translates models into its "binary" or hologram language for improving its inner communication functions.

Let's define what we mean by discrete and holistic. Discrete could be defined as a single member of a choir singing a solo in tenor. This singer can make many melodious sounds or vibrations in the air for us to hear. If sounds are on key and in rhythm, we hear beautiful music that may inspire love and faith.

Holistic is described as a choir of 500 members singing in perfect harmony. Some sing tenor, some sing base, and others sing in different parts. Individuals sing differently, but there is no individual standout. All members are equally important and fill the air with integrated holistic vibrations.

What happens to the air? Each voice causes air vibrations to expand outward in all directions. All vibrations are integrated within the air to make holistic sounds of music. Holistic means integrated and complete. There is a feeling of completeness in hearing the integrated sounds of a large choir.

Holistic could also be a meaningful word. Suppose I gave you a telephone number and you did not have a pen. The number is: 800-738-3725. You could integrate several digits into one meaningful word: 800-SEVERAL. Remembering one, "holistic," word is easier, and we have a formula to retrieve the numbers.

Let's look at discrete and holistic thinking. Each localized trauma network contains a discrete highly emotional memory of a hurtful experience. Trauma memory activations conflict with and detract from the normal holistic symphony of activations throughout the brain.

The holistic mind is like the voices of the 500 member choir. "Vibrations" or synchronized firings of billions of neurons throughout the brain construct beautiful symphonies for creative ideas and lives. Right-brain dominance, for most people, includes repetitive and long-range planning. Mechanics of repetitive right-brain processes and their goals are remembered. Individual repetitions are not remembered. Billions of neuron activities are coordinated to organize thoughts for controlling our lives. Wow!

Our brains and bodies work holistically in many tasks. For example, walking involves integrated coordination of millions of nerve and muscle cells. The subconscious mind and nerves coordinate muscle cell activations. Consciously, we only need a vague idea for moving each leg forward and backward. Each leg movement requires millions of muscle cell contractions and relaxations. Essentially, we only need to concentrate on the sound of the entire choir and not individual voices. Macros, or specialized groups of interconnected neural networks, become organized to efficiently coordinate repetitious brain and muscle cell activities.

Let's take our description of "discrete" one more step. Let's look at the discrete vibrations or firings of one neuron. This neuron fires with approximately the same frequencies with the same chemical and electromagnetic energies. Similar to one discrete choir member's voice being integrated within the music of the choir, each neural network produces a part of an integrated hologram that constructs our thinking or composing inner music.

The brain has inner processes to organize and compare mental holograms for creating a symphony of subconscious and conscious resonances. The integrals of fast resonances manage subconscious processes, and integrals of slow resonances, the conscious mind, manage conscious activities.

Without emotional and trauma design limits, the brain would attempt to holistically think of all aspects of this universe each moment. That is, without brain design limits, we would attempt to "think" like God, with unlimited "thinking."

Mental functions can be divided into two parts: physical sensing and processing and pure analytical processing independent of body actions and reactions. With mental reconstruction, analytical processing should attain significant improvement. Motor-neural networks can be reprogrammed and re-grow for improving body control and reactions.

"Flash" scenarios normally were subconscious processes which developed the unusual reflex that saved me from certain death. In normal thinking, it is difficult to understand how disconnected emotional scenarios caused the precise jerks of the steering wheel to save my life. Hologram processes must work in spiritual time without the slow process of developing words.

Words were developed to communicate ideas between individuals. When communicating within ourselves, we should not limit thinking to word processes. Learning to manipulate images within scenes and other wordless processes restructures the brain to improve thinking.

Speaking includes formation of words with physical movements of the throat, vocal cords, jaw, lips, and tongue. Physical movements slow down thinking. I estimate it takes one thousand times more energy to say a word than it does to think of that word. In a similar manner, it takes at least one hundred times less energy to process a word subconsciously than consciously. We should learn to develop input, process thoughts subconsciously, and then review process results consciously. It is the energy-efficient thing to do!

For solving difficult problems, organize input and relax before sleeping. Wake up the next morning with problems solved. It was solved with less energy while dreaming during the night!

Minds love energy efficiency. For example, speed reading is an example of energy efficiency. By not forming words with the mouth and throat, reading rates soar.

All of our conscious thoughts and feelings have been subconsciously compared to our emotional limits. Is there a life threatening emergency? Emotional limits are developed in neck, throat, brainstem, and other areas of the brain by early and erratic trauma experiences. Even genetic limits can become more organized and efficient.

Traumas disrupt normal subconscious processes. Mentally organizing helter-skelter occurrences was impossible for a baby's young brain. Normal and trauma memories are stored within refined high-energy resonance levels. This explains the lightening recall of highly-emotional, high-frequency "Flash" memories.

There are energy strata of memories and limits governing human behavior. For example, higher emotional mental limits are activated as we get closer to the edge of a cliff. Emotions also get higher lifting increasingly strenuous weights.

If a limit is surpassed, we become irrational. The brain is no longer able to maintain its logical set of operating procedures and activates its faster responding, rugged reactive system. Even though trauma limits during childhood were constructed for immediate mental safety, they limit analytical capabilities.

Meditation and sleeping relax waking emotional limits. Thinking becomes creative when subconscious processes extend to genetic limits.

At the beginning of mental reconstruction, we might model a trauma energy-release as drops of water from a faucet every one tenth of a second when stimulated by one neck exercise. There is a brief initial resistance within the neck when performing a conflicting exercise. Only a small amount of energy is released from one trauma neural network with early exercises.

Toward the end of mental reconstruction, sensations are more like opening the faucet fully and closing it quickly within one second. Healing accelerates as more trauma scar energy is released with similar exercises. Resistance to releasing trauma energy lessens over time and with practice.

Here is a theory of consciousness that determines what is real for us. Individual neuron firings are too fast to be conscious. We know that subliminal messages can be blinked on a screen so fast that we are not conscious of them, but our subconscious minds are aware of them. This process shows that the subconscious mind recognizes images faster than the conscious mind.

Let us explain this phenomenon. If internal or external stimuli become strong enough, a related neural network in the brainstem promotes a dominant resonance throughout the brain that is strong and long enough for consciousness. The minimum human conscious period corresponds to the ability of eyes to recognize image changes.

Let's say it takes twenty consistent firings within one network to promote a "fast" conscious resonance. Consistent "repetitive" firings create long lasting electromagnetic resonances throughout the brain for consciousness.

If our senses perceive an image too briefly, we do not become conscience of that fast stimulus. Our conscious resonance limit was not met. Mental reconstruction widens visual limits.

Since limbs move so slowly, slow resonances within the brain are needed for monitoring and controlling at environmentally survivable reaction rates. Consciousness developed from senses allows us to go about the tasks of our lives.

During REM sleep, the reticular formation initiates faster resonances for managing dreaming functions. Having less energy, dreams are not usually remembered upon slow, restful awakenings. When dreaming, consciousness may be forced upon us by stimuli – such a loud noise.

What are feelings? Let's add an intermediate subconscious processor. My reason for this addition is that, when we spot someone we like, we obviously don't consciously recall all the good things we have done together. Consciously, that would take too much time and mental energy.

At subconscious low energy-levels, significant interactions are integrated, and an averaged subconscious result or "feeling" is constructed and recalled. Our subconscious mind has saved lots of conscious work. All we really needed initially was good (or bad) feelings about someone or some experience.

Let's study conscious and subconscious thinking. We look from a stage into a crowd of hundreds of people. They are all just faces. Each unknown face is a subconscious thought. Suddenly, we recognize a face we know well. Memories of activities together become conscious. Activities of others create no memories.

I know nothing for sure, but if I make models I feel more confident of my understanding. I place my mind on frontiers between consciousness and "subconsciousness" to gain mental confidence for performing efficient inner thinking. Fragmented inner processes create extreme thoughts and behaviors.

Aggressive people will abuse kind, loving people as long as their behavior is rewarded. As a country, we are made up of the good, the bad, and the ugly. The "ugly" are controllers who force the "good" beyond limits into retaliation and psychological destruction, and into criminals. The "ugly" are not guilty of crimes but commit slow murders. Our system does not prosecute such criminals. The "guilty" remain free to destroy again.

The "bad" commit obvious crimes. Our legal system often convicts the "bad" unless they can hire expensive lawyers.

The "good" are at the mercy of the "bad" and "ugly" unless they mentally reconstruct. Childhood traumas, power, and wealth create the "ugly" and the "bad," with corrupted minds and souls.

Manic-depressives become so involved with inner thoughts and dream worlds that loved ones become less important and are sometimes abused. Rather than isolating manic-depressives in hospitals and subduing them with chemicals in hazy semi-stable states, therapists should begin therapy while patients are manic. Therapists should calm patients down with minimal prescribed drugs. The goal is long term healing. Therapists need to teach calming techniques early on. Less drugged, mentally alert patients can learn techniques to calm themselves down more efficiently. Lamaze breathing techniques may help calm patients.

True healing should be the goal, and not simply minimizing erratic behavior. Patients should be encouraged to write and justify "forced" manic thoughts to them selves. After refinements, patients should briefly discuss writings in group therapy. Therapists should guide thoughts in group therapy sessions. They should promote patience, participation, and reason.

Zombie psychiatric drugs should be a last resort. With guidance, manic-depressives should take charge and reconstruct their own minds for stability. Eventually, young children should mentally reconstruct so they can protect themselves from abusers, and society can become more love based. Concerned neighbors and professionals should help abusers heal themselves. It takes a village for good mental health. This book was written to help prevent slow mental murders.

I encourage buying one mind improvement tool, a larger Holusion similar to the one in Figure 7.4. It is easier to work with. Mental excitement increases when working with Holusions.

Focus long-distance beyond the surface of the Holusion, and the right-brain gains dominance and holistically senses all detailed images of the two-dimensional pattern equally.

Rapidly, the right-brain integrates the two-dimensional lines and colors into a three-dimensional image deep within the Holusion. I distinctly see a three-dimensional image of the thinker. I move my head, and the thinker moves like viewing a three-dimensional hologram or normal person. I am amazed by how my subconscious right cerebral hemisphere has brought this three-dimensional image to virtual life. The right subconscious brain has made sense of a confusing two-dimensional picture to construct a virtual or "spiritual" three-dimensional Holusion.

I am able to sense left to right brain dominance transition as the detailed two-dimensional surface transforms into a three-dimensional image. Holusion practice improves brain dominance control. This exercise often causes a flurry of creative ideas.

Experiencing God is similar to viewing Holusions. Relax the mind and surrender focus. The mind integrates three-dimensional details into higher spiritual dimensions.

Mental reconstruction is similar to understanding the two-dimensional fabric of a Holusion with the left-brain and integrating it into long-range spiritual dimensions with the right-brain. Working with Holusions increases awareness of spiritual dimensions with feelings of completeness.

We strive for higher mental or spiritual dimensions. Practice creating a three-dimensional Holusion image from memory. Switch between the two and three-dimensional visions with eyes closed.

When un-focusing through a computer monitor, we see all words holistically or equally. When a baby is very young, he imprints all scenes he sees into his memory holistically. In early life, he evaluates all images with equal importance. Later, he learns to focus on parents' and moving things' actions and reactions. High energy actions and words are stored and repressed as trauma scars.

We should un-focus at times to experience right-brain dominance as when babies. Early right-brain dominance explains why we do not remember early childhood easily. Dreams and right-brain thinking build subconscious structure. Processes are quickly forgotten. Focusing with left-brain dominance developed later in baby's life. Humans remember details more with the left-brain.

If experiences are normal, signals from nerves are synchronized throughout the brain. If a trauma occurs, high-energy nerve energy is "focused" toward one reactive localized neural network. This energy overwhelms the reactive network's membranes and physical structure. Excessive energy makes things rigid. Later, traumatized network membranes absorb additional chemicals, emit and reflect greater electromagnetic radiation, and have greater influence on the brain than normal networks.

Neural networks produce a relatively slow transmission of chemicals throughout the brain, but transmit electromagnetic radiation at the speed of light. At any point in time, the coordinated symphony of mental activities creates charge contours on the surface of the brain. Traumatized high-energy activities degrade synchronized charge contours on the brain's surface.

Consciousness is a resonating symphony of electromagnetic activity within and on the surfaces of our brains. Activities must vary slowly and last long enough to produce consciousness for us to navigate our environments.

The brain's surface charge contours vary with perceptions and analytical activities. Each glance we take causes a symphony of changing neuron activities for a flowing awareness. Consciousness is constructed by chemical activations, in neurons, producing charge and voltage variation, within and on the surfaces of the brain. Brain and neuron surfaces are not perfect conductors. They have some resistance to electron flow which allows for discrete, localized charge distributions and detailed thinking. Without resistance, neuron activities dissolve into meaningless smooth charges on the surfaces of the brain.

Intricate charge distributions on three-dimensional irregular brain surfaces are dominated by energetic resonances. Erratic high-energy trauma networks degrade influence of normal resonances. Normal processes must increase their energy to override erratic trauma energy.

Everyone has freedom to make their own models of the brain. Consciousness is also structured on surfaces of the brainstem and other brain components. Reflexes may depend on the charge distributions on the surfaces of the brainstem and limbus system. Thinking is influenced by the shape of our brains which reflects the contours of our faces.

Working models allow us to think about our brains and minds and improve quality of life. The brain produces relatively high energy and low frequency resonances to control muscles. Upper brain networks produce higher frequency and lower energy for refined analytical processes.

Awareness consists of millions of frequencies. The brain has capacity similar to the Internet. With one search phrase, the Internet can find millions of matches in seconds. The brain can make as many subconscious comparisons in seconds. The brain and the Internet used together wisely are powerful tools.

Neurons fully discharge rapidly and recharge more slowly. After firing, traumatized neurons repeatedly over-charge. Only recall therapy or mental reconstruction can reduce trauma firings back to normal levels.

Each trauma scar contains the basic reflexive message: "I am hurting. Help me! Here's the pain!" Traumatized networks communicate in a semi-conscious reflexive baby language.

We are smarter with more wrinkles on the brain and fewer wrinkles on the face. A wrinkly brain has complex surface contours for more detailed electromagnetic configurations and complex thoughts.

With more wrinkles on the brain, we enjoy new things with low mental energy. Specialize in things interesting to you for success. We only need to pass kindergarten to be happy.

Let's look at feelings and emotions. Differences between feelings and emotions are simply a matter of energy. Emotions add energy potentials to mind and body.

The subconscious mind iterates to integrate many detailed low-energy resonances for holistic feelings. It integrates high-energy resonances to generate a specific emotion. Higher energy levels produce intense emotions with less detail. Good emotions are wonderful and do not need to be highly energetic.

Reading emotional and creative ideas develops self-reflection. If ideas are truly creative, readers will seem to have known them for a long time – maybe for 13.7 billion years! Received spiritual messages also feel as if known for a long time.

Awareness is different from consciousness. For example, we are aware of knowing someone's name but not conscious of the name. We may have awareness of knowledge but are not conscious of that specific knowledge. We may be able to recall it later.

There is a relationship between nerves and neurons. Each physical bruise and scar causes a physical bruise and scar within a related area of the brain. Bruises heal in the flesh more quickly than in the brain. Psychological bruises are more global and heal more slowly. Mental scars can be healed by psychophysiotherapy.

Our subconscious minds are unbelievably powerful. We see a wide view of the mountains. Years later, we recognize the same view. Stimulation lets us recognize things once long forgotten.

Sleeping and dreaming are free of waking thinking restraints. During mania, the mind is not as constrained by waking processing limits. One might have brilliant ideas, but have less everyday judgment, and do embarrassing things.

We lose abilities if they are not used. Skin sensing abilities are being lost by wearing clothes. The air inside our homes, even with a fan blowing, feels so dead. Outside, the air feels alive to the skin. There is a feeling of acquiring subconscious knowledge when skin is exposed. The breeze through the trees breaks the air into refined pressure fabric that speaks to the skin. The holistic air pressure fabric on our bodies stimulates a similar electromagnetic fabric in our brains.

Caveman knew his environment. Skin sensitivities, which are subconscious to us today, were conscious to Caveman. They complemented his other sensitivities. Through genetics, we have inner awareness of Caveman's sensitivities.

Genetic intelligence constructed by our ancestor's historical experiences and memories built our young minds and bodies with greater intelligence than we acquire during our lifetimes. Minds and bodies are integrals of our, and of our ancestors', experiences.

Memory allows recollection including a sense of timing. Memories have only spiritual existence in spiritual time. Mental holograms are spiritual and virtual building blocks of ideas. The brain is physical. The mind is spiritual.

The cosmic sound is an inner sound we can become aware of by reducing mental energy through meditation. The name, cosmic sound, was probably chosen since it is somewhat like "cosmic noise." Cosmic noise is unidentified celestial radio-frequency radiation originating from outside the Milky Way. Calming the mind, broadening the face, and focusing long-distance with eyes closed often initiates the cosmic sound within my mind. The cosmic sound is background interference of trauma scars conflicting with the normal symphony of the brain.

We and our minds search for completion in everything we do. We talk and write in complete sentences. Depending upon reasoning abilities and inner peace, we should complete everyday and some challenging, long-range goals.

Chapter 13
Mental Reconstruction

"Some men see things as they are and say why. I dream of things that never were, and say why not."

Robert F. Kennedy

We can break the mental chains of childhood traumas and indoctrination to expand mental limits into the universe and to God. We need to develop methods to reconstruct the mind.

Mental Reconstruction includes physical and mental adjustments after traumatized local neural networks are stimulated and ruptured to release energy. Releases are stimulated by psychiatric exercises and guided by subconscious understanding of mind models. After releasing excess emotional energy, erratic networks mend and again become part of the brain's symphony. Little used nearby neural networks become more active and grow stronger. A purpose is to document the processes and sensations of mental reconstruction.

Mental reconstruction is a long and unusual process but has reestablished mood control and prevented recurring manic episodes. Healing processes are not easy but may heal reader's debilitating disorders. Preventing insanities of mania may be worth any price.

Child rearing and genetics develop emotional and mood structures within the brain. A child needs two role models – a mother and father interacting and reasoning together. Single parents cannot do nearly as well.

A single or arrogant dominant parent often feels like he/she is in total control and answers to no one. Children miss the negotiating and reasoning between parents. As adults these lost children display the self-centeredness of their single parent. Counselors are trained to pick up the pieces.

We must nurture confident childhood minds. Genetics and childhood develop the fundamental structure of the brain. This structure remains throughout life unless having experienced significant emotional events. Psychotherapy and processes in this book stimulate significant emotional events that essentially replace the original emotional limit system.

Parenting formerly included physical, psychological, and spiritual guidance until maturity. If we neglect our children, morals are not developed. Quests for corporate power reduce time with children limiting future generations. The higher up the corporate ladder; the more egotistical we become. Children learn that power replaces morals.

Mental reconstruction improves translations between subconscious and conscious processes. The reconstructing mind builds improved control structures at emotional limits. Becoming more comfortable with our own minds is part of the cure. Believing in the powerful abilities of subconscious minds and mental reconstruction improves confidence and creative ideas.

Consciousness begins at conception. The embryo is excited about growing faster and bigger as cells divide. Cells share holistic awareness. The embryo is aware of every cell dividing and every neuron connection being made. It is excited about forming the skeleton and body, and plans for, and looks forward to, the future.

As grownups, we are also most excited when planning for the future. Remember how excited we were as children when we looked forward to some anticipated event? Those times were the best of times. Being an embryo within a non-alcoholic, non-drug, and non-smoking mother was the best of times.

An embryo's "mind" is aware of its internal growth history every step of the way. The young embryo "thinks" so fast. Initially, he does not have to worry about controlling slow-moving arms and legs. The embryo's "mind thinks" as fast as dreams.

As the embryo matures, emphasis is directed toward preparing the senses for awareness of the external world. That fast-reacting brain must learn to wait for feedback from developing slow-moving arms and legs. The brain learns to wait for feedback.

This patient waiting is developed mostly within the brainstem. Waiting for and feedback from slow moving limbs, body, and, eventually, sight and hearing, slows mental processes to form a new consciousness within the embryo and young baby's mind.

As a mind matures and learns to respond to environments, it builds normal consciousness. The embryo's early awareness of internal activities remains as baby's developing subconscious mind. As senses become more capable, external activities become the focus of conscious processes.

As embryos we were aware of our mother's heartbeat and breathing rhythms. Mothers' rhythms give embryos an overall feeling of comfort. We were integrated as one with our mothers. As adults we can only regain that feeling of oneness with God and, for some through, Jesus.

Babies must react to diverse, random, and sometimes harsh environments. They build neural network structures for active and reactive thinking. Active thinking integrates sensed and historical resonances to create new ideas and memories for guiding future activities.

Early iterative subconscious processes, reacting to conflict, converge to build an amazing neural structure for external thinking. An embryo must remember his developmental history in order to develop future growth. The embryo's thinking and internal brain development history occurs so fast the growing baby has the feeling of living for a long time.

The growing brain slows to process body and neural growth. A baby retains a sense of internal physical and mental growth and spiritual history. But, is he ready for an inconsistent external environment?

Conflict should be gauged. Babies should be exposed to very little conflict. Growing children should be exposed to increasing conflicts and resolutions. Children should be trained to confront conflict with reason and broad consideration. Children observing parents working together develop reasoning processes. Parents should teach options in solving problems and conflicts as children grow.

Minds were not designed to stay as even keeled as required in today's education, family, and business environments. Minds should be briefly extended to limits at times to maintain working order. Sports help children make decisions and control emotions.

Like babies, we need to experience emotional highs and lows at limits for mental health. We are healthier with periods of creativity, occasional high emotions, and sufficient relaxation. Analytical limits should be experienced at times. A strong, versatile brain structure is developed near, or at, emotional limits.

When manic with right-brain dominance, we tend to concentrate on the "big picture." We lose left-brain reasoning and generalize that even adverse things have equal importance. Right-brain thinking contains seemingly irrational dream characteristics.

We become more spiritual but lose normal reasoning when the right-brain is dominant! Gaining control of left- and right-brain dominance, improves reasoning skills and helps reduce mania.

Reconstructing the mind slows the aging process. Aging is an accident and tragedy for all living things and should not occur. Repressed trauma effects damage the brain and degrade cell division. Medical and nutritional progress is slowing aging today. Aging will be "cured" in this century.

In psychoanalysis, we recall repressed trauma memories and reveal them to a therapist. Repressed energy and guilt are released. A patient becomes less emotional and more rational.

An intense remembrance releases local neural network energy. The patient begins to understand reasons for negative feelings and fears, and improves thinking. He no longer relives semi-conscious negative emotions of recurring repressed partially recalled trauma memories.

With therapy, high-energy trauma memories are recalled and reduced to normal memories. A trained minister, psychologist, or psychiatrist can assist recall and healing.

All victims feel guilty that traumas have happened to them. Inadequacy is a horrible feeling and is present in baby trauma scars. When nursing, a baby feels in control of his mother's soft body and could not feel more powerful. A young baby cannot distinguish his mother's body from his own. He thinks the two bodies are one when nursing.

Let's watch baby learn. His brain functions are electrical and chemical. His mind functions as fast as chemical explosions. Baby throws a temper tantrum because his mother leaves him in his bed for the night.

A night is an eternity for a baby's fast mind. He learns to wait so long. His life's history is so short. He fears his mother is leaving and will not "re-appear." The fear is as great as an adult running for cover while being attacked by a machine gun.

We received traumas scars as infants before learning verbal language. These memories are not stored so we can recall and verbally describe them to a therapist. These memories are stored in the non-verbal right hemisphere. Without words, we can purge energy from infant trauma memories with exercise therapy.

When reducing energetic trauma memories to normal memories, we transform subconscious processes into conscious processes. A reconstructed clear mind uses less energy and thinks faster, more creative, and smarter. If mentally reconstructed, we disconnect analytical processes from sense and physical activities to reduce subconscious wait states.

Mental reconstruction processes free the brain of more excess energy than psychotherapy alone. After reconstruction, one often feels like a different person. The goal is to release all historical trauma effects and then release new trauma effects daily.

When trauma effects are reduced to daily background levels, we have become truly "normal with clear minds!" Thinking becomes refined with less conflict. Life becomes a higher normal.

When high-energy trauma occurs, the brain does not have time to react normally. We do not know what to do or say. Our minds become right-brained and emotional. The reactive right-brain is inadequate to process fright or trauma data. The upper brain momentarily shuts down in a moment of insanity.

The brainstem activates the fast response limbic system. The face, neck, and jaw muscles tense and prepare to react. The slower left-brain is overridden by reactive functions of the limbic system and right-brain. Thankfully, our subconscious fast response system reacts. We are saved from a "certain death" car accident.

I am a physicist, not a chemist. I attack manic-depression from an energy-balance standpoint. Traumas are mostly absorbed by localized fast-response neural networks. If a stimulus is too powerful, the brainstem and limbic system are unable to communicate, or resonate, with the refined analytical upper brain.

If someone abuses another's analytical thinking, trauma scars are ingrained in the left cerebral hemisphere. The left-brain incurs verbal or analytical trauma. A blow to reasoning abilities can cause a sense of failure and a reasoning trauma scar.

Personally, I do not think psychoanalysis can release even five percent of our trauma scars. Most traumas occur between conception and two years of age. During that time verbal and analytical left-brain functions have less influence than right-brain functions. Babies think holistically without works and record conflicting activities of the gods, their parents, in the right-brain.

Muscles affect nerves and brain cells, and brain cells affect muscles. PPT uses energy and force more than psychotherapy. I believe that PPT can release the remaining ninety-five percent of trauma and emotional scars which are inaccessible through words or psychotherapy.

Unique exercises stimulate the subconscious mind to release trauma memories experienced before verbal skills were developed. Non-verbal memories compose the majority of trauma memories and include pre-natal fear, pain of birth, the first breath, infant wordless fears of being left alone, loud noises, hunger, falling, injuries, etc.

Sporadic trauma activations create the bizarre disconnected qualities in dreams. With trauma effects released, dreams become more connected. Fortunately with psychophysiotherapy, PPT, we do not need to recall trauma memories when releasing their energy.

Normal brain symphonies have learned to work around trauma scars. Without these mental cancers, the brain no longer needs to avoid them and develops emotions more appropriate to "current" situations.

There are poor souls who continually look either worried or threatening. They are either in the retreat mode fearing degradation or in the attack mode daring anyone to knock fragile egos off their shoulders. Sunken upper cheeks often relate to the extremely abused who are reduced to survival thinking to the point they will annihilate anyone in their path.

Some are afraid of, and constantly looking for, the next blow to a fragile ego. They are usually reluctant to make eye contact. Their faces show the influence of trauma in their lives. The severely abused have rigid neural networks and rigid behavior.

Mental health professionals should relate facial muscle structure to traumas incurred to facilitate mental healing. Semi-conscious trauma memories develop so many unhappy faces. Reactions to historical trauma events are posted on affected faces.

We can feel a touch on a thigh and sense if the touch moves up or down. Similarly we can sense locations of energy-releases in the neck, throat, and brain. Some traumas cause extreme neck tensions. Healing releases become easier with practice and time.

Computer manufacturers intentionally stress or limit test mainframe computers periodically during maintenance. This process stresses weakened parts to fail during maintenance tests. Diagnostics tests are made and all damaged parts are replaced during maintenance down time rather than sporadically failing during operation. Psychiatric exercises stress local, rigid neural networks beyond limits. We want to promote activations so they do not disrupt thinking processes during normal processing.

Can we explain traumatic energy releases? The metallic ping occurred in the brainstem where sound is processed. The number of trauma network ruptures does not have to be large if in the most sensitive auditory formations. After releasing localized auditory trauma energy through SCAPS, processing timing gets off. A dramatic energy-release realigns timing.

How can we explain the mental nuclear explosion? In a model similar to the metallic ping, visual neuron networks within the occipital lobe of the cerebral hemisphere release trauma energy and visual networks lose synchronization. The occipital lobe is the visual processing center of the brain.

Traumatized networks in the most sensitive parts of the visual formations realigned and caused the mental nuclear explosion. The extremely bright yellow light exploded into my attention, but there was no sound.

What could generate enough energy to produce such a violent display of powerful yellow light that appeared to expand outward at the speed of light? Dreams are mostly visual and the reticular formation is exceedingly active during REM sleep. The aminergic neurons are mostly active during the waking state and consciousness.

I was overwhelmed by a highly unusual phenomenon. A trauma rupture occurred in the most important area between the reticular formation and aminergic cluster. The area is important to the timing between normal vision processing and dreaming.

When the rupture occurred, both reticular formation and aminergic cluster neurons drastically fired competing for dominant timing sequences. If both reticular formation and aminergic cluster neurons fired simultaneously at full speed, that activity would "blow" your mind, or nothing would.

The mental "nuclear" explosion was a show of power with both systems working frantically attempting to dominate while releasing unusual amounts of repressed energy. These brainstem neurons may have activated all brain cells. Brain activities exploded that night, but the mind amazingly recovered.

The yellow light was the color of the sun. In trauma, the mind presented the most powerful color. I was aware of the maximum amount of yellow light energy possible. For a moment, I thought all the nuclei in my neurons had blown their neutrons.

I have performed a dreaming while awake experiment. If I close my eyes, relax, listen for the cosmic sound, void my mind of words, and wait, eventually I can create visions of a big old dragon coming toward me. Boy is he scary! He gets closer and closer; the dream disappears. I did not remain calm enough and the scary dragon dream was gone in a poof - like Puff the Magic Dragon!

I didn't give up. After much practice, I learned to stay calm so the dragon would not "poof" away. I finally mastered this task. What do you think happens?

Well, either one of two scenarios happens when the big, mean, and ornery dragon comes to get me. He gets closer; I feel the closeness! I wince just a little; he gets me. There is a brief emotional black out. I am a goner for sure! But wait! The next thing I remember is sliding down the dragon's throat. The dream ends and I can't stop laughing. The dream vanishes, but I continue to laugh.

Why do I laugh so? The reason is genetically and throughout childhood we have been taught to avoid sharp teeth. Staying calm during the dream attack, tricked the subconscious mind and forced it to continue the scenario.

My subconscious mind logically placed me in the throat. I was no longer afraid because from childhood on I have only been afraid of sharp teeth and not of being swallowed. It is so funny because it suddenly becomes obvious as the dream image dissipates that a dream dragon cannot really eat you. Rapidly releasing inner tension, adds to the humor.

That brief blackout created an "unconscious moment" and trauma scar during my dream trauma. The subconscious mind momentarily did not know what to do. After recomposing, it had me sliding down the dragon's throat.

Oh, yes, about the second scenario! This scenario is simpler. The big, mean, ornery dragon comes to get me. He gets closer; I feel the closeness! I try to be brave but still wince a little. The dragon suddenly looks sheepish, quickly gets smaller, turns, and runs away.

I cannot predict which scenario the dragon will choose. Slight differences in facial expression may affect my subconscious mind and its dragon vision. I used calmness and imagination to explore subconscious emotional limits by briefly making them conscious.

I close my eyes and become calm. A kaleidoscope of colors eventually begins to flow when dreaming while awake. I slowly increase the speed of movement of the kaleidoscope of colors without thinking in words.

With increased speed, I calmly, but rapidly, move my eyes from side to side and slightly flutter my eyelashes to imitate Rapid Eye Movement (REM) without thinking in words. The right-brain becomes dominant. Thinking in words would lose control to the left-brain. What do you think happens?

The whole body begins to twitch. I am on the edge again and have fooled my subconscious mind. Here's what happened. My eye movement, fluttering the eyelids, and the kaleidoscope of color variations, simulated REM dreaming. I have done the reverse process of being abruptly awakened during sleep. I was abruptly "asleepened" by my subconscious mind while awake.

This funny little reversal shows how different our English language words are developed for active and passive attention. We might say that while awake and visually stimulated I was quickly nodding off to sleep. While awake, my body twitched as I repeatedly quickly fell asleep and awakened.

From a neurological standpoint what has been happening? I'm awake and aminergic neurons within the brainstem are firing like crazy as they should. I create excitement of REM dreaming with eyelid fluttering and rapid eye movement. The reticular formation is excited by "the dream stimuli" and begins firing like crazy. This excitement suppresses aminergic and body sensory activities.

Muscles relax and begin to go limp as I momentarily fall asleep. This muscle relaxation causes body movement that stimulates the aminergic cluster. Muscles reflex, and I awaken with a twitch before falling asleep again. I have discovered a new limit.

We can use many techniques to make our dream world more conscious. We become more aware of limits between waking and dreaming. Dreams become more structured with improved subconscious processing. Experiments can extend subconscious processes into consciousness.

Let's dream up other theories. From conception to seven years of age, emotional experiences dominate genetic development for future generations. Traumas reduce thinking processes and narrow genetic limits. Mental reconstruction and positive emotions expand thinking processes and widen genetic limits.

Babies and young children experiment to explore arm, leg, and body limits, and their mirrored mind limits. If a young child is subjected too often to "sit down and be still like your big brother," he may limit his movement experiments and even mental abilities.

Sadly, two year olds learn to act like adults and limit physical activity thinking processes. We praise nice quiet two year olds for having such good behavior. We ease child-rearing burdens but limit developing physical and mental abilities. No wonder the human race is so uncoordinated. Careful child rearing with lots of fun, and reasonable conflict and risks, expand abilities.

I have also experienced distinct energy-releases upon completing seemingly profound thoughts, which sink deeply into the mind. This is exciting. After significant conscious thoughts, my subconscious mind confirms it as true with a SCAP. I have developed a subconscious feedback system for judging emotional and possibly spiritual truths! This unusual process occurred only with profound thoughts and lasted only a few months.

I have had other unusual sensations. With a creative thought, the sides of the upper brain become flush with excitement. There are goose bumps and my hair stands on end. The heart beats faster. Sensations occurred during experiments over a year or two.

During periods of unusually high SCAP activities, I refrain from resistance exercises as they increase the rate of mental reconstruction. With high reconstruction activity, I become aware of soreness surrounding my brainstem and upper neck.

Increasingly pleasant feelings and mind control confirm that energy-releases heal and expand the mind. I have experienced countless mental activities and continue to feel more capable.

Emotional limits constrict and confine thoughts during depression, and are shattered in manic episodes. Shattered limits reduce reasoning abilities but increase spiritual communication. Unrestricted manic emotions extend thinking abilities to genetic limits. Mental reconstruction expands emotional limits for spiritual activities and lives.

Without an organized, complete set of emotional limits, thinking becomes faster, and less controlled. The mind processes frantically as subconscious processes lose resonances when un-reflected by missing emotional limits. Eventually, the mind can no longer develop consistent decisions or complete thoughts.

An energized manic-depressive develops vaulted goals of solving long range global problems. However, eventually, the mind works so fast he is no longer able to determine what makes sense. He cannot distinguish between dreams and waking life.

Without normal subconscious resonances and limits, the manic-depressive believes any "dream." Manic thoughts are not compared to, and resolved with, historical memories for sanity.

If the manic mind can be calmed down and controlled at reasonably high levels, fast subconscious processing can increase mental abilities. Control of fast thinking is one of the best benefits of mental reconstruction. The process is exciting and dramatic. Since 1995, I have had confidence of controlling moods and no longer worry about manic episodes or needing to feel normal.

The brain is not so different from the body's protective systems. Stress can overwhelm the brain and seriously affect its functioning. As in immunization, controlled doses of stress or simulated stress can prepare the brain for higher levels of stress.

The brain's immune system to stress can be developed just as the body's immune system can adapt to combating infectious diseases. Forcing the mind to limits is much like working out with weights. Afterward, daily physical activities seem relatively easy.

After briefly pulsing the brain and mind to limits with psychiatric exercises, stress during normal activities is more reasonably controlled with less negative health effects. It is better to have brief pulses of stress at mental limits rather than enduring lower levels of stress for long periods of time.

Looking forward to brief stress-pulsing sessions becomes similar to looking forward to physical workouts. Minds are not designed to be emotionally consistent. Humans were designed to spend time relaxing between action-packed, stressful events.

The left-brain directs normal everyday activities needing detailed attention. The right-brain performs flowing, repetitious, holistic, and futuristic processes. Accomplished thinkers have more right-brained reality than those of us who always worry about the present. If we plan holistically for the future with our right-brains, we do not need to worry so much about the complexities of the present.

Long distance, dream, and repetitive functions do not need to be remembered as strongly as up-close detailed left-brain activities. We do not need to remember individual repetitions. We just need to know how to perform such activities. Long distant thinking does not need immediate action and its memories are not as pressing. Subconscious dream processes are also not as necessary to remember. We can increase right-brain to left-brain transfer processes to improve memory.

Our sleeping reality is fundamental for structuring mental functions to meet present and future challenges. Subconscious reality includes organizing and associating trauma and normal memories into dream logic. We need to reconstruct subconscious processes as much as we need to reconstruct waking functions.

In reconstructing the sleeping brain, the goal is to make the subconscious mind energy efficient, confident, and more conscious when phasing in and out of sleep. Due to sporadic baby and childhood attention and perceptions, the original development of subconscious processes is disorganized. Reconstructing these processes makes thinking easier and more efficient.

Thought development is a non-linear, iterative process. When meditating, I have had feelings of subconscious processes converging into thoughts. To achieve this iterating sensation, I broaden the face and keep the mind and body relaxed.

Less research is directed toward understanding the holistic right-brain. We go to church and listen to a minister tell us how we should worship something that we cannot see and may not be able to feel. Parents may be afraid to discuss holistic matters in depth with children.

At church, we learn of goodness and kindness and of fitting into something bigger than mother and dad. Feeling part of a church or extended family develops holistic, right-brain thinking. We are the lucky ones. Group spiritual activities encourage right-brain thinking as we look beyond ourselves.

Over the years, I have developed methods to improve the mind. Readers can use models to construct their own healing models and activities. The National Institutes of Mental Health only fund research by institutions. This attitude suppresses individual contributions. Individuals must partner with research institutions to get funding. Government leaders think only institutions can contribute to mental health.

Normal minds develop one idea after another for problem solutions. A restructured mind holistically fits pieces into a puzzle until the hologram puzzle or solution is complete. When the puzzle is complete, a new creative idea is born.

Two figures illustrate my sensed energy-release history. Figure 13.1 illustrates the relative energy-releases of SCAPS over seventeen years. The Series 1 curve shows the initial SCAP as having a relative energy peak of "1." The Series 2 curve represents an average SCAP after nine years as having a peak of 0.1 but lasting longer than the initial SCAP. The Series 3 curve represents an average SCAP after seventeen-years with a peak of only 0.01 but lasting six times longer than the original SCAP.

The X-scale is in seconds. The total energy for each SCAP released is represented as the area under each logarithmic curve. The energy peak, Y-scale, is an arbitrary gauge of sensed SCAP energy released. There is a large difference in the energy profiles between initial SCAPS and those near the end of mental reconstruction. This illustration presents relative sensitivities based upon "inner feelings." One day, researchers may be able to measure the energy of inner releases.

SCAP energy peaks declined over seventeen years. During this period, feelings often occurred that mental reconstruction was ending until another energy shell was ruptured with many slightly lower energy SCAPS released.

Figure 13.2 provides some idea of the relative energy-release differences between the initial SCAP, Metallic Ping, and Mental Nuclear Explosion. As seen, the metallic ping and mental nuclear explosion have estimated energies of one thousand times that of an initial SCAP. The mental nuclear explosion lasted much longer than the metallic ping.

Integrated SCAP energy-releases, over a nineteen-year period, are shown in Figure 13.3. Feelings of creativity have roughly increased along this same path. SCAPS have had rather erratic release cycles. I roughly describe sensations so readers may know what to expect.

At 4:45 am on May 30, 2005, Labor Day, I was awakened with a vision. I saw an older lady with a scarf. Her face was hardened from years of hard work. I was frightened to see her so real and so close. I had not seen her face before. There was a brief second when I thought she was real.

Abruptly, I felt a slight slip between my left and right-brains. My whole brain became flush with excitement. Most people would have fear with such an unusual sensation. With so many unusual sensations I no longer fear inner changes. I am excited about mental reconstruction.

High levels of excitement lasted almost five minutes. Slight feelings of pressure occurred on the top and side surfaces of the brain. The pressure was not unpleasant but a little shocking. I had done a lot of creative writing in previous days. Writing promotes inner excitement and change. I anticipate adjustments, but seldom can predict the nature of major changes.

This sensation nearly rivaled the Mental Nuclear Explosion in importance. During this mental reconstruction, I never worried about insanity. My interpretation of the dream lady was that she mirrored my feelings of hard, laborious work with expectation of change. At times since this dream, I have had rather pleasant flush feelings at the top and side surfaces of the brain that occur during mental excitement.

When frightened or emotional we get goose bumps as the skin tenses. I performed another exercise. I broaden the face for right-brain dominance and think about my entire skin. I quickly tense the throat and create goose bumps all over my body. This experiment was done without thinking of anything scary. A simple mental and throat exercise produced another limiting response.

A notable mental reconstruction event occurred on June 26, 2007 while practicing non-resistant exercises. My body jerked followed by awareness of a circular pinkish-red vision expanding from the center of my brain to several feet beyond my head. I interpreted this sensation as inner awareness expanding beyond the limits of the brain. The mind extends beyond the brain's boundaries.

The author has questioned several middle aged individuals. All were experiencing SCAPS with normal neck exercise. I conclude that most individuals are affected by trauma scars which need to be purged of energy to attain the clear mind. I have proven it is not harmful to purge trauma energy but is mentally healthy.

I am amazed at the dreaming brain's sense of timing. At times dreams seem to drag on forever with self embarrassment. Once awakened, dreams were obviously untrue but have created threatening or pleasant emotions as if they were true. Dreams prepare us for waking situations.

Energy during dreams is less than waking energy. With less energy, dreams process faster. This lower energy makes recalling dreams difficult. Actually, this is good. Otherwise, it would be difficult to distinguish between waking and dream memories. Dreaming is an inner process of accepting ourselves.

Most of us need a spouse or significant other to feel accepted unless they have treated us so badly that we have rejected them. In this case we usually have a hurtful, unrealistic opinion about ourselves and others.

I try to like everyone I meet. I like and respect everyone who is good to me but do not respect those who act superior. We should never act superior to anyone. However, it is difficult not to feel spiritually superior to those who act superior. We need to be vigilant and careful in helping not hurting others. Superior acting people are usually insecure but can be very damaging.

My inner work convinces me that no one is spiritually superior. Upon conception we were equally, perfectly spiritual.

Acting superior with verbal and body language degrades observers. Confident people recognize degrading perpetrators. Unfortunately, some do not, accept feeling inferior, and aggrandize false superiority. From my experience, those who have never worked and unaccomplished heirs show false superiority.

Perpetrators, acting superior, degrade confidence, abilities, and limit thinking of others. No one needs to be degraded. Solitude is often necessary to recover inner abilities. Mentally lessen thought destroyers' importance.

Thinking channels include everyday tasks, creativeness, love, spiritual communication, and anger. Each channel has a different energy level. All machines and the brain have optimum resonances and energy levels for different modes of operation.

Reactions from, and responses to, psychiatric exercises, add unique memory action potentials to refine the fabric of the brain. Repressed localized neural network energy, and overall brain energy, is reduced.

Intelligence is the ability to think of creative options and select efficient ones for actions and solutions. With genetic and spiritual guidance, babies make sense of new environments. Babies' minds make comparisons of sensed environments to their "genetic data and spiritual communications" faster than grownups.

Babies' minds synchronize environmental awareness resonances with their genetic and spiritual resonances for early learning. Comparison processes amplify specific genetic and historical resonances to increase their importance for new memories and abilities.

Outdoor naked experiments make global changes and restore the skin's holistic awareness abilities. Outdoor air carries active information for the skin to absorb. One should be careful in outdoor experimentation to ensure privacy as the curious will trespass from miles away to degrade perceived odd behavior. It is the nature of the shallow-minded to degrade anyone they perceive as odd or inferior.

Can the abnormal become normal? If there is a cut on the skin, mind and body focus to make the skin normal again. Healing is not perfect. Scars are left. If a trauma or emotional injury occurs, the brain works to make its self normal again. With mental healing, the brain can become better than its original trauma infested self.

For thirty years my laboratory has been my own mind and body. Experiments have resulted in many unusually pleasant feelings and very few headaches.

Many of us have headaches. We are aware where the pain is located. Sometimes the pain migrates. At times I experience unusual "headhealings," which have some characteristics of headaches. But, healing feelings are pleasant and slowly migrate from the front to around the sides of the cerebrum. Feelings give a subtle sense of wonder and joy rather than painful feelings of thinking closing in.

We frown and narrow faces at frights and disagreements. Due to social pressures, we disconnect facial expressions from true feelings. This self-deception produces inner processing distortions and associations. Reasoning conflicts are widely-dispersed within the brain. Releasing reasoning tensions produces sensations around the top and sides of the brain, and, hopefully, is near the end of energy to be released.

The human eye is specialized in receiving and passing information on to the rest of the human organism for benefits we only partially understand. With specialized senses, the whole becomes greater than the sum of its parts.

During sleep, subconscious processes integrate conflicting light frequency and resonance information into memory action potentials for memory and waking actions. For every conscious thought, there are millions of subconscious activities.

At times, near the end of mental reconstruction when awakening, brief feelings of mental agility and joy become almost overwhelming. I have had experiences never thought possible.

Our minds are the flowing and integrated result of shared activities between billions of neurons. Without sharing there would be no human awareness and minds. The mind integrates disconnected, discrete ideas for reason and spiritual completeness.

The written word has a spiritual quality. Its message remains constant and independent of time, whenever read. Vast changes through neural network energy releases over the years are difficult to believe unless having had similar experiences. Let's review reasons for continuing this inner journey into the unknown.

An important early prediction was that, if neck and throat sensations were caused by localized trauma energy releases as a result of exercises, sensations would migrate. Traumatized neural energy would decrease over time.

After four months, this was definitely found to be true. Increasingly exciting sensations were incentives to continue exercises for seventeen years. Having experienced amazing sensation changes within the neck and throat, I predict that releasing all trauma effects will uncover an amazing "clear mind."

Sensations are difficult to believe unless experienced. Perhaps, only manic-depressives are able to experience dramatic trauma energy releases.

We do not truly understand difficult times unless having experienced them. Teenagers do not understand older peoples' physical struggles.

In 2009 when thinking or writing creatively for an hour or so, occasionally, I have had feelings that the left and right brains are working together, holistically, as they should. The scalp and face felt flush, but not unpleasantly so. Energy releases in the upper neck and throat felt spread out and flowing. At this time, I felt close to the evasive end of mental reconstruction.

Figure 13 .1 History of SCAPS: Initial, Middle, Last

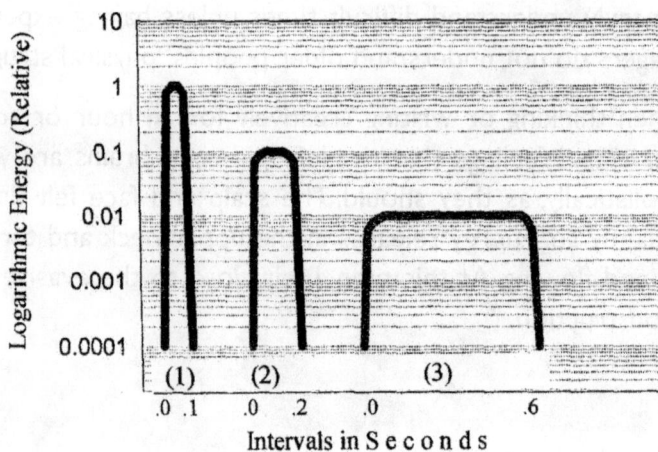

Relative SCAP Energy Peak and Longevity in:
(1)   1990
(2)   1998
(3)   2006

Note 1: Y-scale for Relative peak energy is logarithmic

Note 2: Peak energy of (1) is 100 times that of (3) and longevity of (3) is six times longer than (1).

Note 2: Total energy of each SCAP is given by the area under the curve.

Figure 13.2 SCAP, Metallic Ping, Mental Nuclear Explosion

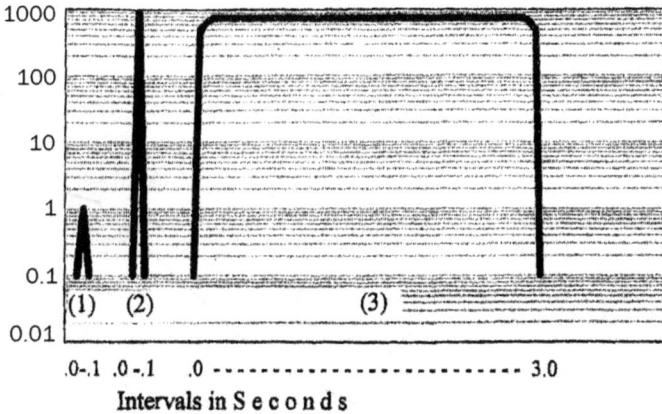

Relative Energy Peak and Longevity for: (1)   Beginning SCAP in 1990
                                         (2)   Metallic Ping in 1989
                                         (3)   Mental Nuclear Explosion in 1989

Note 1: The Y-scale for Relative peak energy is logarithmic
Note 2: The peak energy of the original metallic ping and the original mental nuclear
     explosion are 1000 times greater than the initial SCAP peak.

Figure 13.3 Integrated Yearly SCAP Releases

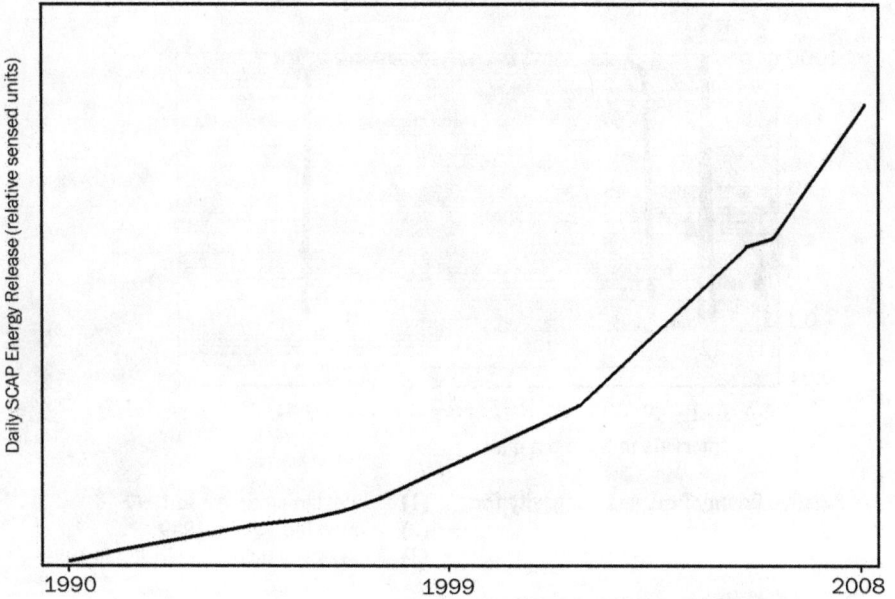

Note 1: SCAP energy is relative as estimated from inner sensations.

Note 2: The total energy released each year is the area under the curve.

Chapter 14
The Clear Mind Procedure

Sound and Light

When normal, I hear sound and see light;
My senses let me know things are right.
Inner sound and inner light bring change,
The brain and mind must rearrange.
Hugh Fulcher, 2005

The Serenity Prayer

"God, grant me the serenity to accept the things I can-
not change,
The courage to change the things that I can,
And the wisdom to know the difference."
Reinhold Niebuhr (Theologian)

The author studied the mind in depth as it was cleared of trauma scars. Guidance for healing processes was feedback from inner and spiritual sensations. Models are intended to promote future research. Later models often refine earlier models. Processes at mental limits improve thinking and refine beliefs.

A goal is for everyone to understand and use their minds efficiently. "I have a dream, I have a dream, I have a dream;" Dr. Martin Luther King, Jr. The better inner understanding we have, the better we are able to understand others. People who understand themselves are relaxed and reach out to others. Those who do not understand themselves are more likely to abuse others.

The clear mind subconsciously processes with greater detailed, clearer holograms. Trauma scars reduce clarity of mental holograms. Dreams, with a clear mind, are similar to high-definition, rather that analogue, television, and possibly as detailed as "flash" visions. It requires greater effort to understand less clear pictures.

When trauma energy is released, neural networks re-grow. The brain reconstructs former traumatized networks into more normal networks. With continued exercises, subconscious processes become more adept at re-growing a creative brain structure.

Thinking and feelings after years of mental reconstruction, activated by psychophysiotherapy, PPT, are very different than before manic depression. I felt normal before becoming bipolar. Inner feelings when not performing exercises or experiments are calmer than earlier normal feelings. Pleasant feelings increase. The abnormal becomes a higher normal.

Genetics and growing are amazing things which occur in all living things. God seems to be a magician. Growing occurs as slow, proportional analog or smooth processes. SCAP sensations are discrete, not normal, and should not occur. If we sense a click in a joint we know something is not working right. If we sense SCAP releases, we know something is not working properly.

If we hit our hands with a hammer, the mind is forced to think about the hand. In traumas, stronger, more resilient nerves of the neck and throat, and neurons within the thalamus, absorb energy and protect delicate analytical upper brain neurons.

After years of exercises, creative idea development becomes easer. Psychiatric sensations and spiritual feelings must be experienced to be believed. People tend to think everyone thinks similarly until someone develops a noted reputation.

Einstein was slow learning language. Thinking in images or pictures longer when young may have helped him develop picture models for his impressive discoveries. Picture thinking may be more distributed and important than I originally thought.

New discoveries must begin somewhere. This work has been so overwhelmingly successful for the author that clinical trials should be performed to prove results with others who suffer bipolar disorder. If successful in clinical studies, processes should be expanded to everyone including children.

My contention is that all of society could benefit by reducing trauma energy from neural networks. When beginning processes, there was concern that sensations of presumed breaking neural networks might not be beneficial. A thought was that breaking networks might lessen mental abilities. After seventeen years of extensive exercises, I have proven this is not the case. Excitement about life and abilities has increased. A positive attitude was maintained during this long process.

I am unaware of similar mind/body research using unique neck, face, and throat exercises to promote mental healing. Generally, there is psychiatric benefit to all exercise, if not over done.

At my uncle's (a neurosurgeon) house when growing up, there was always a book on display, "Laughter is the Best Medicine." I do not recall the author of this book. After manic episodes, it was beneficial to be able to laugh at myself.

Each exercise provides a sense of excitement and feelings of incremental accomplishment and confidence for controlling the mind. In limit experiments, excitement was elevated to brief feelings of uncertainty. The mind was calmed with breathing exercises.

It is difficult to measure results of individual exercises. As a whole, exercises have added control in defending against elevated moods that earlier erupted into manic episodes and insanity. Manic uncertainties often required surrendering decisions to God.

SCAP sensation analyses guide exercise regiment and model development. Making models gives confidence of understanding and excitement for healing. Psychiatric exercises should be practiced a few times a week and inner healing progress reviewed monthly, if one chooses mental reconstruction.

A basic model is that low-energy thinking is high-level thinking. High-energy thinking, such as anger, is low-level thinking. In anger, we think of only a few options. With low-energy thinking, we can think of many creative options. Brief controlled levels of mania increase creative thinking, when followed by calming the mind.

Christianity teaches surrendering control of lives to God. Have you seen the smiling faces? You can see their deep happiness due to their beliefs that Jesus is in control of their lives! There is less conflict and guilt in decision making.

That face, get rid of it! Relax and smile and your subconscious mind will relax and work faster with less energy. Smiling initiates psychiatric changes. With meditation and relaxing the face, the left-brain relaxes into right-brain dominance. Thoughts feel light and flexible. A slight smile during meditation sets the mind free for relaxed pleasant dreams.

There are so many suffering people that could benefit from this work. While exciting and encouraging, processes take a long time. Research needs to refine processes for results in a shorter time frame. This is a challenging task that fits into the relatively new category, "mind/body/spirit," established by the National Institutes of Mental Health, NIMH.

Beliefs and spirituality are an important part of mental health. We hold on to early learned emotional and spiritual beliefs until we have a significant emotional event. This event may be a relationship with Jesus or other emotional events.

We like people and things that are predictable. It is heart warming when someone is better to us than expected. We do not like unpredicted bad things. We know something about how our friends think and act. Sometimes we like to be unpredictably nice to those we love. It warms hearts of both givers and receivers.

Scientists develop theories to predict and control new things and environments for human benefit. It is human nature.

Neuron axons and dendrites have characteristics similar to muscles. The more they are used, the thicker and more efficient they become. Thicker axons and dendrites channel chemicals faster, and its neuron becomes more important in thinking processes. There is competition between neurons for importance within the brain. Nothing happens within the universe or the brain without conflict. In solving conflict, the brain re-grows and we get smarter.

Why is the mental reconstruction process so long? When there is a rupture in emotional processing limits, original limits cannot be mended. All old limits have to be purged. After purging all emotional limit structures, only genetic limits remain. Brain processing expands to its wider, more logical limit structures.

A physical rupture within limiting neural networks causing manic depression is more realistic than a chemical imbalance. Something must cause the chemical imbalance. Manic depression requires physical structure healing and not only chemical therapy.

Over fifteen years of practice, sensations have been dramatic. I suggest advanced imaging of the brain, throat, and neck to identify neural network effects after psychiatric exercises. Patients with severe, frequent, or cycling manic episodes should be the first to benefit from this technology.

At times, excitement from psychiatric exercises is intense. Rates at which exercises are performed need to be gauged. Going too fast could lead to mania. This author has had thirty years of successful experience with psychiatric changes including fourteen years with resistance exercises. We must live on the edge to be creative. However, we must approach limiting exercises with caution to avoid over-excitement or injury.

With respect to environments and history, caveman was much smarter than we are today. He had a clear mind and used his entire brain. The entire human brain evolved and was constructed by this more global use.

Today, human brains and minds are cluttered with disruptive trauma effects. Adult lives do not frequently experience severe traumas or naturally purge their effects. Brains and minds are seldom forced to limits for critical decisions and maintaining creative brains. Humans use only a fraction of their brains today. Generations are losing earlier developed emotional brain functions.

With early mental reconstruction, children may live lives using their entire brains. They will be creative with inner peace. Widespread mental practices could promote world peace.

Medical professionals take an oath to do no harm. We must be careful to do no harm. Researchers will gauge PPT application.

Inability to handle conflict started this PPT process. I've seen fire and I've seen rain that I thought would never end. In the depths of depression, the mind cannot develop a single thought or make simple daily decisions. Surprisingly, returning to thoughtless times initiates creative thinking. One has to experience difficult times to appreciate successful, enjoyable times.

Difficult times promote spiritual transitions. Spiritual feelings or ideas are received during depression with temporary losses of physical and mental abilities, during manic episodes with high, creative excitement and sporadic losses of mental control, and by spiritually surrendering emotional decisions to God, Jesus, or other spiritual leader. Most people do not accept that those close to them can improve spiritually in other than traditional religions.

In the worst of depressed times expecting imminent death, I experienced a holistic, limiting sense of life escaping. My body and mind evaporated into the universe. I briefly sensed true awareness.

Do not be afraid to relax mental control. Some people never relax the face and brain. Relaxing the brain before sleep may seem frightening to some with fear that disturbing memories will emerge. Recalling intense memories becomes less threatening and normal with practice. Creative ideas fill a relaxed, dreaming mind.

Mental health researchers, who do brain scans, should also scan the neck and throat. I propose a scan machine that holds the head still and moves the body. SCAP activities and other brain functions during exercises would be monitored. Movements should be tested slowly at first, before scans, to test flexibility of and protect the neck. The machine must monitor and prevent pain.

When practicing non-conflicting neck exercises, energy release sensations are increased by stiffening the throat and neck. Tensions, within the tongue, throat, and neck, are varied to excite nerves and related neurons to limits. Unique exercises appear unusual, so practice in seclusion to avoid adverse attention until methods become more widely known.

Trauma scar shells are organized by energy levels or activation cliques, rather than by physical position within the brain. Exercises develop resonances that activate and reduce local trauma scars with similar resonances. The brain responds to exercises with its rhythms. It has a subconscious mind of its own.

Each external stimulus activates nerves with a specific frequency. This frequency is transparent to neural fabric until its energy is absorbed by, and activates, neural networks with similar resonances. If having high enough energy, the stimulus ingrains a repressed trauma scar.

Normal people seldom think about mechanics of their thinking. If anyone studies and learns, thinking improves. If we practice a particular sport, thinking improves for that sport. Exercises, models, and thinking about inner processes improve thinking efficiency.

The subconscious mind promotes long-lasting resonances for conscious thinking, and recursively, the conscious mind redirects subconscious processes. Together, the brain and mind are an iterative feedback system. However, the subconscious mind has difficulties understanding its own processes.

Emotions played a big part in writing *Bipolar Blessings & Mind Expansion*. After writing, we must refine. Hopefully this book is an example of reasonable communication. Making models and writing ideas for this book improved thinking about the mind.

Careful listening helps others develop ideas and control emotions. Recognize who is building your confidence. Later and when calm before sleeping, think about interactions. The subconscious mind can help evaluations. Pay attention to feelings. Frequent negative communications and actions from significant others may cause depression. They should have less significance.

Detailed physiological models of the brain are too complex to stimulate emotions for psychiatric healing. I make physiological models, only detailed enough to stimulate change and healing in subconscious processes.

Let's make a simple model of our brains that give feelings of understanding consciousness. Our conscious minds provide feedback, or are the mirror, for the subconscious mind to understand its own processes. In turn, the subconscious mind is a multi-level reflection of conscious thinking that makes us who we are. The subconscious mind needs feedback to understand itself. Mental problems occur when the conscious mind denies reality and does not provide a true reflection to the subconscious mind. Psychiatrists, and simple mind models, provide feedback for understanding and healing subconscious processes.

Practice and repetition gives confidence to perform in real life situations. We must frequently judge repetitious actions and thoughts to improve thinking. We repeat important tasks many times to ensure we perform well. Some of us work twelve hours a day to become experts and not fear failure or layoffs.

There is comfort in repeating uplifting rhymes and spiritual rituals. Recitals increase comfort and confidence as we get older. We like to be part of important ideas by repeating them with like minded believers. We need to believe in something beyond self.

Repetition can increase emotions, importance, and heighten moods. Poets have known the power of repetition for centuries:

> "Once upon a midnight dreary,
> While, I pondered weak and weary.
> There came a rapping upon my chamber door,
> Perhaps, the wind and nothing more."
> The Raven, Edgar Allen Poe

Unfortunately, cruel and damaging people learn the power of false ego phrase repetition. Their psychological control falsely increases the self-esteem of audiences. To be well-adjusted, we must understand falsities in emotional repetitions. We must learn to defend against false reasoning from others.

Subconscious emotional limits reflect neural processes until they iterate and converge into feelings, thoughts, and solutions. Without limits, the brain cannot converge to logical thoughts. Without limits, engineering systems and minds cannot be stable and self-destruct. Expected mental inputs converge into desired thoughts as outputs. More sophisticated systems accept broader inputs and produce wider, acceptable outputs. A reconstructed brain accepts higher emotional input and produces more diverse and logical thoughts as output.

Individual neuron activations produce varying electromagnetic resonances. Consciousness begins when an active neural network promotes dominant resonances throughout the brain. Conscious resonances include harmonics which allow us to see and hear many things at one time, and have complex thoughts.

Let's look at design from a physics and engineering viewpoint. We want stable engineering and brain systems. With acceptable inputs, an engineered system should converge to produce expected, stable results. Outputs should be consistent with acceptable inputs. With inputs within emotional limits, the brain should converge to reasonable thoughts and solutions.

The soul is the spiritual communication system. It is a part of God within us. I once modeled the soul as within the original cell of conception in the brain. This model was easy to think of as an unchanging, spiritual component within minds.

Some people lie to themselves about who they are and what they have accomplished. The problem is that the conscious mind thinks one thing and the subconscious mind and soul know better. There is conflict because subconscious processes normally iterate to produce consistent conscious thoughts. Degrading another's reasoning confidence is the worst of psychological abuses.

Many like to think of heaven as a wonderful place. Others think heaven is a myth. With spiritual thoughts, the mind and creative things flow.

I perform humility, power, control, and pride exercises. To appreciate one emotion, we must experience its opposite. In depression, I was humbled and helpless with little thinking ability. This experience keeps me humble and in perspective.

Superior feelings should not be allowed to last long. We see the extreme joy when athletes make a winning endeavor. Feelings of superiority can assist work or sports. However, long term superior feelings lose spiritual focus and degrade others.

As in other experiments, I have briefly taken emotional superiority to limits – through imagination. I never intentionally act superior to any one. My parents' training would not allow such a degrading thing. Power or imagined power over others strikes a resonance in the brain and develops the sin of pride.

I experience pride for brief periods, then experience past feelings of depressed helplessness. This experiment was designed to learn to enjoy brief periods of success and keep pride at low levels. Controlling pride is one of the best things to control. Nonsense, humor, and light thinking, including hobbies, provide escapes from needing to control.

Laughter releases tensions as repetitive mental jogging. We need to study our laughter and determine what makes us laugh and why things are funny. We need to be sure we are laughing with and not at people. If we are laughing at others' misfortunes, we need help in a hurry.

Laughter is rooted in established values, and the breaking of those values. Laughter forms slow relaxed rhythms and resonances in the brain. We like those who make us laugh and give us joy. Joy is a deeper emotion. I practice feeling and sharing the joy of others, especially, when there is no direct benefit to me.

The purpose of analyzing dreams is to find meaning within bizarre visual content. Determining the meaning of dreams includes connecting previous day events and related historical experiences within emotional limits. Sigmund Freud developed dream analysis for this purpose.

Compare dream emotions to your honesty in caring for others and honesty you feel others have in caring for you. Dream emotions often amplify historical, current or expected emotions. Reasoning through troublesome circumstances reduces negative emotions. Brainstorm and pray for creative solutions and positive relationships.

Dreams exaggerate feelings and emotions. Feelings are integrations of thoughts about particular things, actions, or persons. Sometimes only one good act or memory of that act develops good feelings. Feelings have a subconscious dream quality. Sometimes we can analyze feelings to understand them. Feelings are low energy, integrated ideas on the edge of consciousness. One negative response or action can negate all positive feelings.

Before football games, players' emotions become high. Players do not recall all previous practices and past experiences they have had. They experience high energy, integrated feelings of knowing what to expect and how to execute. High-emotions help us react to fast, threatening situations. Emotions have fast repetitive qualities to intensify reactions.

When beginning to play football, a young player might have fears of death during initial practices. With successes, confidence overcomes fear. All emotional endeavors at limits reconstruct the mind and add action potentials to develop "can do" adults.

I had a surreal occurrence when highly manic in Phoenix, Arizona. The memory function is sophisticated. With human sight, we see images that last for a split second and then vanish into the next visual image.

I wandered where people were dancing. To my amazement, I saw images of dancer's previous feet and leg images trailing their most recent image positions as they fast danced. The tailing or "slowly" disappearing images looked liked fast action cartoons. I worried only briefly and theorized this strange sight was caused by my mental reconstruction. I did not think reality had changed. In this unusual experience, overlapping, trailing images lingered longer than usual. This occurrence happened only once.

Some techniques for learning names use exaggerated visual associations. If your name is George, I can visualize George Washington's head upside down on your head. The vision is so ridiculous that the image of George Washington's face and your face is easily remembered. This image lingers until normal memory is established. I have activated analog non-verbal abilities of my right-brain to remember names.

The subconscious mind manipulates pictures - mental holograms - even when reciting the alphabet. Study the structure and meaning of images in our lives, and our subconscious minds will love us for it.

Much, of our mental abilities, is used for language. Cultivate visual and dream processes to complement language skills,

Learning languages using images reinforces foundations of dream processes. Younger generations will have a stronger thinking foundation through creative image processing. They will think faster with more depth. Complex ideas, developed through image association, will make more sense. Foundation pictures should be associated with letters and words in early grades.

As babies become aware of environments, things are perceived in a flighty, confusing order. Babies develop emotional limits from repressed trauma scars. Memories of previously limiting experiences provide guidance in judging and predicting new experiences.

The best thing for baby is to be cuddled by his mother with a soft reassuring hum or song. Repeated sounds and nursery rhymes develop rhythm for developing right-brain resonances. Babies learn to predict what comes next. Predicting the future is important throughout life. Resonating sounds are spiritual experiences for baby.

Mixed messages by a parent or an important person tear a mind apart. We need to cuddle babies to reinforce embryonic feelings and emotions. Dreams will become less fragmented and easier to analyze.

The subconscious mind processes pictures as foundations of thought. Languages mold the human brain's fundamental conscious structure and processes. Chinese writing includes more visual processing, and repetitive, rhythmic sounds than English. Chinese are good at remembering details due to the structure of their language.

With experience, a nuclear engineer becomes confident he can design and predict successful operation of a nuclear power plant. Confidence for large accomplishments is developed through repeated smaller successes.

There is a level of uncertainty in all things. God is a perfect recorder of physical uncertainties throughout the universe and integrates all uncertainties into perfect spiritual certainty. Physical, mental, and spiritual processes are iterative. There are no fixed solutions in the universe. Thoughts iterate searching for solutions. God continually iterates for completeness throughout the universe.

If we work to understand God, our holograms become more integrated and clearer. Not doing so darkens or hazes our holograms. God is a Crystal Clear Hologram. Light of all colors integrate to construct holograms of pure clear heavenly light.

God is electromagnetic radiation, EMR, or Light. Light striking an atom gives it momentum, energy, and a relativistic increase in mass. Heated or high energy atoms give off light energy. It is undeniable that Light or Spirit can increase mass energy, and mass or atoms can give off Light. Heaven and the universe are in synergy and interchangeable.

Faint light from all stars interferes with light from other stars. Low-energy light meeting low-energy light produces God's awareness or complete spiritual Hologram even in outer space.

Spiritual and complex mental holograms have some qualities of simpler commercial holograms constructed with split and re-converging coherent laser light. See Appendix B for discussion of commercial hologram models.

My models were developed by elevating the mind briefly to manic levels, taking notes, and then calming down with meditation and breathing exercises to refine writing. Writing enhances detail learning about self and searching for limits to explore and expand. The mind is more complex than originally thought.

Writing builds reflective and recursive processes for connecting words into ideas. Repetitive writing processes synchronize muscle and neural network activations. Reflective writing develops awareness of physical symmetries in the universe, and spiritual symmetries within our minds.

Subconscious processes "parse" flowing mental hologram images into meaningful words, sentences, gestures, and facial expressions. Gestures are under-appreciated by many speakers. Smooth and continuous motions of the hands and body coordinate listeners' left and right brains for powerful learning and memories.

Right brain memories are recalled more easily by sight stimulations. Faces create flowing memories. Left brain memories of names are more difficult to recall. Connecting face images and names unites both memory functions. Genetics has established brain structure for learning from sight and other senses.

For inner thinking, we reduce energy within the brain and body to minimize interference from sense activations. Activations, from sense processes, overwhelm higher reasoning and spiritual abilities. Thought iteration, or development, rates vary with emotions. Slow, low-energy iterations produce in-depth, creative thoughts. Memories exist in spiritual space independent of physical space and time. When normal, minds iterate to complete thoughts.

We must distinguish between detailed-holistic thinking, sleeping-waking, relaxation-emotional thinking, and body-mind coordination. Converting uncertainties-to-certainties develops faith in self and God for mental health.

If striving to be upwardly mobile in careers, we must think positively and creatively. In notifying bosses of potential problems, upward thinking employees must always present possible solutions, or identify needed resources, as early as possible.

I dream about healing and improving the mind constantly. Today's best medical practices were yesterday's dreams.

Chapter 15
The Brain "String" Theory

"This above all: to thy own self be true.
And it must follow, as the night day,
Thou canst not then be false to any man."

Shakespeare: Hamlet

Our goal in this chapter is to construct an intermediate model of the brain and mind. Let's begin by studying water waves as an analogy to simplify thinking about electromagnetic waves and mind models.

Observe a pond when two rain drops make colliding waves. The smooth rings of highs and lows traveling outward from each wave source meet and are broken up into distinct vibrating peaks and valleys. Additional raindrops cause additional waves and more interference. As rain becomes heavier, interfering waves create a frenzy of vibrating peaks and valleys.

A similar process occurs when electromagnetic waves from neuron activations meet at the speed of light within brain cell membranes. From our water analogy, water drops represent neuron activations. Water waves or ripples represent electromagnetic waves from neuron activations.

Electromagnetic radiation, EMR, is reflected back and forth within membranes forming detailed resonances similar to the interference between water waves.

Rather than water waves expanding and interfering in two dimensions, electromagnetic waves within the brain expand and interfere with each other in three dimensions. The mental EMR picture is more complex than the water analogy, which we can visualize more easily.

During neuron activations, negatively charged electrons are lighter and explode outward faster than positive charged nuclei producing electromagnetic radiation, EMR.

EMR explodes outward at the speed of light, and chemicals flow along axons. EMR is absorbed, reflected, diffracted, and transmitted through neuron, glia, and brain surface, membranes to create four and possibly higher dimensional mental holograms. EMR passing through brain cell membranes are diffracted into distinct spectra to form detailed resonances and mental holograms for thought and memories. Integration of all neuron activities is somewhat similar to all voices of a 500 member choir integrating to form coherent, beautiful music.

EMR from a neuron activation or spike is partially absorbed within its own body, reflected by its own inner membrane surface, resonates between its inner and outer membrane surfaces being partially absorbed each iteration. Some EMR escapes and resonates between membrane surfaces of other neurons and glia support cells. EMR, created from one neuron activation, creates millions of reflections and absorptions by membrane surfaces to form specific distributed aspects of mental holograms. Near neurons are affected more than distant neurons within the brain.

Resonating electromagnetic waves die out as their energy is absorbed by, or escapes from, the brain. Awareness dies out and is reborn as new electromagnetic waves are created by new neuron activations.

For incoming light, brain cell outer surfaces either reflect or refract light. Refracted light within membrane surfaces resonates with widening angles at each reflection creating an increasingly detailed imprint. Transmitted light continues on to filter throughout many different brain cell membranes. Resonances in cell membranes continue until a single quantum of energy is deposited within a membrane atom or molecule. Light or EMR continues with less fractal energy as it travels through more distant neurons. The first incoming light beam entering a cell membrane becomes the "reference beam" for subsequent reflections and resonances within that membrane.

Sense nerve cell action potentials initiate subconscious resonances and other brain activities. Each distributed memory hologram has its own action potential. Consciousness depends upon strength and duration of internal and external stimuli. High-energy holograms have greater influence on culturing thinking.

For understanding multiple reflections within a membrane, let's look at fractals. An example is the Sierpinski Triangle in Figure 15.1. Repeated mathematical, geometrical, and reflected processes build fractals. In the figure, there is an overall triangle, with a black secondary triangle one fourth the size of the original in the center. Initially the other secondary triangles were white. But then we continue the process by placing tertiary black triangles of one fourth the size inside at the center of the remaining white secondary triangles. This process could go on indefinitely.

EMR, reflecting back and fourth inside membranes, continues until the last photon is absorbed by a single atom. Mental holograms are constructed by quanta of light absorbed by membrane atoms and molecules. Our visual and computer monitor images are constructed of small dots and seem smooth and continuous due to our limited vision abilities.

Each neuron has unique activation characteristics. EMR spikes from each neuron are different like snow flakes are different. The outgoing EMR forms the most energetic component of a distributed hologram on its own membrane. This cell's membrane is also affected by incoming EMR from other neurons firing during the same spike time. EMR spikes usually do not completely overlap. EMR reflection and absorption itera-tions culture increasing hologram details throughout the brain. EMR becomes less as it threads through distant nerve cells. Eventually, EMR is split into "Strings" of light that affect individual atoms.

This process is similar to triangles within triangles becoming smaller and more detailed. EMR absorbed by distant membranes corresponds to smaller Sierpinski Triangles. Multiple diffracted and reflected EMR has less energy but refined details. Highly reflected EMR adds holo-gram definition by overlaying refined imprints on current membrane imprints. Each brain cell membrane atom constructs a piece of each mental hologram.

If photographic film can absorb light energy and store images, then certainly DNA within membranes can absorb EMR and store imprints. Mental holograms are stored similar to pictures on photographic film.

The fabric of brain cell membranes has amazing properties. Memory holograms are much more complex than laser holograms. EMR, and light, spectra are hitting millions of membranes at many angles, intensi-ties, and frequencies each second.

The smallest mental "Sierpenski" triangle, consisting of three atoms, absorbs light. Each reflection within cell membranes occurs at slightly widener angles. This phenomenon produces detailed three-dimensional holograms on all membrane surfaces within the brain. EMR of one re-fined frequency, filtering, through the brain, constructs one distinct ho-logram.

Physical processes within neurons develop chemical and electrical potentials that keep brain cells firing and brains active. Routine elec-tromagnetic activity continually reads from and writes to brain cell membranes – similar to reading from and writing on computer CDs.

EMR absorbed by less fixed neuron body fluids has less influence on brain activities than that absorbed by cell membranes. EMR absorbed by brain cell nuclei also influences thinking. Our three-dimensional "photo film" neural membrane imprints are always there, as are family photos, ready to be viewed at any time.

Let's refine our model. Since reflected and diffracted EMR strike membranes at slightly different angles, subsequent smaller fractal triangles appear less than equilateral when absorbed. The smaller more reflected triangles are distorted more as repeated diffractions and reflections produce wider angles. Smaller triangles provide higher definition and dimension than the original triangle for constructing mental holograms.

Rather than distinct triangles, the mind works with mental images, produced at all angles, with wide spectra of light energy. Membranes of complex brain cell systems correspond to the intricately woven two-dimensional Holusion designs. The brain is more complex. Our brains construct higher-dimensional virtual holograms on a complex three-dimensional membrane system of "photo film."

Our subconscious minds make millions of decisions at fractal levels for each conscious thought. In reverse, subconscious processes build increasingly larger fractal triangles to create a big triangle of conscious thought. We are not normally aware of smaller fractal triangles. A goal is awareness of the next lower level of fractal triangles for added control in culturing thinking.

Truthful EMR resonances are referenced to resonances within our souls, or the refined array of smallest "fundamental fractal hologram triangles." We have a guiding light to live our lives by when conscious thoughts are referenced to wisdom within our souls. Unfortunately, trauma scars haze over communications reflected to and from our souls.

Repeated thoughts make corresponding holograms brighter and clearer. Similar visions and experiences develop similar resonances. "Triangle holograms" are imprinted on every solid surface in the brain at every angle. There is so much EMR traveling at all angles that some EMR hitting membranes are coherent at differing angles. Coherent light with slightly differing angles and resonating within a cell membrane has more influence than diverse light waves in constructing mental holograms.

Pondering specific in-depth thoughts over long periods of time develops strong, specialized resonances for creative ideas in chosen arenas. Einstein pondered for long periods of time on similar concepts resulting in his prestigious discoveries. He developed a detailed, precise symphony of mental holograms.

Each brain cell membrane contains imprints that refine light, which is integrated with all other light within the brain from different perspectives. Each brain cell membrane receives EMR from even the most remote brain cell. All brain cells, free of trauma energy influences, would construct a clear hologram with higher spiritual abilities. Trauma networks degrade clarity.

The brain consists of 50 to 100 billion neurons with 10,000 dendrites per neuron and several kilometers of dendrite fibers per cubic millimeter. Is it not amazing that this intricate brain structure and activity allows us to focus on one thing!

Electromagnetic spikes from neurons have unique energy characteristics and shapes. Electrical and chemical pulses sent along a neuron's axon to dendrites of other neurons also have a distinct characteristic. This footprint is recognized by billions of other brain cells. Brain cells refer to both neuron and glia support cells. The electromagnetic footprint is filtered through many membranes before reaching distant neurons. Neuron firing sequences are influenced by electromagnetic and chemical transmissions from sense nerves and their connected neurons.

Neurons reacting to sight seem to be the fastest firing neurons. Neuron spike intervals can be as fast as .15 seconds. Under the most stimulated conditions, neurons do not fire or spike more than 100 times per second. These firing or activation intervals are not nearly fast enough to produce the "certain" death flash described in Chapter 4. There are residual effects from neuron firings. Neuron spikes produce delayed influences along axons, through synapses to connected dendrites for influencing other neurons. Timing and coordination of neural activations are fundamental to learning, memory, and other mental functions.

Negative potential impulses from some neurons slow down potential chemical buildup and spike rates of connected neurons. The timing and integration of concurrent EMR spikes from all neurons produce four-dimensional mental holograms. Integrating repeated neuron activations produce consciousness.

Mental holograms and the alphabet are building blocks, for human language. Comparing and integrating mental holograms construct inner language for conscious thought. Inner processes are more complex than verbal and non-verbal thinking. Understanding inner processes, improves language.

Researchers are studying human neuron firing potentials, electromagnetic frequencies, spike shapes, and connectivity to understand brain functionality. Researchers are not yet studying neuron and glia membrane fabric as foundations of thought. Researchers need to analyze membrane fabric to discover mental holograms. Diet supplements may enhance membrane abilities.

Cosmological calculations require several additional spatial dimensions to combine atomic sized quantum theory with general relativity theory to construct the integrated "unified field theory." Physics calculations require that six or seven additional dimensions of freedom are needed to explain existence. Some of these additional dimensions are needed for thought. Most of these addition dimensions are spiritual dimensions. We should not be so egocentric to limit God to our meager thoughts and existence.

Distributed neural membranes throughout the three-dimensions of the brain compare to the detailed two-dimensional surface of a Holusion. From neuron activations, EMR writes to and reads from trillions of two-dimensional imprints on complex and diversely oriented membranes, structured in three dimensions, to produce higher-dimensional mental and spiritual holograms.

Trillions of memory imprints on neural membranes throughout the brain are stored with unique refined frequencies for promoting specific resonances. Thinking is a virtual process beyond our sensed three dimensions. Spiritual dimensions reside, or are integrated, within, physical dimensions.

Neuron spike profiles can be measured with micro-technology. In the future, brain scans will correlate neuron fabric, mental hologram characteristics, and thought construction.

Small, closely placed micro-sensors inside neurons will increase detailed knowledge of the brain. It will be interesting to analyze differences between those who have and have not practiced mental reconstruction. Eventually, we may analyze how the subconscious mind constructs "near-death flashes" so quickly.

Let's summarize the brain string theory. Upon firing of one neuron, there is a pulse of outgoing electromagnetic energy in all directions. This light is: 1) reflected by its inner membrane surface, 2) transmitted though its inner membrane surface, 3) absorbed in the fabric of its own membrane, 4) reflected by its own outer membrane surface, 5) repeatedly reflected between inner and outer membrane surfaces imprints higher refinements with less energy each reflection, 6) transmitted through its outer membrane surface, 7) reflected by another cell's outer membrane surface, 8) transmitted through another cell's outer membrane surface, 9) absorbed by another cell's membrane, 10) reflected by another membrane's inner surface, 11) this process continues throughout all brain cells, 12) and some energy escapes the brain. More distant brain cells receive less energy. Light is refracted or bent by membrane surfaces. Light frequency and directions change when hitting surfaces at other than 90 degree angles. All these characteristics add to the diversity of the light energy absorbed in its own and other brain cell membrane fabric.

EMR travels and deposits energy along a zigzag path through cell bodies and membranes as it is refracted, diffracted, and reflected. EMR paths in the brain are referred to as, light "strings." Even when neurons are not firing, their membranes are absorbing and reflecting EMR and defining resonances.

Fractal levels of reflections essentially digitize EMR absorptions. From television, we have learned how digitizing signals can increase EMR data transmission capacity.

The mind consists of millions of mental resonances vying for importance. Many subconscious resonances are integrated for increased energy to become conscious resonances, which are reflected back and forth through brain cell membrane and brain component surfaces. All mental processes are iterative. Longer resonances are reflected between brain component surfaces. Mental holograms contain time stamps for organizing memory and may be a reason for aging.

Diverse neuron shapes and sizes create diverse three-dimensional electromagnetic radiation profiles for constructing mental holograms. Each neuron footprint is recognized by, and uniquely influences, other brain cells. Some segments of neuron spike profiles may be independent of distances between neurons. Two radios tuned to the same station will receive the same music at different distances from the station.

There are trillions of communication paths between dendrites and axons and refined EMR paths traveling at the speed of light. Each neuron is a mental radio station and a mental radio.

A goal is that "brain string" theory and other models are realistic enough to dissolve trauma scars and inspire mental reconstruction and future experiments. Emphasis should be placed on studying brain cell membrane properties and how mental holograms are constructed and processed by the brain.

With consistent feedback from parents and environments, conscious processes tend to converge into acceptable ideas and behaviors. Our three-dimensional neurological web-like fabric is extremely diversified and different within each person. Human brains produce extremely different subconscious processes that cultivate similar conscious processes when individuals are doing or observing similar things. Subconscious and conscious processes are more diverse for individuals with different languages, conflicting values, and varies environments.

Much of our thinking processes seem to be analog or continuous processes. With analog thoughts developed, a writer or speaker has to cultivate discrete words to communicate analog ideas to others. Some of us receive spiritual feelings. We must energize our souls and subconscious minds to translate analog spiritual messages into discrete words truthfully.

People, including spiritual leaders, are basically self-centered toward their investments in effort and money. If we choose our own creative path of spiritual enlightenment, most religious leaders will degrade our efforts. "Superior" dogmatic religions have caused more pain and deaths than other causes.

The medical profession has done little in analyzing how manic thoughts lead to spiritual enlightenment. From my research with a few manic-depressives, it is amazing that spiritual thoughts have such similar themes; however, words are different depending upon experiences and vocabularies. Researching manic episodes, we may discover the universal nature of the inner mind, prove God exists, and define His nature.

Let's make an inference. God's awareness is stored within and on the surfaces of all living and inanimate things that absorb and reflect light within this universe. Our minds are a small part of God's reflections and wisdom. Every reflection and absorption of light has meaning to God.

Physical structure and chemical activities construct the mind and soul. Mental holograms communicate with God in higher dimensions through the soul's resonances.

Ponce de Leon traveled to Florida in search of the Fountain of Youth when he only needed to stimulate his longevity genes. Researchers have discovered longevity genes in lower life forms such as yeast. They are searching for master regulator genes for cell dividing processes, which may influence life spans. Longevity genes are related to natural defense mechanisms, aging, and stress resistance. A goal is to enhance stress reducing abilities and slow aging. Emotional and trauma limits, developed as babies and during childhood, build our defenses against stress.

Without conflict, nothing occurs within the universe. Electromagnetic radiation is the conflict from and awareness of exchanging physical and spiritual energy. There is no awareness without conflict. Traumas conflict with our security and guilt of being inadequate or in the wrong. The birth of, and all actions within, the universe were created by conflict. God's constant physical and spiritual laws were reactions to conflict of non-existence. We can increase abilities to control conflict.

Figure 15 .1 Fractals: The Sierpinski Triangle

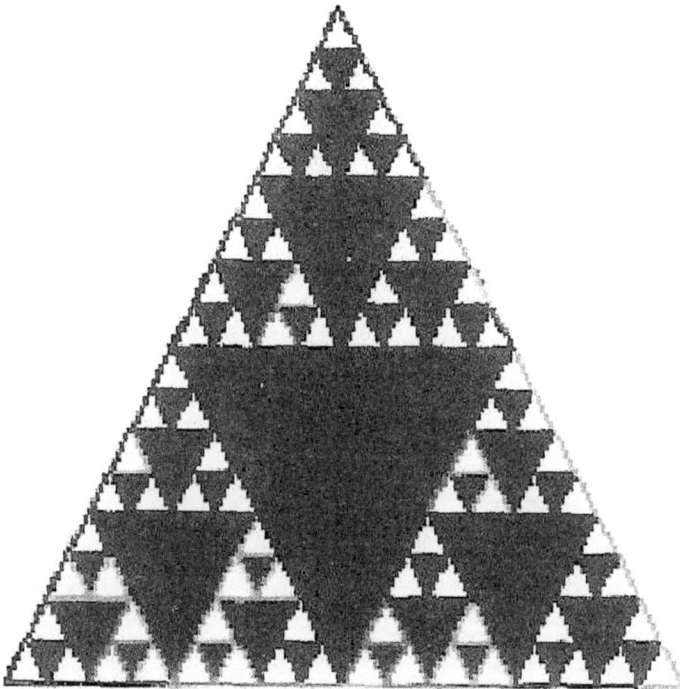

Without conflict, nothing occurs within the universe. Electromagnetic radiation is the conflict from, and awareness of exchanging physical and spiritual energy. There is no awareness without conflict. Trauma is conflict with our selves and guilt of being in disharmony in the whole. The birth of and after life within the universe were traced by conflict. God's constant physical and spiritual laws were traced to a conflict of non-existence. We can increase abilities to control conflict.

Figure 15-3 Fractals: The Sierpinski Triangle

Chapter 16
Abusive and Abused

Only a life lived for others is a life worthwhile.

Albert Einstein

Marriage and sex make the lesser equal to the greater. We should never feel greater or less than our spouses. Doing so is spiritless.

Love and caring build character. Thinking of one's power is uncaring of others. Love and closeness are not truly invented between some husbands and wives and between some parents and children. However, it is not too late. Mutual forgiveness creates miracles and is the secret to successful relationships.

Friends give, take, and suggest but do not control. It is easier to agree than disagree. If we agree too much we lose our freedom. If we disagree, we may expose our ignorance. For our own mental health, we must learn to disagree wisely. Disagreeing can cause arguments.

At the beginning of adult arguments – **STOP!** Agree to discuss issues the next day. Stay emotionally apart until then. When apart, list conflicting issues. Grade issues from 1 to 10. Rationally explain ratings of each issue. Write down actions needed to reduce issue ratings. Combine lists and work together to reduce issue ratings. Both must learn to compromise.

Keep records of each person's willingness to compromise. If working on issues causes other issues, add them to the list for the next session. Each individual should be proud of, and document, their willingness to change. Lasting relationships are developed with reason, not emotions.

In life and arguments intelligence is not memorizing and stubbornly sticking to a single routine. Intelligence is the process of and integrating old and new ideas rationally for direction in one's own and others' lives.

If one combatant changes very little, records of issues and changes will be starting tools to assist counselors. If one spouse does not cooperate, rate your own and his perceived list to discuss issues with a counselor. Work on small issues before they become big issues. Discuss emotional issues only when both parties give "absolute attention." Don't nag. Discipline for correcting behavior succeeds only if we are reasonable and consistent.

We have to earn our children's respect daily. Otherwise, they become defiant and uncontrollable. In order to correct children's behavior, we must spend more time having fun with and praising them in enjoyable activities than in time punishing them.

The early years are crucial in developing versatile methods for getting along with others. Parents, or single parents, must take responsibility for each child's mind and body development. Safety and confidence building are most important. Destructive behavior toward or by a child must be addressed immediately. Find out inner reasons for behaviors and discuss them.

If a parent or older sibling is physically or psychologically abusing or bullying a child, they are severely wounding and limiting that child's mental abilities for life unless he has psychotherapy or practices mental reconstruction. The abused child "knows" his parent's do not care about him and his suffering.

An abused child is constantly aware he is helpless and cannot defend himself. This deep down helpless feeling limits normal curiosity and mental abilities. Abusive effects remain throughout life and the abused becomes passive or learns to control and abuse others. It's normal.

False egos of abusive parents or siblings force them to act superior to the abused. Abusive parents and siblings must have counseling to learn patience and understand why they are abusive.

Parents should punish abusive children with longer time outs until abuse stops. An abusive sibling will learn to live the easy or hard way, and will find out that respecting younger siblings is better than sitting alone without toys or television for hours.

His suffering and crying will help him understand his younger sibling's suffering and crying. An older sibling needs to know he is important but no more important than younger siblings. Parents should not comment on crying until time out is over but then compare his crying and discomfort to his sibling's crying and discomfort. He will learn concern for others' suffering.

Be vigilant. It is parents' responsibility to sew seeds of caring behavior. If an older child cannot be trusted with a younger sibling, keep them separated when unsupervised. Be strict when necessary. In today's and tomorrow's world, your allowing sibling bullying may eventually lead to campus murders. Bullies and parents of bullies may be as responsible as abused victims who murder. Persistent bullying can make life no longer worth living and can trigger an attack on society for letting abuse happen. The news media should not just report on shooters psychological problems but also on shooters' persistent abusers and their parents to help this society understand and heal. Bullies and lack of parenting are a basic cause for innocent people being murdered.

Superior acting people enslave with psychology and subtle threats. Older siblings mimic parents' superior attitudes and behavior and abuse weaker, younger siblings. Parents should promote an atmosphere of not feeling superior or inferior to anyone, or younger children will feel inferior to abusive older children.

Bosses who degrade subordinates in front of their children are damaging to those children. Almost nothing is worth degrading someone in front of their children. In today's fast paced computer environments, it is difficult enough to maintain a child's respect. The dumbest people pretend they are superior and enjoy making others feel inferior. Heaven does not wait for such abusers.

If a sibling abuses a younger sibling, older neighborhood children will also think the younger sibling is inferior and abuse that child. Their parents also have not taught respect for younger children. Early competitions and play should be structured with mental and physical achievements for everyone. A six year old should be handicapped so a four year old wins at times.

There is a genius in every child. Parents have responsibility to nurture abilities and prevent mind limiting abuses. However, labeling a child as a genius adds stress to and corrupts a child's relationships with others. Before every moment of genius, there are hours of inconclusiveness beyond reasoning limits.

Drunk drivers are abusive and dangerous to other drivers. Laws are passed to prevent inebriated drivers. Similarly, laws may be required to educate and punish parents and older siblings, together, if parents let children continue to abuse younger children. Children's behavior is parents' responsibility. Don't have younger siblings unless prepared to protect and nurture them also. "Persistent" abuse is so destructive to the mind and ego and limits abilities for life. However, brief, even difficult, challenges build creative minds and character. Parent should be ready to provide assistance but only when needed.

There is a huge difference between reactions to brief and persistent stress. The subconscious mind has an innate ability to meet brief, even severe, challenges. It cannot understand or cope with persistent abuse that causes feelings of helplessness. The mind is programmed to attack or retreat. Persistent abuse and fear, without a reasonable way out, destroy fragile minds.

If we have fought in wars with persistent stress and fear, we could be labeled as having post-traumatic syndrome. If we have had persistent abuse or fear of abuse as children we are simply labeled as dumb. A young child's daily stress from an older sibling causes fear equal to that of a soldier in combat. A traumatized mind is a terrible thing to waste!

Eighth graders and high school students should pass parenting courses, beginning with caring for new born babies and extending to caring for and managing teenagers and older adults. Few families teach responsibilities. We can bring out the best in our students. Currently, we only psychiatrically treat, and attempt to heal, the most poorly parented, usually, after it is too late.

Students and parents can work to reason together, be a team, correct mistakes, gain confidence in their own thinking, and begin emotional healing together. We must recognize and correct destructive student and parent behaviors early. America is spending unnecessary resources on prisons.

Important new jobs are needed to develop parenting skill infrastructure. Too many children are "trained" by self-centered movie and television characters. Parents should be children's best stars. Teachers should be creative in promoting respect for parents.

Dreaming processes have fewer inhibitions and are more emotional than most waking experiences. Dreaming activities amplify and extend abusive experiences to emotional or mental limits. Dreams prepare the brain for waking activations, even traumas, and long range memory construction and integration.

Some areas of the brain are blocked or hidden by trauma scars and can not be activated. Disorders become degrading when traumatized areas of the brain are so severe dreaming processes can no longer prepare these areas for waking activations. With severe trauma damage, the mind can become divided into split personalities. If waking events become more emotional than dreams, repressed trauma memories are ingrained.

Adverse social interactions cause so many dysfunctional minds and illnesses. A false-hearted lover, spouse, older sibling, or bully can cause so much pain and misery.

A bullied or deceived spouse should not hide abuse but reason with her spouse and tell supportive friends. (Don't become isolated!) If things don't improve seek counseling together if possible, if not seek counseling alone. After a year if the abusive, bullying spouse's behavior does not improve, and you have tried very hard, the constant abuse will ruin your health. Split. Long term abuse causes painful stress disorders.

Parents must be harsh when siblings harshly abuse or bully younger siblings. Possibly, hours of time outs standing in a corner without toys are needed. If necessary, place young older siblings in a small space for brief periods of time. This may prevent some from incarceration later on.

Let *them* cry for abusing younger siblings. Ensure older siblings that they must be good to younger siblings or endure severe punishment. Make sure they know it is *their* choice to have either punishment or freedom to play and have fun. Respect and love must be taught and learned.

It is difficult for gentle, loving parents to punish children for sibling abuse, but everyone in the family will become healthier, smarter, and more sociable in the long run. Dysfunctional families are ruled by power, control, and deception.

We are not being good to our abusive children to allow them to abuse. Abusers develop a superior attitude and often become too smart to learn in school and stop listening to parents.

Students and workers should report bullying and abuse of others and themselves. Persistent kidding should be reported as abuse if not in a positive light. Administrators or management should define abuse in their arenas. Observers should be punished if observing bullying and do not report it. Isolate the bullies.

I cringe when I hear a mother of father say, "I can't do a thing with him!" Well, you should not have had children if you are irresponsible! We must start early with discipline. It is the parents responsibility if an older sibling ruins his and the lives of younger siblings. It is "all <u>our</u>" fault! There are so many tools you can use to correct bad behavior. Having a sense of humor with children and having them laugh frequently is good for everyone.

It does not help simply asking a child, "What did you just do?" or "Why did you do that?" A child cannot explain why he hurt another child. Parents must help older siblings learn, and correct, there inner reasons for abuse. It has everything to do with parents' behaviors.

Children are taught to play baseball. They anticipate and hit or catch a ball. Anticipation and success develops brief feelings of control. Some older siblings' sport becomes to hurt their younger sibling. We need to correct long-range, right-brain abusive thinking more than correcting the left-brain "hit" thinking. An abusive sibling gets a pulse of control and a lasting feeling of superiority when hurting "an inferior" sibling.

Current American culture and laws no longer permit parents to physically discipline a child. In most cases this is good. Parents must be more creative with their discipline. Look for creative disciplinary limits to explore. If we physically discipline a child, social services will take our children away as the older child continues to torment the younger sibling.

When you catch an older sibling hurting a younger one, very slowly ask the older and younger one what the older has done. Help them explain what occurred. Look stern and have the abuser do the same thing to you. Have him do it again. Let he see your displeasure and anger. Ask him how he feels about what he just did? Then ask him what you should do to him.

Do a similar thing to him with some degree of discomfort with an angry, stern face. Show no sympathy. Force him to think about what he has done with left and right-brains. Explain why his thinking and actions are wrong, have him "stand" in a corner for an appropriate time, and have him write his "inner" reasons for his selfish abuse an appropriate number of times.

We must learn how our children think of our and their limits. Discipline should be at children's thinking limits. The mind grows and expands at limits. "Briefly," stress children toward proper, creative limits so minds grow in a positive direction.

A younger sibling should not be made to say he loves an abusive sibling. Encouraging false childhood feelings may cause an abused child to take abuse from others and in marriage. We do not need to love someone who is abusing and controlling us. A controlling, abusive person does not truly love those he abuses.

However, we should approach everyone with love until they abuse us. Unfortunately so many abusive people are incarcerated because they had no parenting or love when young. There are too many single parents raising children and too many ill trained and irresponsible men disrespecting women, their children, and themselves. Without respect for self, people take the fast way out. They use alcohol, drugs, and crime to find false self-respect.

If you cannot correct a young child's bad behavior, you will not be able to correct an older child's behavior. If you do not discipline your child, get a head start and have your city or county prepare more space in the jail or penitentiary for your child. It is your fault! Most people in jail have been neglected or abused.

If you and your children are away from home and your darling abused his younger sibling, right at that time determine his punishment. Tell him he owes you punishment level X when you get home or at your first opportunity. Keep a list with dates to frequently remind him of his misdeeds. Punishment slowly gets worse. Always keep a record of what he owes you. Hard work can be substituted two hours for one hour standing in the corner. Make sure he works. Hard work never hurt a healthy child.

For severe abuse, make him dig 2 x 2 x 2 foot hole and bury a plastic envelop with hand writing describing his abuse and reasons for not abusing again. Measure the hole. If he continues abuse make him dig up his writing and add to it. Dig deeper and rebury. In digging a hole, he has time to think about what he has done. Check on writing and digging progress at times. Persistent abuse of a young child is very serious. It wrecks younger siblings' mental abilities and lives. He is a failure each time he is abused. This digging method works in the military.

Persistent abuse mentally damages at any age. If someone did to you what your older sibling does to the younger one, you would accuse him of physical assault or mental assassination, have him incarcerated, and sue his pants off. My older sibling has been an only a child! Children will be children! Meanwhile, the younger child lives in a war zone unable to dodge mental bullets.

Abuse and uncertainty in young lives develop low self-esteem. It is written on faces of grownups, which have experienced "persistent" abuse when young. It does not take a rocket scientist to understand that persistent abuse develops inner stress and narrows thinking limits. The abused are less analytical and creative with higher probability of stress and other disorders.

Reactions to some original traumas caused devastation, others anger. Anger related trauma scars contain extreme repressed anger. If activated by a stimulus, uncontrollable anger recurs. With psychotherapy and psychophysiotherapy, trauma anger energy can be released. Alternating, between high and low emotional levels while recalling causes of anger, can help purge excess energy. As healing progresses, alternate reactions to adverse situations can be discovered or learned from others.

People with anger management difficulties are too serious about them selves and their egos. They seldom find humor in life, except at others' expense. An important healing process is developing a sense of humor, which is not at another's expense. When by myself or with others, I enjoy thinking of funny things.

We must try to have patience and love everyone. Anyone can have a bad day. A rule of three seems appropriate. If someone abuses me and makes me feel second class three times, I avoid them if possible.

If necessary, I still treat them with courtesy but no longer respect them. They make amends by showing remorse, love, or concern. We should not be treated second class unless paid, or we volunteer to serve. If abuse continues, we must describe inappropriate behaviors and its effects to abusers if wise, or to authorities if necessary. It is everyone's duty to stop bullying and abuse.

Chapter 17
Integration of Mind Models

We learn of the world and universe
through imprints on fragile brains
to discover God is within.

H. Fulcher 2008

Are we positive about ourselves and others? Are we judging who is confidence-building for us and others? Do we build our and others confidence? With confidence, we can integrate our skills and purposes for helping ourselves and others more. At times, we should evaluate our thinking.

Life and the universe would have no purpose without uncertainty. If we always knew what would happen, we would be predestined without options or judgments in life. Competitions have no purpose with certainty of results. Curiosity searches to make uncertainties known.

The physical brain is stationary. Relative to our brains, mental holograms are constructed while traveling at the speed of light in all directions. The brain exists in physical space but the mind exists within relativistic spiritual or virtual space.

Our minds "parse" flowing subconscious holograms into words, sentences, and gestures. Good diction, enunciation, and gestures make compelling communications.

Gestures and expressions are powerful communication tools under-appreciated by many speakers. Coordinating gestures with speech activate the emotional right brain to add to the communication process. Listeners' left and right brains become synchronized creating powerful emotional memories.

Memory is developed by filtering neuron light through a myriad of neuron membranes to form hologram awareness and consciousness. Mental holograms are spiritually alive. God is a living higher-dimensional Hologram framed by all electromagnetic and other field force activities throughout, and relativistic to, the physical universe, creating perfect consciousness.

EMR in the brain initiated by senses are cultured with past histories. For refined inner thinking, we reduce energy of the brain and body to minimize sense activations. When normal, minds iterate to complete thoughts. Speed varies according to emotions. Memories are stored in chemical configurations on brain cell membranes. Memories create their own spiritual space and time independent of physical space and time.

Our minds are shared activities between billions of neurons. Without sharing, there would be no human awareness or minds. Subconscious processes integrate diverse experiences into holistic thoughts allowing unity of purpose. God integrates all universal activities into oneness for spiritual purpose.

The brain is constructed by a labyrinth of neuron networks for practically unlimited thought. I estimate we use less than one billionth of our neural channels for creative thought. Our minds are a bridge between the physical universe and spiritual oneness.

Two-dimensional Holusions are amazing tools. Relaxing focus, a three-dimensional image appears. This is similar to life. Observing three-dimensional views, we yearn to relax and understand higher spiritual dimensions.

Artificial intelligence suggests constructing a semi-artificial and an artificial mind. For the semi-artificial mind, researchers could use a few hundred brain cells from a young pig in a solution to keep them alive. With neuroscience technology, cells could be activated and coordinated. Researchers could study the firing profiles of these neurons. With knowledge of electromagnetic firing profiles, researchers could alternately force weak then stronger love and then anger human resonances. Changes in timing of neuron activations could determine learning.

An artificial human mind could be constructed using advanced artificial materials with absorption and reflective characteristics similar to nerve cell membranes. This material would be similar to photo film but with curved surfaces having some resemblance to neuron three dimensional shapes. At artificial brainstem locations, EMR frequencies of various emotions would be introduced with laser beams and fiber optics for simulating neuron activations. The test for "artificial thinking" would be if dominant new longer lasting frequencies are constructed from several overlapping and varying shorter input frequencies.

The clinical term for hearing unexplained voices through the ears is called auditory hallucinations. Hearing inner voices is referred to as thought intrusions or insertions. With controlled levels of mania, I am able to receive inner, positive voices and assign them as blessings from God.

Traditional spiritual words received were also thought intrusions or insertions. God speaks to us today as He did in traditional spiritual times. Prophets probably had bipolar disorder. Psychologists and psychiatrists today would say traditional spiritual leaders had mental disorders and had auditory hallucinations or thought intrusions and insertions. What was spiritual in the past is still spiritual today.

In is important to write down and recall events or pressures that caused manic episodes. After episodes, explain initiating events and how thinking could have been calmed earlier.

Sunlight can help regulate moods. From genetics, eyes were formed by responses to sunlight. The frequencies of sunlight can help regulate frequencies and resonances within the brain. Too much sunlight can cause an onset of mania. Regular sleep promotes efficient resonances for managing subconscious tasks.

A key in supporting manic-depressives is to distinguish between bipolar motivated speech and actions and normal activities. If thoughts are manic oriented, support persons should say, "Your thinking and actions are caused by mania. Do slow breathing while I get you to your doctor or the hospital." If thoughts are depressed sounding such as, "No one cares about me. I have no reason to live." Get help early before things get worse.

At times a cognitive therapist may help change suicidal or manic thoughts. Individuals in depression or mania can be guided toward listening to and caring for others. Depression and mania cause self-centeredness.

When able, tell your doctor effects medications are having on you. With your input, your doctor may suggest changes to your medications. Discuss attitudes and thinking. Ask what you can do on your own to help yourself. Discuss what or who is causing tensions and anxieties. Explain what triggers mania and avoid these situations.

Predicting the future gives us confidence and stability. Bipolar thinking and actions are predictable to some extent. At the beginning of each manic episode, many statements and actions are similar. Recognizing manic actions and speech, supporters can get help early on and save a lot of pain and expense. Predicting manic behavior gives hope of improving and controlling behavior. Managing bipolar disorder is discussed by Julie A. Fast and John Preston in *Take Charge of Bipolar Disorder* [1].

At times, I have felt frustrated by the long effort to complete mental reconstruction. Normal adult brains are highly infested with trauma scars. I felt compelled to make mental reconstruction a way of life. With amazing trauma energy release sensations, I have rushed toward the clear mind for fifteen years with excitement and wonder not knowing the final result.

We have described the mind as travelling in all directions at light speeds relative to the brain. Also, we have modeled the mind as existing in spiritual dimensions, including dark energy, which may integrate meaning throughout the universe. Our minds have wide spread holistic or spiritual abilities which may influence the universe and God.

Figure 17.1 is a picture of some mind functions. Each mind exists as its own universe. Picture functions, "A" through "G," as vibrating at various physical and spiritual distances within and/or beyond the brain. "G" may vibrate with extremely low frequencies to and from the edges of the universe for communicating with God.

A. Mental communication back and forth with vital organs is repetitive and, when healthy, is direct.
B. Dreaming and mental organization make spiritual sense of daily activities by integrating them within long range memories and our souls. The ovals are genetic macro-functions connecting diverse ideas and dream scenarios. "B" may vibrate considerably beyond the physical brain.
C. The rectangle represents genetic functions for awakening from sleep into consciousness with body control. The mind zigzags while navigating varied daily activities within up close and long range environments.
D. Efficient processes are developed for routine, macro, and repetitive activities within "C" above. Thinking becomes more organized and direct.
E. Analytical thinking extends to extremes or mental limits at times to relate new concepts to established thoughts. Thinking extends beyond the brain into spiritual space.
F. Reflex thinking reflects genetic and emotional processes to trauma limits. Up-close reflex thinking consists of high-energy

short wave vibrations for fast reactions. The Flash is the limiting reflex process.

G. Surrender and spiritual thinking extend beyond free will thinking. We must think humbly and holistically beyond self into the universe. Adult minds with even normal egos, unless having experienced near-death, may have resistance to spiritual surrender. "G" shows resistance to and then expansion into spiritual thinking. The oval represents parallel, holistic, and flowing processes for spiritual thoughts beyond space and time.

Think of "A" through "G" functions as vibrating in spiritual dimensions. We need imagination to understand our own minds. Imagination is everything.

Figure 17.2 shows mind functions cleared of trauma effects and prejudices. All processes are straight forward. "G" shows no resistance to spiritual surrender with constant God consciousness. Spiritual processes convert worries and uncertainties into certainty.

Young babies need lots of certainty to build confident minds. Weak, dying persons need certainty of having lived purposeful lives for attaining spiritual existence.

We cannot determine or feel which of our 50 to 100 billion neurons activate for constructing thoughts, but, from experience, we are usually sure of consistent thoughts at reasonable speeds and energy levels to perform normal conversations and activities.

The brain continuously generates millions of subconscious resonances available to be amplified into consciousness. One sensation or random neural network activity can tune in a specific conscious idea. The more we exercise specific neural networks, the easier it is to recall, understand, and have faith in that channel or thinking arena.

We must analyze ourselves for nearsightedness, narrow-mindedness, and prejudices to become complete and truly spiritual. I work to be a world ling. A less global mind is prejudiced. Even with unusual mental reconstruction, I'm not yet concerned about the welfare of outer-space and inter-galactic aliens. However, I continue with disappointment of not supporting my parents enough on earth or in heaven, or God, as I should.

REFERENCE:

1) Fast, Julie A., and Preston, John, PsyD, *Take Charge of Bipolar Disorder, A 4-Step Plan for You and Your Loved Ones To Manage the Illness And Create Lasting Stability, 2006,* Wellness Central, Hachette Book Group USA, 237 Park Avenue, New York, NY 10017, New York, Boston

Figure 17.1 Normal Mind Processes

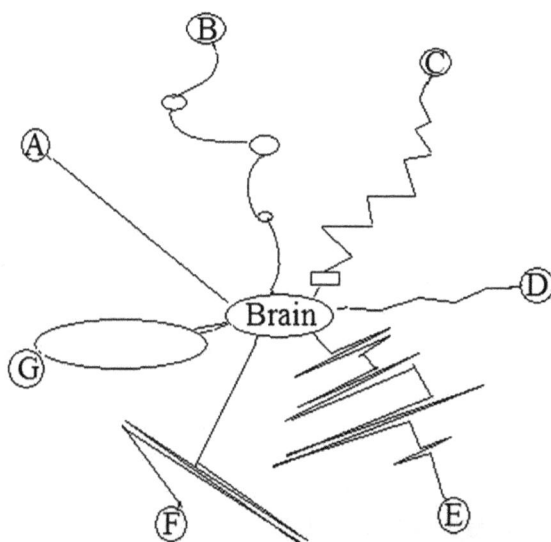

A. Subconscious Vital
B. Dreaming & Mental Organization
C. Flash to Consciousness & Body Control
D. Routine
E. Analytical
F. Reflex and Limit
G. Spiritual Surrender

Figure 17.2 Clear Mind Processes

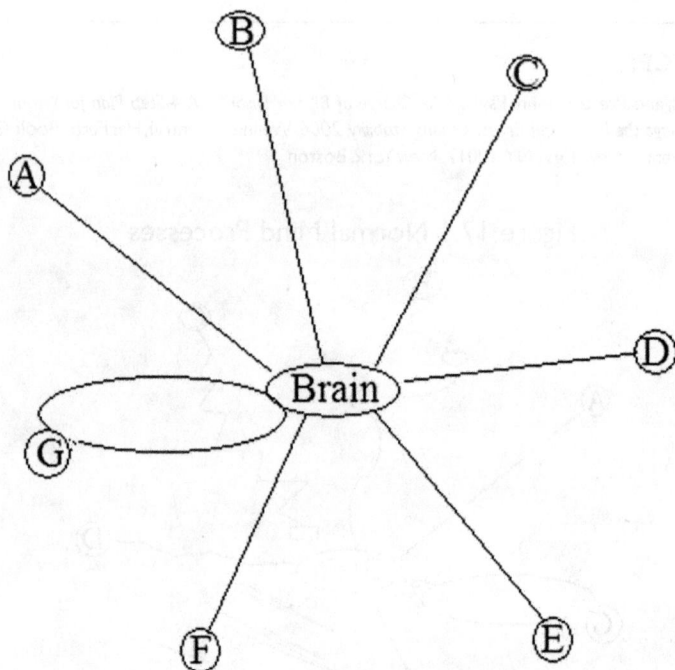

A: Subconscious Vital
B: Dreaming & Mental Organization
C: Flash to Consciousness & Body Control
D: Routine
E: Analytical
F: Reflex and Limit
G: Spiritual Surrender

Chapter 18
Conclusion

"At the end of all our exploring
Will be to arrive wherever we started
And know the place for the first time.

T. S. Eliot

America was founded by amazing leaders. Unlike many countries, no tyrant formed a dictatorship and abolished freedom of thought, speech, and religion. I am proud of our founding fathers who respected fellow countrymen and their freedoms. In earlier times subjects were forced to believe as the king or queen believed.

I have felt frustrated by the long effort to complete mental reconstruction. I felt forced to make it my life. Normal adult brains are highly infested with trauma scars. I have had amazing trauma energy release sensations and have rushed toward the clear mind for fifteen years with excitement and wonder not knowing the final result. Faith has carried me through rough times and humbled me during exciting times.

Writing itself is an adventure into the mind. With persistent work in the same arena, God provides amazing ideas never thought possible. Inner feelings and thoughts received from God frame the fundamental purpose of life. Mental and spiritual freedoms beckon.

Build relationships with those supporting your freedom to change and improve. Do not trust those who confine positive freedoms. Suggest changes with care. Be supportive of others decisions in accepting or rejecting changes or improvements.

True mental healing increases our freedom and can be only our own responsibility. No one else can heal our minds but us. Living on the mental edge with its uncertainties beyond normal mental confinements is a path to inner freedom.

Be cautioned. Once you begin your inner search, it is difficult to accept life in the cave again or be accepted by the cave dwellers with their egos in "judging shadows on the wall." Take your mind to limits briefly, at times, to expand mental freedoms and receive spiritual messages! God usually speaks to us softly, but sometimes astonishingly. Creativity attracts spirituality, and spirituality is the foundation of creativity.

Through trials and errors, I hope to help readers experience their own minds more fully. I stress that my methods and models are certainly not the only paths to heal the mind or experience God. Through your personal relationship with God, construct your own healing and spiritual experiments and practices.

I am proud of having been a manic-depressive and having cured my own bipolar disorder. I have endured unbelievable experiences. Constructing foundations of creative, certain thinking from manic uncertainties is spiritual. I fought an inner war, with the fears and risks, and survived.

Successful efforts have developed unique exercises and mind models to clear the brain of trauma effects and improve mental processes. Mental reconstruction has continued for thirty years, and has accelerated over the last fifteen-years.

Purposes and processes were so unusual they were kept secret until mental goals were accomplished and spiritual channels were reopened. Daily trials and errors were not disclosed to avoid distractions and misunderstandings. Initial processes were focused but without supporting confirmation. In my case, sanity and creative advancements were worth the long effort. As societies learn of benefits, mental reconstruction can become more open.

A long-pursued cure for bipolar disorder, with higher mental states at times, has been accomplished. In early and lonely struggles, goals were only a faraway dream. Mental changes, and their sensations, have converged to a more relaxed, efficient brain.

Thinking and life are mostly iterative processes. Happiness is enjoying interesting uncertainties and challenges each day with hope for exciting uncertainties and challenges in Heaven. Heaven with absolute certainty would be Hell. There would be no reason for eternal life without looking forward to exciting heavenly experiences. Heavenly duties may include monitoring uncertainties in the universe.

Evaluate feelings with positive thinking. Imagination creates exciting lives. Work to make thought patterns positive until they become part of you. With practice and patience, we can restructure fundamental mental processes to accomplish any goal. Be grateful for what you already have. Being consistently positive and grateful attracts blessings through spiritual frequencies. Visualize goals coming true to guide your future. *The Secret* [1], by Rhonda Byrne, focuses on developing positive mental resonances for attracting spiritual frequencies from the universe and God.

Today, Americans use computers for many purposes. We learn electricity can be used to search millions of servers to find millions of matches for selected topics in seconds. Our brains are as amazing. They can also search millions of memory files in fractions of a second for matches to current thoughts and experiences. Both are unbelievably fast.

A clear mind freed of trauma effects will be more aware of inner processes for solving emotional and other problems. We will have a deeper purpose in life. When the clear mind is accomplished, it will have three hierarchical improvements:

1. Neural fabric refined by adult consistent and meaningful experiences rather than constructed by only original infant and childhood helter-skelter, less meaningful awareness and experiences;

2. Faster analytical processes separated from sensing and muscle controlling processes;

3. And improved God consciousness for receiving spiritual communication in "words."

If cultured, analytical processes can attain the speed of dreams. Thinking would be in depth with expanded memory and abilities. Reading speeds and comprehension would increase. There would be less emotional resistance to creative thinking beyond normal boundaries. Many with less trauma effects than my own may have attained the above levels with less effort.

What may happen in the third level? There would be greater spiritual communications to attain God Consciousness whenever lowering or raising emotional energy levels beyond the normal. Spiritual communications would be received more in discrete words rather than feelings. Spiritual words will promote higher levels of understanding. Spiritual reason and purpose will be shared and grow throughout the world. The subconscious mind will become more capable in healing its body and mind.

Throughout this work, importance of physics analyses is emphasized. There are important biochemistry advances in brain research. We learn that stress hormones prepare the body to deal with stressful situations.

Prolonged stress during depression results in a deficiency of the neurotransmitter, norepinephrine, in certain areas of the brain, while mania results in an overabundance of norepinephrine. Lack of proper levels of serotonin in depression disrupts normal mental processes. Exercise is important and can increase serotonin to regulate the brain's activities.

In recent years several other hormones have become better understood. More recent research on corticotropin-releasing factor, CRF, shows that medications blocking actions of CRF can reduce affects of depression. These insights may lead to new options for prevention and treatment.

"CRF also sets off a sequence of events that include the release of two other stress hormones, adrenocorticotropic hormone (ACTH) and cortisol. These hormones arouse various body systems and prepare them to cope with challenges. They also facilitate the body's return to a normal state." Stress hormone advances reference *Depression and Stress Hormones* [2] by Leah Ariniello, October 2001, *Brain Briefing*.

Most of us need seven to eight hours of sleep each night. Prolonged lack of sleep increases stress and the cortisol hormone. High levels of cortisol increase chances of heart disease. Advanced chemical analyses can help us avoid risky health conditions. Biochemistry is showing promise in improving thinking processes for overstressed minds.

Work with mice by Joe Z. Tsien, "The Memory Code," [3] Scientific American, July, 2007, has developed methods of digitizing brain responses to traumas. It has been known for some time that the hippocampus is instrumental in developing memory. Experimental methods included placing over 200 electrodes in CAI neurons within the hippocampus. Monitored neurons are divided into "cliques" activated by the same event categories. Staging experimental traumatic events for mice and recording neuron clique responses allows digitizing of mental processes. Digital response information can be analyzed by computers.

Clique activations and their follow-up harmonic activations support my theory that subconscious activities and consciousness are developed by resonances throughout the brain. Hippocampus activities initiate many resonances throughout the brain during the same time. Electromagnetic waves, from clique activations, integrate to form mental holograms, which are foundations of mental processes.

Dr. Tsien's work may have far reaching importance. Near the end of future generation lives, people may have their neuron activities monitored and digitally stored into advanced "personal" server memories with sensing devices. Physical bodies will die but minds may live forever in simulated mental processes and memories within "personal" servers. "Computerized" minds may provide guidance for their great . . . great grandchildren. In the distant future a parent might say, "I don't know, log on and ask your great . . . great grandmother. When you are through, don't forget to turn her off." Computerized minds "born" of human minds may continue to learn with original personalities and skills.

As with scientific discoveries, I initially made educated guesses with a small amount of data. With a physics background, I predicted that slight sounds, or SCAPS, during neck exercises were releases of relatively high-energy from repressed trauma memories. Confirmation of my theory was that SCAP sensations did change in both character and position over time with exercises. This has definitely occurred. Individual release sensations have lasted longer than expected and have become exciting and pleasant throughout the years. After years of experimentation, the entire mind feels excitement of shower cleanliness after exercises.

Nothing occurs in the brain or universe without energy transfer. Recollection requires precise energy to activate specific memory resonances. It takes repeated exercises to release localized trauma energy and dispersing that energy as normal distributed memories throughout the brain.

More children and adults will be affected by bipolar disorder as they are exposed to greater reasoning challenges with less physical exercise. Mental pain and emotional tragedies may be reduced by exercises, mental reconstruction, and releasing, repressed high-energy action potentials early in life.

Repressed trauma activations increase emotional energy throughout the brain and distort reasoning abilities. Partially releasing repressed, trauma action potentials is the erratic driving force behind fast, emotional, and manic thinking. Complete release of localized, repressed trauma energy through unique exercises or psychoanalysis is true mind healing with increased abilities.

Our youth experience so much pain because societies have not developed a simple language for discussing inner thoughts and analysis. Hopefully this work will be of some assistance.

During years of mental reconstruction, sensations from psychiatric exercises feel more global with less energy. The years of psychiatric exercises, needed to reconstruct the brain toward the clear state, confirms the intricacy of traumatized networks within the fabric of the brain. So many energy-releases have been followed by neural network reconstitutions. Hopefully, this book attests to benefits toward developing a clear mind.

Consciousness, throughout the universe, is developed with iterative and recursive processes. Refining these processes broadens spiritual abilities. God has given humans free will for us to choose to communicate with Him.

Children can be protected from bipolar disorder with normal exercise, and unique exercise, programs when emotional energy potentials are less set and can be purged more easily. Psychiatric and normal exercises reduce trauma action potentials. With lowered energy, the young mind becomes more confident, reasonable, and spiritual throughout life.

Unfortunately repressed trauma scar potentials become more engrained within adult necks, throats, and brains. Considerable research is needed to improve healing methods, and prevent or cure adult manic depression.

We need faith in predicting environments to survive. My religious approach is similar to my approach to science. Individual thoughts and activities have uncertainty, but integrated together throughout the universe, they create a certain belief in a higher power and awareness.

Without the mind, the brain has no purpose. Without EMR activities within the brain, the mind is nothing. The brain and mind can have synergy.

All activities within the universe create God. God controls the universe. Without God the universe has no purpose. Without physical activities within the universe, God is nothing. God and the universe are in perfect synergy. The brain and mind, and the universe and God, are recursive, iterative processes.

My prayer is that readers will use their most precious gift, their minds, to the fullest extent possible. A mind is a terrible thing to waste. I want each person on this earth to receive wonderful spiritual messages daily. What a grand world that would be! Everyone has the ability to become humble messengers of God.

If chemical and electromagnetic energy within our brains create awareness, nuclear, chemical and electromagnetic energy throughout the universe can create a higher awareness, God!

Additional details of mental reconstruction events are available in my "*Mental Reconstruction Log*" under separate cover for researchers. This log contains sequences of psychiatric and spiritual events and may be useful for researchers developing psychiatric experiments and models.

Work to expand your free will. Also, work for spiritual thoughts to extend your existence into the universe independent of space and time. Long range goals for future generations should be:

- Improve and practice mental healing and research in early and later life;

- Culture minds to love, care, and share globally, as the world becomes connected and smaller, for peace;

- Promote spiritual research to deepen and expand God Consciousness to advance spiritual understanding and love with reason and more controlled emotions.

Since using my physics background to heal my bipolar disorder, it became clear I should use physics to bring science and Christianity together. Models of faith are developed by writing, praying, and using the Bible, other religious books, physics, and other sciences toward understanding God. I was forced into a mental healing struggle that extended into a personal spiritual path.

As very young children, parents were perfect and powerful. We grew up to know better. We regain feelings of being cared for by religious models. These feelings give us importance and confidence in life, and after-life.

Some spiritual leaders enjoy power over others using association with God to earn respect and a good living. Some claim they are speaking God's perfect truth. God is perfect with His perfect flowing communication. Mankind can only translate God's perfect flowing language and message into imperfect "manmade" words. Religions and religious leaders are imperfect.

Words and human language have different meaning to different listeners and readers. *God, the Universe, and You!*, 2nd Edition, attempts to translate my personal messages from God truthfully with limited abilities.

I can never repay the debt to my parents and God for my life and their love first given to me. My parents' and God's love saved me when in despair. All I can offer are praises within fragile prayers.

Attaining a clear mind is spiritual. A future book, *The Clear Mind,* is expected to include spiritual definition, hope, experiences, and challenges from readers and this author. A guide for healing feedback from readers is detailed in the epilogue. We need faith, but with scientific facts we need less faith.

We should not be afraid to be wrong. Fantastic mental adventures develop mind models that inspire new models.

Mathematically modeling five neurons and four glia support cells within an enclosing semi-reflective boundary and two nerve cells beyond that boundary might be a starting point for modeling biological intelligence. Cells may be modeled with "half silvered" reflective membrane boundaries. Sharing biological information is an intelligent, spiritual concept.

Inspiring the physics community to develop models of the mind and God, and the communication structure between the two, is a future goal. In time, we may create models with physical, chemical, cosmological, and spiritual synergy.

It is difficult to conclude such an unusual work. I am grateful for having, and being cured of, bipolar disorder and receiving spiritual ideas and blessings. I have presented ideas as truthfully as I understand them and will continue toward improving healing processes and spiritual communications. With careful attention to the inner self, healing and spiritual processes should also benefit readers.

An important conclusion is that with depression or mania, we can go beyond free will thinking limits with an unusual opportunity to experience spiritual communication. Free will is for normal human thinking and activities independent of God's guidance. Surrendering control with low energy, and sometimes with truthful, emotional thinking, invites spiritual blessings.

Practicing psychiatric exercises and processes may prevent, or cure, bipolar disorder, and relieve fears of manic episodes. The author is concerned about the mental health and well-being of others and about NIMH and mental health researchers who ignore experiences and ideas of cured suffers. The author's amazing bipolar disorder cure is understanding, and releasing, neural network tensions.

God views the universe from a holistic perspective. Man's purpose is to reflect detailed local ideas and activities, in the form of mental holograms, to God for him to integrate them within Himself and reflect them throughout the universe.

Individuals or societies forcing their "beliefs" by threats of harm, or loss of eternal afterlife, are tyrants. There are religions and religious universities in America, which are intolerant of beliefs other than their doctrines.

We choose freedom of thought, action, and beliefs or allow others to dictate our thoughts, actions, and beliefs. Indoctrination by some political and religious groups is rigid and meant to intimidate followers and non-followers. Religion is an escape from daily toils and uncertainties. True religions expand, others suppress, freedom of thought. Families, societies, and religions must do more to protect gentle, loving minds from mind predators.

Corrupt political and religious leaders gain control using crowd-aggrandizing influences, bigotry speech, and false promises. Political or spiritual power corrupts concern for others. False leaders cut off communications to divide, isolate, and suppress opposition. Dictators and false spiritual leaders would kill much of their own population and all other populations to maintain power and prove their (false) spiritual superiority. They weave fear and false pride into followers' minds. Some priests have used their position to isolate and sexually abuse young believers.

My mind and spiritual models use established science, but reach for imaginative steps beyond current discoveries. The author explores science and religion to unite them when possible.

Understanding science and the physical universe develops spiritual reasoning. My work is directed toward developing spiritual reasoning without repetition or indoctrination.

God "reasonably" created this universe and its laws. My book, *God, the Universe, and You!*, 2nd Edition, uses science and metaphysics for developing models of God and His universe.

Thank you for being a part of this mind adventure. We have taken a path less traveled. My prayers are with readers and their interpretations for improving their minds and this work. In this world with so much hate, please keep love alive. I am proud to be an earthling searching for unity and meaning on earth. May God bless you and your spiritual purpose!

REFERENCES:

(1) Byrne, Rhonda, *The Secret*, 2006, Atria Books, New York, NY.

(2) Ariniello, Leah, October 2001 issue of *Brain Briefing, Depression and Stress Hormones*, Science Writer, Society for Neuroscience, 2001, 11 Dupont Circle, NW, Suite 500, Washington DC, 20036.

(3) Joe Z. Tsien, July, 2007, "The Memory Code," Scientific American, New York, NY.

Epilogue

Create universal love that binds,
With caring and refined minds.
Writing with love for the Lord;
The pen is mightier than the sword.

Hugh Fulcher (1995)

Emotional Mind Modeling and *The Clear Mind Procedure* were foundations of *Bipolar Blessings & Mind Expansion*, 2nd Edition. Updates and refinements for this book were researched and written during 2008 and 2009. *God, the Universe & You!* was published in 2008 also. Its Second Edition will also be published in 2009. It will update, refine, and include spiritual aspects from *The Clear Mind Procedure.* Another project entitled *The Clear Mind* will be written after experience with the clear mind.

We have free wills to discuss science procedures and logical discoveries without offending anyone. If we use our free will and apply science logic toward spiritual models of God, traditional religion believers stigmatize us as sinners or dogs. Fundamental religions force followers to believe only what they believe. They want followers to memorize their traditional doctrine and believe no one today could receive a profound spiritual message on their own. Historically, kings forced subjects to believe as they believed.

Feedback from readers receiving unusual, traumatic words, or visions from God is requested. One does not need to be a spiritual leader to receive strong spiritual messages in feelings and words. Please, include exact words of your messages from God. What were dates, ages, and circumstances? What were feelings, emotions, and conflicts before and after spiritual messages? What life changes occurred? When and in what location did messages occur? Why are you sure you had a message from God?

Significant spiritual research and advances are also requested. Don't be afraid to let your inner self out. Be absolutely truthful or you may hurt others. If you wish, give your religion. Spiritual messages from all faiths are welcome. The goal is to integrate spiritual messages received by readers to develop spiritual communication technology and reason.

Your feedback from significant emotional events, extreme traumas, and their spiritual effects will add to analyses. Also, please provide effects of exercises and mental reconstruction on mental disorders and normal minds. Send information only in which you give permission for me to integrate into a spiritual log. Designate if you want material to be anonymous. The author cannot guarantee using submissions or timing for another book. Be truthful about your experiences. They may help many people.

Please make submissions concise. Let God be your writing guide. Have a friend edit and comment on your writing. It may seem difficult, but allow a month of refinement before sending in submissions. Indicate number of refinements. Compositions must be **three** pages or less in **12pt. font**. Submissions may be condensed for publishing. If your work is extensive, publish your own article or book. Sorry, I do not have time to decipher poor writing.

Include your email address. Work must be in English. Acknowledgments depend on time available. Have a spiritual brain day, and pass the "biscuits" please!

Send submissions to: *The Clear Mind*
                              P.O Box 1278
                              Forest, Virginia 24551

Appendix A

Dr. Fee In 2084

I dream of Dr. Fee and his "Unified BrainMind" theory. It's the year 2084. You are not getting along with your spouse. He (or she) intimidates and manipulates you until you just can't take it any longer. You are normally mild and meek but finally lash back. The dominant spouse reacts. You have suppressed anger for all your life and are not accustomed to being angry. Your wonderful, loving childhood did not include arguments so you never learned to argue or control anger.

You are now very different than your normal self. Your aggressive spouse is an expert at anger and the control it can give. He declares you, "crazy." Well, by now, you are crazy. You are beside yourself, out of your tree, and beyond emotional limits.

Realizing that anger has gotten you in trouble with an anger expert, you retreat from your own home. There is no escape from high controllers. As you walk toward a safe haven, police and emergency personal search for, this "crazy" person. Your spouse declares you insane with indignant hopes of getting rid of you. As you are "jailed" in a psychiatric ward, your spouse is feeling powerful, righteous, and ashamed to be stuck with a weak spouse in a psychiatric ward.

Controllers respect only strength and discard those they have weakened. In their lying eyes, they are perfect and always right. Your being in the psychiatric ward proves it. He has saved himself from his burden of weakness without sympathy.

Love is just a word to a controller. He has repressed love as you had repressed anger. He does not feel love for himself or you.

By this time, he is scheming of legal ways of getting rid of you, dumping you in the garbage heap, and greedily acquiring all joint material property for himself. Power-based people have an insatiable need for power, security, and material wealth.

People who have been hurt badly in childhood will discard a spouse's loving soul to increase their elusive security. Even though you have loved and supported an unloving person for so long, you, yes you, are in the mental trash heap for finally being assertive.

And now, flooded with out-of-control emotions of hurt and anger for years of being controlled and deceived, no one can recognize you from the rest to the emotional trash. As good as you have been you have just realized you cannot survive with a spouse from an abusive childhood. You have wasted so much of your life for apparently little reason. How could you have stayed with a spouse so long who showed deceit, suppressive control, and no love? Controllers learned deceit from damaging alcoholic parents.

Well, being in a trash bin is better than being with someone who falsifies statements to destroy you and ensure his security in his twisted life. Your spouse has mentally murdered your ego and you ended up in the can. Where do you go from here?

The morning after being drugged into a stupor of semi-restful sleep, you wake up. It's time for your visit to the analytical artist. Later you will see the powerful mental reconstruction psychoanalyst (MRPA, for short). This is your first visit to an MRPA. You have heard they are awesome dudes. But do you really want anyone this powerful messing with your mind?

You may be better off keeping the mess you've got! Well, what the heck! You are not so sure you like your mind that much anyway. Maybe it's time for a mental checkup, and this hospital has a special on "Mind Adjustments (MA)" this month. With the new health plans, the medical profession has become competitive with specials every month. Physical, chemical, electromagnetic, and heat migration abilities, within the brain, will be analyzed

The first session includes a computer with a large, three-dimensional holographic screen. The analytical artistic asks you to think of first rec-ollections and helps "return" you back to early times. He asks you to describe your childhood house and neighborhood. He shows pictures of insides and outsides of houses; he does a binary search of houses. A binary search is very fast. You choose images closest to your remem-bered experiences. He asks what needs to be changed and uses com-puterized artistry to complete images of your childhood. He completes images of this early period.

Next he asks about people important to this period and how they looked and acted. After finding near matches, he uses his computer programs to complete likenesses. He works with you on how these people moved, walked, and talked. Images are animated.

When you no longer make suggestions, images are checked off as suffi-cient. Processes are continued for all significant emotional times during early life. Voices are selected for important people in your life. Things are so automated and specialized that this exercise takes only a few days. Images of your life are in the computer and set up so the MRPA can manipulate your mental life.

After image therapy, you enter this white room. The physical therapist will take you on the ride of your life. They strap you into the brainmind analyzer (BMA).

Your hands and feet are inserted into gloves and shoes that are con-nected to movement and resistance machinery. Hips and shoulders are strapped for a full range of back, side, and stomach resistance with forced exercises. The head is strapped for head and neck resistance exercises. Supports are placed on the bottom teeth and on the chin so jaw muscles can be forced and resisted. Sensors everywhere will record all movements including eye movements and pupil dilation. Your mind will be analyzed including at limits.

On each side of the large holographic screen, there are square banks of smaller holographic screens. On the left side are neurotransmitter analysis screens, and on the right side are energy analysis screens. Screens can display local temperature, electric and magnetic field strengths and their migrations. Other holographic screens measure electromagnetic energy throughout the brain. Advanced scanning machines are put in place.

Left screens display detailed color-coded neurotransmitter slices of the brain at various angles. Holographic screens are able to display color-coded flow contours of each neurotransmitter throughout the brain. Combinations of local transmitter fluxes can be color coded and displayed. Any data can be displayed on the large three-dimensional screen to be closely analyzed by the doctor. Microscopic areas can be blown up on the large and smaller screens for problem analysis.

In the BMA machine, your physical analyst has you move each body part to limits without risking injury. He has you twist your back in all directions. He has you exercise your neck, jaw, tongue, and throat in all possible directions. He records initial chemical and energy data for each slice of the brain during each exercise. Data gathering is very fast with futuristic sensors and computers. The physical therapist records correlations between body movements and electrical, chemical, and energy or heat contours within the brain. Exercises are repeated with various levels of resistance.

Next, all movements are carefully forced to their limits with data recorded. Pain monitors ensure physical exercises do not cause injury. Computers develop correlations between resistant and forced exercise data and brain scan data. Data includes physical and neurological correlations for the MRPA.

The next morning you are again hooked up to the BMA. To this point, you have only worked with the junior staff. Your primary doctor, Dr. Freud E. Einstein, comes in. He has a reputation for getting at physical and mental truths within the brainmind. I refer to him simply as Dr. FEE. He has reviewed the image, response, and physical data. Together, you go through the important images and emotions of your life. Dr. FEE uses computer animation and "going back" technology to review your important trauma experiences and dream relationships. Some scenarios are viewed at faster than normal speed to amplify subconscious and emotional responses.

With Dr. FEE at the helm, the real analysis begins. All sensors and screens are switched to real time. Dr. FEE analyzes the detailed holographic chemistry, electromagnetic, and energy migrations within your brain as you discuss and re-experience childhood and adult life.

He takes you back to strenuous times. Trauma scar effects are shown on the large screen with translucent holograms. Translucence is varied so all areas of the brain can be viewed, or enlarged and viewed. With his guidance, you relive important traumas. Dr. FEE hears your descriptions, monitors truthfulness, and watches the same picture unfold on the screens. He simulates worse traumas and has you describe the severe trauma experiences. He is taking you to and expanding mental limits.

He has the computerized machine move the head, neck, and jaw in various directions. You surrender to Dr. FEE's hypnotic commands. He adjusts holograms and movements to purge local trauma energy. You repeat movements freely and then with increasingly conflicting resistance.

The doctor analyzes the effects of amplified traumas and their effects on trauma energy releases. Then Dr. FEE purges less severe trauma energy. The process is repeated until most major trauma memories have released excess energy. The doctor prescribes an exercise program to release pre-verbal trauma and emotional scars. He locates trauma hot spots with high energy and neurotransmitter fluxes.

After finishing, he gives you a machine to take home that keeps track of your psychiatric homework. Dr. FEE is very strict about your prescribed homework therapy.

On the next visit, the doctor tests reasoning and emotional stability with stimulated composite trauma experiences and asks you to resolve conflicts. You use controls to manipulate scenes, yourself, and others within scenes. The emotional experience is between dreaming and consciousness to strengthen communication between conscious and subconscious processes.

Dr. Fee operates a machine that converges ten laser molecular beams to change chemistry and structure of troublesome localized neural networks. Lasers can guide and insert needed molecules into focused microscopic locations. Other laser beams in opposing directions can stop molecules at precise locations. Dr. FEE seldom prescribes pills. Most oral pills went out years ago. He repeats this procedure several times to get you chemically balanced for the short term.

Next, the doctor takes you to socially-accepted emotional limits and assists you in establishing a new set of wider, stronger, kinder, gentler, and more consistent mental processing limits. Dr. FEE and you work out the levels of emotion, logic, and social reason you wish to have for professional, social, and limiting situations. Dr. FEE inserts local computerized macro logic into your right hemisphere to assist you in expanding your most stressful emotional limits. You now have proven computerized macro logic at your command for traumas.

Macro logic is similar to that of signing your name without consciously thinking about the details. You will have logical and confident reactions to severe trauma and emotional situations.

May I-err-call you, Dr. Spock. Oh, excuse me! You left some emotions in your decision-making processes. Well, it is 2084. Did you expect anything less?

Dr. FEE assures you that new limits contain a carefully thought-out mixture of emotion and logic. With homework, you will have a clear mind in a few months.

You will think fast as lightning, stay cool in pressured and emotional situations, and make wonderfully considerate decisions for your and others' benefits. You look to the future with love, hope, and a reasonable amount of doubt. You are a gentle person but are now ready to interact reasonably with selfish controllers.

When quietly meditating with eyes closed, on pure darkness, your EEG shows a pure sine wave and its harmonics from the prefect symphony of a holistically functioning brain. Normal thoughts show less complex waves with various amplitudes.

On your next checkup, Dr. FEE prepares you for your toughest challenge so far. He places electrodes throughout the head and body. He has emotionally strengthened your mind for this test. He zaps you. Your neck and shoulders compress. Your face grows pale and lifeless. Your heart stops. You scream! You have just relived a difficult simulated birth! Dr. FEE jumpstarts your heart. You almost died during childbirth. The deeply repressed birth trauma" is now a less energetic subconscious memory. The birth trauma establishes reference energy levels of mental holograms.

Your greatest hurdle is about to begin. Your mother and father were distant cousins, and two of your gene pairs were equally dominate. Upon conception, there were, relatively, long emotional battles to determine gene dominance. This extended conflict left emotional scars imprinted within two DNA genes.

Dr. FEE injects you with trillions of strong reconstructed genes attached to cultured nano-particles. With designed resonances, they attach to defective genes. Dr. FEE zaps you with precise radio frequencies that release all defective genes. You scream and collapse. The reconstructed genes replace DNA vacancies. The separated nano-particles, old defective genes, and excess new genes are purged in a few days. You are now smarter, confident, and creative! But who are you?

You are a grown baby ready to learn with an exciting new mind at the speed of dreams. You are in for some awesome previously mind boggling experiences. Life is not easier. Higher capabilities mean attacking higher-level, more difficult problems. You will not let these newly developed capabilities and talents atrophy back to normal. You will accept higher responsibilities as the next Plato and climb out of your modern cave to refine the direction of philosophy and human thought for understanding God.

Technology has evolved as the unified brainmind theory. Dr. FEE knows every important thing about you. His instruments can locate points initiating each thought. With his instruments, he can be aware of all subconscious candidates that develop each conscious idea. He knows more about your thinking than you do.

Dr. FEE prescribes more personal thinking in images. It produces faster, fuller, and more consistent thinking. He prescribes methods for efficiently converting dream image language into verbal language for understanding yourself. He emphasizes that verbal thinking should be performed mostly when practicing communication skills or communicating with others.

Energy efficiency has been improved over the years in many machines. Why not increase energy efficiency in the human brainmind where benefits can be improved by huge factors?

Dr. Fee has been very observant of your face. He learns very fast and has the entire structure of your brainmind within his mind. You can't hide your thoughts. Dr. FEE can determine your thoughts by carefully observing your face and eyes. He no longer has to ask what you are thinking. Facial muscles and the eyes are intricately controlled by the conscious and subconscious minds.

Lookout, Big Brother is here (1984, George Orwell!) Dr. FEE can completely simulate the personalities and behaviors of his patients. How does Dr. FEE know everything about you? He has a bionic right eye and left-brain. Bionics is the field for engineered devices that simulate living functions. With his bionics, he detects slight eye movements. Small eye movements, or microsaccades, provide changing retina activations even when staring on a fixed spot. They provide Dr. FEE a window into your subconscious secrets. You are an open book to Dr. FEE. The only thing left is to pay Dr. FEE's considerable fee.

Criminals and false accusers would have to tell the truth to Big Brother, (Dr. FEE.) Judges would no longer have to listen to the horrendous lies the guilty and their attorneys perpetrate.

Appendix B
Holograms

"I write for the same reason I breath - because if I didn't, I would die"

Isaac Asimov

Commercial holograms are made with coherent laser beams that have been split into two beams by half silvered mirrors. Neuron membranes also split light beams into smaller beams in many directions within the brain. Mental holograms are much more detailed than commercial holograms constructed by only two laser beams. With so much electromagnetic radiation reflecting within the brain, coherent light affects each neuron membrane.

A commercial laser beam is focused on a half silvered mirror at a forty five degree angle. Half the beam goes through the mirror and the other half is reflected. Both beams are again reflected and then magnified.

One, the reference, beam, is directed to a photographic plate, and the other beam is directed toward an object to be photographed. The light from the object is also reflected onto the photographic plate. The light has taken two distinct paths. The laser beam originally had coherent phase angles. The split laser beams have traveled different path lengths and now have different phase angles. The phase angle differences between the two split laser light sources are kept constant during exposure of the target.

The reference and image reflected beams interfere with each other as they are absorbed into the photo film surface. Light interferes with light on the film surface like a diffraction grating splits interfering light into smaller beams for refined imprints. Light overlaps light at different angles within holographic film.

A diffraction grating is a tool for measuring wavelengths of light sources and consists of a large number of very fine equally spaced parallel grooves on a glass plate cut with a precision ruling machine. A light source is split into a large number of equally spaced light sources by the diffraction grating. Resulting smaller, closely adjacent light sources interfere with one another and light is deflected at angles depending upon light wavelengths and spacing of grating grooves.

A diffraction grating causes light to separate into bands, lines, or fringes of colors. Interference causes groupings of different light frequencies or colors. Dark bands occur when waves with different identical wavelengths but at 180 degrees out of phase cancel each other.

Photographic film absorbs light as it is reflected back and forth between its front and back surfaces. Interfering light waves deposit energy on the photographic material at different angles to produce three-dimensional images. When light meets light there is awareness. This awareness is saved on the photo film. We can view this stored awareness whenever we choose. Stored holographic memories on membranes within the brain can also be recalled if we have good memories. With improved memories, we should enjoy life and not take ourselves too seriously.

Physics for Scientists and Engineers [1] by Paul A. Tipler was a physics reference for holograms and much of the science presented in *Bipolar Blessings & Mind Expansion*.

REFERENCE:

1) Tipler, Paul A. 1991. *Physics for Scientists and Engineers,* Worth Publishers, New York, NY

Bibliography

The Holy Bible -New International Version - Disciples' Study Bible,
1984, Holman Bible Publishers, Nashville, Tennessee

Ariniello, Leah, Science Writer
2001- October. *Depression and Stress Hormones,* Society for Neuroscience,
11 Dupont Circle, NW, Suite 500, Washington DC, 20036

Babyak, Michael, Blumenthal, James A., et al..
September/October 2000. *Exercise Treatment for Major Depression: Maintenance of Therapeutic Benefit at 10 Months. Psychosomatic Medicine.*

Blumenthal, James A., Babyak, Michael A., Moore, Kathleen A., Craighead, W.
Edward, Herman, Steve, Khatri, Parinda, Waugh, Robert, Napolitano, Melissa A.,
Forman, Leslie M., Appelbaum, Mark, Doraiswamy, P. Murali, Krishnan, K. Ranga.
October 25, 1999. *Effects of Exercise Training on Older Patients with Major
Depression.* Archives of Internal Medicine.

Byrne, Rhonda
2006. *The Secret* by, Atria Books, 1230 Avenue of the Americas, New York,
NY, 10020

Chabaneix, P.
1897. *Physiologie cerebrale: le subconscient chez,* les artistes, les savants, et
les ecrivains, Paris.

Fast, Julie A. and Preston, John, PsyD
2006, Take Charge of Bipolar Disorder, A 4-Step Plan for You
and Your Loved Ones To Manage the Illness And Create Lasting Stability,
Wellness Central, Hachette Book Group USA, 237 Park Avenue, New
York, NY 10017, New York, Boston

Freud, Sigmund
1899. *The Interpretation of Dreams,* translated by James

Strachey as: *Sigmund Freud: The Interpretation of Dreams*, Avon Books, 1965.

Fulcher, Hugh Drummond

1995. *Emotional Mind Modeling*, H D Fulcher Publishers, Inc., Lynchburg, VA.

Fulcher, Hugh Drummond
2007. *The Clear Mind Procedure*, H Fulcher Publishers, A Division of Wide Acceptance Financial, Inc., Lynchburg, VA.

Fulcher, Hugh Drummond,
2008. *Bipolar Blessing & Mind Expansion,* H Fulcher Publishers, a Division of Wide Acceptance Financial, Inc., Lynchburg, VA.

Fulcher, Hugh Drummond,
2009. *God the Universe, & You!,* 2nd Edition, H Fulcher Publishers, Lynchburg, VA.

Harris, Thomas
1969. *I'm OK, You're OK*, Avon Books, NY, NY.

Hubbard, L. Ron
Dianetics (The Modern Science of Mental Health), Bridge Publications.

Krauss, A.
1858-59. *Der Sinn im Wahmsinn, Allg.* Z. Psychol.

Spitta, H.

1882. *Die Schalf- und Traumzustande der menschlichen Seele*, Tubingen. (1st ed., 1878)

Styron, William
1990. *Darkness Visible A Memoir of Madness*, Vintage Books (A Division of Random House, Inc.).

Tipler, Paul A.
1991. *Physics for Scientists and Engineers*, Extended Version, Worth Publishers

Tsien, Joe Z.
July, 2007, "The Memory Code," Scientific American, New York, NY

Woititz, Janet Geringer
1983. *Adult Children of Alcoholics*, Health Communication Incorporated.

Glossary

10^{-35} seconds = 0.00000000000000000000000000000000001 seconds; a very, very small fraction of a second

aberration – malfunction of the mind distorting true mental images and memories, failure of normal recall, loss of truth in memory reduces instinct to survive

aberee – a person with mental dysfunctions or aberrations

adrenaline – epinephrine; a hormone of the adrenal gland that acts on smooth muscle and causes the narrowing of blood vessels; increases blood pressure

Adult – a psychological state free of restrictive childhood behavior and free from historical parent controlling thoughts and actions. (Dianetics)

aminergic cluster – brainstem neurons predominantly in the dorsal raphe nucleus that are most active during waking and tending to suppress reticular activation

analytical mind (Dianetics) – the logically perfect mind

antidepressant – a prescription drug that relieves negative thinking and can "force" positive thoughts

artificial intelligence – a (robot) computer program that can process sensory and logic input, "learn" to navigate new environments, and make human like judgments

asynchronous – parts of a system not operating at normal frequencies

ATSV – apparent vision time span, "The Flash"

auditory hallucination – clinical term, hearing unexplained voices through ears

axon – a long stringy extension of a neuron that sends electrical impulses and chemicalsto other neurons and nerve cells through their dendrites

"biophysiofeedback" – touching and sensing parts of one's body to enhance feedback and mental reconstruction; a method of enhancing self-awareness

binary language – the language of digital computers; all data manipulations and calculations are performed using the binary number system of ones and zeros.

bipolar disorder – manic-depressive illness; emotional communication disorder in between left- and right-brains; disorder of moods with loss of reasoning

Body language awareness – assigning numbers to body language for comparison with words spoken to activate the left-brain in judging body language

brain – the organ consisting of interconnected and coordinated neuron and nerve cells that create thoughts, judgment, and self-awareness

brainmind – an integrated concept of the brain and mind when physiology of the brain and psychology of the mind converge to form one integrated analysis.

brainstem – part of the brain at the top of the spinal cord that transmits body nerve signals and relays signals to and from the rest of the brain; coordinates and to some extent controls sleeping or waking states

brainstorming – a creative management process allowing only positive ideas and group decisions including a facilitator to ensure avoidance of negative ideas

censorship – activities of the subconscious mind to suppress dream "sub-thought" processes upon awakening, conscious mental process of reining in dream Free Will to conform the mind to conscious responsibilities

cerebral cortex – gray matter neurons beneath the surface of the cerebrum

cerebral hemispheres – the two upper brain hemispheres; the latest evolved areas of the brain associated with human higher reasoning levels

cerebellum – "little brain" at the base of the brain, located over the medulla and pons, contains motor feedback and muscular tone and coordination functions; governs conditioned learning and some reflexes

cerebrum – the two upper brain hemispheres; the latest evolved areas of the brain associated with human higher reasoning levels

chemistry – a science that deals with the composition and structure or materials and fluids and includes their abilities to interact and bind with other materials

Child – a psychological state heavily influenced by restrictive childhood behavior and parental restraints

circular thinking – continually recalling the same old negative thoughts; negative thoughts revolve like a broken record with little success in finding solutions
"Clear, A" – a person with a clear mind free of all trauma effects

Clear Mind – A mind cleared of psychoses, neuroses, compulsions, and repressed and psychosomatic ills, brain free of all trauma and emotional scars or "engrams"

clique – a small group of people sharing selfish interest; a group of neurons reacting to the same stimuli.

codependent – a person controlled by either a power based person or a manipulating alcoholic; a person who enables bad behavior by others.

cognitive science – the science that studies processes of awareness and of being able to make judgments on that awareness, the study of how we and robots learn

consciousness – a state of being aware of one's body, mind, and environment including touch, emotions, and volition (the power of choosing); an integrated resonance of sensory nerve signals and subconscious mental processes amplified for evolving awareness

"controlled conflict" – forcing the mind to sense conflicting signals with conflicting exercises and mind experiments

corpus callosum – massive neural network connecting left and right cerebral hemispheres

cortex – the layer of gray matter beneath the surface of the cerebrum and cerebellum

cortisol – a hormone of the adrenal cortex that is derived from cortisone

cosmic sound – awareness of an inner mental sound during meditation and reduced mental energy, the inner sound is similar to cosmic noise

cosmic noise – celestial radio-frequency radiation from outside the Milky Way

cosmology – study of the origin, structure, and space-time relationships of the universe; relating high-energy properties of elementary particles to near the beginning of the universe

creative idea – an idea derived from subconscious and conscious processes that an individual has not seen or heard of earlier, an idea received from God

"deep structure language" – a part of any natural language that promotes self-reflection, inner awareness, and God-consciousness

dendrite – a long stringy extension of a neuron that receives electrical impulses and chemicals from axons of other neurons and nerve cells

depression – extremely negative thinking about oneself; a disorder of mood

Dianetics (L. Ron Hubbard) – emotionally healing the mind using simplified mind models, an organized method of healing built on definite axioms

diffraction – modification of light as it travels next to and by an opaque object or through a small slit between opaque objects, Different wavelengths (or colors) are bent at different angles.

discrete – consisting of or studying separate identifiable entities or parts, not continuous displacement – an object or image being removed from its normal place; a "remote" awareness viewing his own image in a dream or vision

DNA (deoxyribonucleic acid) – the molecular basis of heredity in living organisms

dream content – animated dream pictures, memories and hallucinations experienced in, and sometimes remembered after, dreaming. Dream animated image content referred here also as mental binary processes.

dream images – images within the dream content

dream thought – integration of recent and early childhood memories that instigate dreams and future wishes. The dream thought is the true meaning of the dream content that must be revealed to successfully heal some overstressed patients.

dream work – mental processing during dreaming; retrieving, comparing, organizing, and storing daily experiences within long range memory; integrating daily experiences into a unified set of emotional or logical life memories

dysfunctional – impaired or abnormal function

EEG (electroencephalogram) – display of brain electrical activity

ego – inner reflection of self and self-worth

Electromagnetic radiation (EMR) – produced by moving or vibrating charges causing alternating electric and magnetic fields to be propagated outward at the speed of light

electromagnetism – the physical science that deals with the relationship between electricity and magnetism; magnetic fields are caused by changing electric fields

elementary particles – the building blocks of atoms and nuclei; the "glue" that holds nuclei together

emotion – mental and bodily reaction marked by strong feelings that prepare the mind and body for action or reaction

emotional scar – an ingrained neural network injury caused by traumas or persistent emotional abuse degrading mental processes

EMR – short for electromagnetic radiation

engram (Dianetics) – source of all mental aberrations, localized trauma scars, mental dysfunction caused by trauma induced moments of unconsciousness

episode – an abnormal or unusual situation for some period of time that is separable from normal continuous life activities

"fast thinking" – thinking as the manic mood evolves, includes "forced" and "strong" ideas that tend to intensify and compel thought patterns and actions

FEE, Dr. (Dr. Freud E. Einstein) – A futuristic mind doctor

"Flash, The" – a near-death experience in which important occurrences in one's life quickly flashes through the mind

flux – the flow and rate of change of flow of a fluid through some channel; some instruments can measure certain chemical fluxes in the brain

free will – God's most precious gift to Man; freedom of thought and choice

"freeze" – a very depressed state in which an individual might stop all movement and remain in any position; a person experiencing only holistic thoughts

frontal lobe – the front part of the cerebral hemisphere

fMRI – functional magnetic resonance imaging, a method of imaging brain activity with higher resolution than PET without radioactive methods. The process uses differences in magnetic resonances of specific nuclei in active neural networks.

genetics – determined from the origin or genes, study of living building blocks

genre – a distinctive type or category of literary or musical composition

glia – structure or support cells within the brain that may also influence on long term memory processes and mental abilities

Golgi Type I – neurons with long axons in the cortex

Golgi Type II – neurons with short axons in the cortex

God – supreme reality and awareness, perfect in power, wisdom, and goodness, worshipped as creator and ruler of the universe, the infinite Mind; Light

googol – an extremely large number; 10^{+100}

gyri – ridges or convolutions on the surface of the cerebral hemispheres

harmonic vibrations – a periodic motion that has a fundamental frequency and amplitude and with lower level corresponding vibrations.

heart – emotional feelings and thinking as distinguished from the intellect; holistic thinking with body, mind, and soul; an organ of the body.

heaven – God's and the blessed Dead's sanctified, joyful structure or home; light and all field forces that are structures for God's Resonance; spiritual stability

Heaverse – term used when integrating heaven and the universe as one entity

heuristic – involved in or serving as an aid to learning, discovery, or problem solving by experimental or trial-and-error methods, exploratory problem-solving utilizing self-educating techniques and feedback to improve performance.

hippocampus – part of the brain resembling a seahorse that is critical to long term memory formation in the cerebral cortex.

holistic – relating to completeness and whole systems; in medicine attempting to heal the whole body; a feeling of wholeness and completeness by perceiving details equally by focusing long distance through visual details.

hologram – a three-dimensional image using interference patterns between two coherent beams of light, the fundamental method of creating memories with electromagnetic interference patterns on brain cell membranes; see appendix A.

holographic film – film used to capture there dimensional hologram images

Holusion – a visual product of NVision Grafix, Inc. A two-dimensional image that can be interpreted by the subconscious mind to produce a conscious three-dimensional image

Holy – exalted and righteous completeness; worthy of humble devotion, continuous or analog thinking

hypothalamus – located below the thalamus, forms the floor of the third ventricle, and includes vital autonomic regulatory centers such as body temperature, blood pressure, and sex hormones

id (Freud) – the subconscious inner driving force from Man's basic instincts

imagination – a process of forming mental images not presently stimulated by, and never before wholly perceived by the senses

insanity – a deranged state of the mind, a mental disorder in which one is not able to cope within his "normal" social environment

integrate – to blend or incorporate into a unified or functioning whole

interbrain – portion of the brain located between the cerebrum and the mid-brain

left-brain – the left cerebral hemisphere controlling discrete verbal and mathematical processes

Light – God; the visible spectrum of electromagnetic radiation frequencies

limbic system – a group of structures below the cortex of the brain that are concerned with emotion and motivation

limits – a boundary beyond which some system or process cannot safely exceed. System and mental processes degrade and may have unexpected operation beyond limits.

lithium – major mood controlling element/ingredient in psychiatric medications

locus cerulus ("blue place") – brainstem neurons containing blue pigment that influence sleep-waking state functions

macro (mental) – a routine mental process that can be performed with minimal consciousness, a signature is a mental macro.

mania – mental hyperactivity including disorganization of thoughts and behavior and elevation of mood

manic-depressive illness – a mental disorder characterized by alternating psychotic depression and mania.

manic episode – the mind attains a "feeling good" or "high" mood with fast, forced thinking that if continued evolves into loss or reason and reality; thoughts include more and more dream processes, so many good ideas evolve that the manic often goes in circles not knowing which to act upon

manifest dream – normal dream images readily perceived or recalled by the mind upon awaking, the easily perceivable part of a dream

meditate – to focus on or ponder ideas while the body is relaxed; to relax body, facial muscles, and eye focus (with eyes closed) to enhance calm holistic thinking; to reflect on inner thoughts of self and God

medulla oblongata – a part of the brainstem that contains the pyramidal motor tract and sends fibers to control larynx, pharynx, neck, respiration, heart rate muscles, wakefulness, and digestion

"mental binary" – the natural, visual language of the subconscious mind, relates to binary language used in computers.

"mental limits" – subconscious processing limits governed by emotions developed mostly during early childhood; transformed to more logical limits through mental reconstruction

"Mental Nuclear Explosion" – extreme holistic mental energy-release with perceived brilliant out-flowing of high-energy yellow light

mental reconstruction – self healing corrective action the brainmind performs after positive stimulation through psychotherapy and psychophysiotherapy

"Metallic Ping" – abrupt reverberating inner ("anvil strike") sound of a large internal energy spike being released

microelectrode – an electrical sensor small enough to be placed in, and monitor electromagnetic voltages from, a single nerve cell

midbrain – middle division of the three primary divisions of the vertebrate brain

mind – the function of the brain and nervous system; functional awareness

mind modeling – processes, patterns, similarities, descriptions, and analogies to visualize and understand mental processes

model – a pattern, similarity, description, or analogy used to visualize and understand some process or system; includes postulates and assumptions as to what is modeled and what is not modeled

modeling assumptions – precisely stated, assumed structure and boundaries surrounding model systems, conditions expected during operation and expected interactions with the environment

monitor (Dianetics) – mental center of subconscious awareness

mood – predominant emotions, orientation, and reflection of self

MRI (magnetic resonance imaging) – a technology for developing images through the response of brain electrons, atoms, nuclei, or molecules to discrete radiation frequencies as a result of space quantization in magnetic fields

MRPA – a futuristic mental reconstruction psychoanalyst

mysticism – direct communication with God as ultimate reality as reported by mystics; inducing a feeling or awe or wonder

narrow-minded – thinking only of old routine and negative ways of responding and solving problems; causes the face to frown or narrow and the brain to tense

neurobiology – a life science that studies the anatomy, physiology, and pathology of the nervous system

neuron – a grayish or reddish granular cell that develops fundamental electrical and chemical processes within the brain; neurons contain stringy appendages, axons and dendrites, that allow communication with many other neurons

neurosis – a nervous disorder marked by anxiety and the use of defense mechanisms to escape the anxiety; especially when there is no defined cause

neurophysiology – study of brain functions including neurons and nerve cells

neurotransmitter – a chemical substance that transmits nerve impulses across a synapse from one nerve cell to another

non-verbal communication – important communication using arms, legs, body, head, and eyes that may conflict with or support verbal communication

noreprinephrene – a neurotransmitter that is the chemical means of transferring chemical information across synapses, a precursor of epinephrine

normal – typical behavior within an environment, conforming to and being accepted in an environment, characterized by average intelligence

NMR scan – nuclear magnetic resonance scans providing images of the brain and other parts of the body so anomalies can be discovered and studied

nuclear engineer – one who designs and verifies safety and performance of nuclear systems, one who interacts with (or as) regulatory authorities to comply with nuclear safety requirements

nuclear reactor – a device for controlling nuclear reactions for experimentation or producing electricity, nuclear weapons, radiation, or commercial products

occipital lobe – the main sight processing center of the brain

omnipresence – being everywhere at the same time; God is everywhere at the same time and is independent of space

omniscient – having infinite physical and spiritual awareness; God is omniscient.

out-of-body experience – an acute awareness of perceptions beyond the ability of the normal senses

"Parent" – imprinted parent behavior by a young child, psychological effects throughout life due to imprinted parent behavior – Dianetics

pathological – study of human diseases and their effects on body and mind

perfect – a term referring to God or unexpected goodness but never to self

PET (positron-emission tomography) scan – diagnostic technique taking image slices (of the brain) using emission of positrons, repeated at different depths.

pharynx – the part of the alimentary canal between the mouth and esophagus

philosophy – all learning excluding technical, art, medicine, law, and theology

physics – the study of matter and its energy; includes mechanics, optics, heat, electricity, magnetism, atomic and nuclear structure, and motion energy.

physics mind model – awareness is created by interferences of electromagnetic resonances interacting with and storing energy on neural membranes – a reflection of the continuous symphony of neuron activations

pituitary gland – master gland of the body; produces its own and influences hormonal production of other body glands

process – a natural phenomenon with gradual changes that leads toward a particular result; subconscious activities that lead to conscious thoughts

prophet – one who proclaims divine revelations for the future

psychiatrist – a physician who specializes in psychiatry

psychiatry – a branch of medicine for healing mental and behavior disorders

psychic – relating to the soul or inner self, lying beyond physical science or common mental abilities

psychoanalysis – method of explaining and treating emotional disorders emphasizing importance of talking freely about conflicts, childhood, and dreams

psychobiology – the study of the physiology of the brain placing microelectrodes in individual cells to correlate neural activity and behavior characteristics

psychology – the science relating mental processes and behavior "psychophysiofeedback" – sensed changes within the brain during psychiatric exercises and mental reconstruction

psychophysiotherapy (PPT) – mental healing through physical exercising of neck, throat, facial, eye, and, to some extent, other muscles, and including forced, conflicting, or resistance exercises

psychophysioanalysis – determining a logical selection of physical exercises to promote psychophysiotherapy and mental reconstruction

psychosis – severe personality disorder characterized by defective or lost contact with reality and often with delusions and hallucinations

psychosomatic – pain or illness affecting the organs, body, and mind that have conflicting and anxiety origins

physiology – biology dealing with structures and activities of living things

pulse – a forced increase of system parameters above normal levels

R-complex – most primitive part of the human brain

Rapid Eye Movement (REM) sleep – sleep state in which the eyes move rapidly during which most dreaming occurs

reactive mind (Dianetics) – the course, rugged, fast, mental response system that is naturally self-centered for protection

rebirth – freed from trauma effects and sin; surrendering one's life to God.

recursive – a procedure that can repeat itself indefinitely or until a specified condition is met; in computer programming, a program that calls itself, iterative

redeem – to free from what distresses or harms; to remove obligations and convert to something of value

reflect – to give or return back an image or outline with possible awareness of that image or outline, to ponder meaningful images

refraction – light traveling in air and hitting a smooth glass (or other) surface at an angle will travel slower in glass at a lesser angle, the angle of refraction.

relativistic – an entity traveling near the speed of light

relativity – a theory based on: the speed of light in vacuum is constant and independent of the source or the observer, and laws of physics are invariant in all inertial systems, which leads to equivalence of mass and energy; relative variation of mass, spatial dimensions, and time with variations near-light speeds

religion – faith in and worship of God or the supernatural, a system of beliefs

repress – to prevent the natural or normal expression, activity, or development of; to exclude from consciousness; to inactivate recall of trauma memories

resistance (mental) – prevent from happening; trauma scars impeding normal mental processes; a hand resisting neck movements and stimulating trauma energy-releases.

resonance – oscillations occurring when a driving frequency equals a systems natural frequency; conditions in which the maximum energy is absorbed by an oscillator (a device for producing alternating current), dominant frequencies from a system, including the brain.

return (Dianetics) – mentally going back in time using a systematic and logical set of previous memories to arrive at earlier memories

rhythm – a pleasing flow of sound and silence including music

right-brain – right cerebral hemisphere containing spatial and holistic processes

RNA – ribonucleic acid for protein synthesis and probably long range memory

sanity – being mentally sound and healthy and able to accomplish expected tasks and communications

SCAPS (Snaps, Crackles, and Pops) – inner localized sounds of energy-releases from neuron and glia cells within neural networks and from nerve cells mostly within the neck and throat

Schizophrenia – a psychosis characterized by abnormalities of thought; interactions and emotions inappropriate to the thoughts or behavior associated with them; delusions; hallucinations

science – systemic knowledge acquisition about occurrences and forces in nature using the scientific method

scientific method – principles and procedures for the systemic pursuit of knowledge involving the formulation and recognition of natural occurrences; formulation and testing of physical hypotheses

scientific notation – short method of writing extremely large or small numbers; eg.: 2000000. can be written as: $2. \times 10^6$; .00005 can be written as $5. \times 10^{-5}$

septal – the front part of the hypothalamus

serotonin – a neuro-transmitter; a powerful vasoconstrictor

Sierpinski Triangle – a method of dividing larger triangles into smaller triangles with a continuous process of smaller and smaller triangles. A fractal procedure.

simile – a story comparing two dissimilar things

soul – the spiritual foundation within human beings, a part of God that dwells within us, the inner most part of humans distributed throughout the human mind

spinal cord – nervous tissue in the cavity of the spinal column that connects the nerves of the body to the brainstem and brain

spiritual – relating to God and loved ones holistically through worship, humility, and love

standing light waves – large amplitude electromagnetic oscillations or reflections when a frequency equals a system's natural frequency; frequencies in which maximum energy is absorbed by atoms, structures, and brain cell membranes, resonating or recursive light processes

stigma – a mark of shame or discredit promoted by the narrow minded.

stimulus-response – analyzing responses after stimuli are applied

strata – roughly parallel layers of substance; neurons with equal energy and resonances

stupor – a state of extreme apathy

subconsciousness – a wide variety of supporting neural processes in the mind below the threshold of consciousness

"sub-thoughts" – supporting subconscious components of conscious thought

sulci – grooves on the surface of the cerebral hemispheres

superego – the subconscious judge of drives from the id; only acceptable drives or processes reach consciousness

suppression – that which is excluded from the conscious mind

synapse – a joint or connector where nerve signals pass from one nerve cell to the other; connection between axon of one cell and dendrites of other nerve cells

syntax – an orderly system of putting words together to form sentences

thalamus – located at the top of the mid-brain; an ovoid mass of nuclei in each lateral wall of the third ventricle; relay station for information entering the brain

therapeutic – treatment of disease or disorders by remedial agents or methods

thorazine – a tranquilizer successfully used by the author

thought – a complete conscious awareness, a discrete entity within an ever flowing mental process; a mental process that has a distinct beginning and end

thought intrusions/insertions – hearing inner voices, or spiritual messages

trance – a state of profound abstraction or absorption

transform – change in composition, structure, character, or spiritual belief

tranquilizer – drug to reduce mental disturbances such as anxiety or mania trauma – a disordered psyche or behavioral state resulting from mental or emotional stress, or physical injury; an injury to living tissue; an experience causing momentary unconsciousness

trauma scar – localized (rigid) neural network injury caused by traumatic overload

trochlear nucleus (fourth cranial nerve) – controls oblique eye movements

undulatory – forming and moving in waves; rising and falling in volume or magnitude, light is formed by moving waves

Unified Field Theory – A predicted theory framing Man's understanding of gravity, electromagnetism, nuclear, and other forces into one consistent theory

vestibular system – system that correlates head and eye movements

"wait states" (mental) – delays in subconscious processing due to sensing activities and monitoring of slow moving body parts

wavelength – the distance between successive wave crests

"what if" thinking – worried or depressed thinking continuingly mulling over things that could have been done differently with little work toward solutions

wholeness – completeness, the same independent of time and space

wish-fulfillment – frequent cause of dreams about things we wish would occur

www.ingramcontent.com/pod-product-compliance
Lightning Source LLC
Chambersburg PA
CBHW052033090426
42739CB00010B/1893